The Independence of
BRAZIL

The Independence of
BRAZIL

RODERICK CAVALIERO

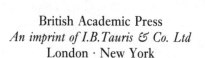

British Academic Press
An imprint of I.B.Tauris & Co. Ltd
London · New York

Published in 1993 by
British Academic Press
45 Bloomsbury Square
London WC1A 2HY

An imprint of I.B.Tauris & Co Ltd

In the United States of America
and Canada distributed by
St Martin's Press
175 Fifth Avenue
New York
NY 10010

A full CIP record for this book is available
from the British Library

Library of Congress Catalog
card number: 93–60104

A full CIP record for this book is available
from the Library of Congress

ISBN 1–85043–661–4

Typeset by The Midlands Book Typesetting Company,
Loughborough
Printed and bound in Great Britain by
WBC Ltd, Bridgend, Mid Glamorgan

Contents

List of Illustrations

Plate 8.   A Bahian family at table, from *Travels in Brazil* by Spix and Martius, showing the slovenly finery of rich Brazilians amid the squalor of domestic slavery.

Plate 9.   A Botocudo family on the march. A watercolour dated 1816 by Prince Maximilian zu Wied-Neuwied, from his *Journey to Brazil*, showing the distended lower lip characteristic of this tribe.

Plate 10.   Dom Pedro I in 1822, from a painting by Henrique da Dilva in the Imperial Museum of Petropolis. Dom Pedro is shown in imperial robes, with the newly made crown by his side.

Foreword

Robert Southey wrote too much. Had he concentrated more he might have written a history that would have ranked with Gibbon and Macaulay. Certainly his industry was enormous and his three-volume *History of Brazil* was for many years the only work in the English language that described the epic Portuguese colonization of Brazil, the unfinished battle between settler and autochthon for land, the enforced migration of entire peoples across the Atlantic and the first stirring of nationhood. His narrative stopped just after the Portuguese court had been chased out of Lisbon by Napoleon and was setting up house in Rio de Janeiro.

That court was escorted across the Atlantic by British warships and lived round its monarch, the King of Portugal, for most of the time that George Canning dreamed of bringing in the New World to redress the balance of the Old. Then, Britain's commercial hold was almost total. Today, very few Britons know more about Brazil than her achievements on the football field and the threat to the Amazon rainforest. At least that is better than thinking of her as the place 'where the nuts come from'.

How that independence came about, and Britain's part in it, is the subject of this book. It is not a string of epic battles or the story of a prolonged guerrilla campaign, for it was achieved with a loss of life and limb so small as to be almost imperceptible beside the blood-bath that gave rise to the successor states of Spanish America. The credit for this must go to the happy combination at the right moment of a pragmatic conservative politician and a liberal-minded prince. The Brazilians and the Portuguese could have slugged it out like their

Spanish-speaking neighbours, since Brazil was a frontier society and both Brazilians and Portuguese had shown by their conquest of the continent and their treatment of Indians and black slaves that they could be as ruthless and brutal as their neighbours. But for all that, there is a tolerant and unvindictive streak in the nature of both peoples, who can fight like tigers when they want to, but who seldom want to. This is an account of one of the occasions when they did not want to.

There have been many books that have explored that phenomenon, but the only one that described its beginning was written by an English merchant in Brazil in 1835. Southey believed that Brazil's political and economic future was rosier than that of the United States of America. Others at the same time feared that the huge colony would Balkanize, like Spanish America, into a rash of Portuguese-speaking but mutually competitive states, north and south, pitting creole Europeans against Afro-Americans under the guns and stock whips of military *caudillos*. Brazil has defied most prophets and she has survived as a colossus without power, a sleeping giant who one day may find her real strength.

Portuguese is a language that presents peculiar difficulties for Britons, but apart from anglicizing the name of King João VI to King John and the house of Bragança to Braganza, I have left Portuguese names untouched. The pronunciation of Portuguese diphthongs is a matter of trial and error for the foreigner, usually error, until he has been some time attuned to them. The most common, *ão*, and its plural form, *ões*, are a nazalization of *ion*, *iones* rendered near enough to p*ou*nd and b*oy*s.

The Brazilians have not neglected their own history and a thriving translation industry over the years has rendered most of the (often extremely rare) travel and other contemporary books into Portuguese, so that they have been far easier to consult in translation than in their elusive original versions. In giving page references to quotations I have often done so, as specified in the bibliography, to Portuguese versions. Also, in dealing with the complex racial cauldron that Brazil has been for nearly four centuries, I have used words which are tainted in modern parlance. But *mulatto, caboclo, mameluco, cafuzo, mazombo* mean importantly different combinations of blood and breeding.

I am therefore happy to dedicate the work to our family's best and most enduring friend in Brazil, Hilda Alves da Conceição, *paseista* with the Mangueira Samba School when she was not minding and feeding us all, one of those 'cheerful, good-natured, stout-hearted and obstinate' blacks who, Charles Darwin devoutly hoped, would one day assert their rights and forget to avenge their wrongs. That day has yet to come, but, thankfully, this is the half of Brazil's population which has produced the triumphs in the World Cup, the *desfila* of the Rio Carnival and the samba. It is not, after all, entirely bad that these are the things for which Brazil is best known, even today.

Roderick Cavaliero
Tunbridge Wells, 1993

1· Nemesis, 1807–8

'Al fuego, al fuego, todas al Infierno' —
> Maria I of Portugal, on hearing that the French
> had invaded Portugal in November 1807, according
> to Madame Junot in her *Memoirs* (1833–5)

'God will not allow the Portuguese nation to suffer great harm
without Brazil coming forward to be her refuge and strength' —
> Ambrósio Fernandes Brandão,
> *Diálogo das Grandezas do Brasil* (1618)

1768.   Captain Cook was on his way to observe the transit of
Venus over the sun's disc, a phenomenon that could be most suitably
observed from a position in the South Seas.   HMS *Endeavour*
made her first landfall *en route* at Rio de Janeiro. The city had only
five years earlier become the capital of the largest colony, then, in
the world, a possession of England's most ancient ally, King José I of
Portugal. A land, not exactly flowing with milk and honey but rich in
gold and diamonds as well as in pumpkins that kept very well at sea
and, though no one knew why, were good for scurvy. He expected a
friendly welcome. His mission was reported to the Viceroy because
it was thought he might be interested. But that dignitary did not
believe that a captain of the Royal Navy could possibly be engaged
on such a profitless mission. No, he must be a trading spy, while
Joseph Banks and the ship's doctor, who applied for permission to
explore the hinterland, must be supercargoes or engineers. They
could not be naturalists, since as Cook noted wryly in his *Journal*,
'the business of such [is] so very abstruse and unprofitable that they
cannot believe gentlemen would come as far as Brazil on that account
only'.[1] Permission refused.
    1800.   The 31-year-old Alexander Humboldt, born the year
after the *Endeavour* had shipped out of Rio de Janeiro, was a year

into the travels that were to take him across the northern provinces of Spanish America and result in the 30 folio and quarto volumes of his historic *Voyages aux Régions Equinoxiales du Nouveau Continent*. Any hope he had of visiting Brazil was quietly removed when the minister for the colonies in Lisbon issued an order that should he come down the Rio Negro from what is now Venezuela, he was to be politely arrested, escorted to Belém do Pará and sent out of the colony. Like Joseph Banks, Humboldt could not just be a man of science. He must be a spy.

And yet the Jesuit missionary, André João Antonil, had stated confidently in 1711, in a book widely read abroad, that Brazil was the finest and most useful of all the conquests of the Kingdom of Portugal. Perhaps that was the trouble. It was extravagantly fine and far too useful to be shared with other, less fortunate nations. Portugal was, or had been, before gold was struck in the central Brazilian highlands, a poor country, which had with difficulty under the house of Braganza thrown off the Spanish yoke and reasserted her ancient independence at the antipodes of Europe. To her nervous monarchs that independence rested on the wealth of her maritime empire, and of that empire Brazil was the richest jewel. She was, accordingly, preserved in almost oriental seclusion, like Japan, and foreigners were not allowed to leave the coastal towns. Even Portugal's ancient allies, the English, could not be trusted. Believing as they did that the safety and wealth of their little island off the Normandy coast depended on the possession of India, they should have been sympathetic to such nervousness, but they resented the fact that they could only trade with Brazil through the harbours of Portugal. In order that a Portuguese monarch could be allied to the Court of St James's, he had once had to part with Bombay. Brazil was not to go the way of India. Trespassers would be prosecuted.

Yet in only a matter of years everything was to change. Brazil was to be rediscovered, just as Spanish America was being rediscovered, with results that were quite unforeseen and strange. A new world was born to redress the balance of the old and it started with the news from Paris in 1791. All witnesses were united in their view that it was the trial and execution of Louis XVI which drove Queen Maria I of Portugal out of her mind. It had never been very steady and the loss, first, of her husband, then of her first-born son and heir had shaken it badly. But throughout the onset of insanity two convictions were never to be dislodged — that heaven and hell were fixed to all eternity and that monarchs were God's vice-gerents on earth. Naturally, as a result, they were of great interest to the Devil. And that dignitary first appeared in the Queluz palace in Lisbon, as soon as he had completed his mischief in the Louvre. On 10 February 1792, his forays having proved too insistent for simple exorcism, the queen's doctors declared her unfit to rule. Her son, Dom John, Prince of Brazil, became her regent.

Dom John was only 25 and, unlike his contemporary, the Prince of Wales, he was most unwilling to fill the role vacated by his mad parent. He was as fat as his royal cousin of England, but there the similarity faded. He was timid to the point of terror, stammering dreadfully when pressed for words, and with his protruding lower lip and dog-like brown eyes some people thought he was not far off being an idiot. Moreover he suffered so badly from erysipelas that, not to put too fine a word on it, he stank and it was torture for him to sit on a horse or a throne as became a monarch, without scratching and fidgeting. But if life had dealt him a hand of shabby cards, it had also given him an exquisite taste and refined sensibility in music. He seized every opportunity to avoid the business of statecraft by escaping to the Chapel Royal to hear a sung Mass or to practise the organ.

When 18 years old, he had been married to a shrew. His 10-year-old wife was Dona Carlota Joaquina, Infanta of Spain and daughter of Goya's unprepossessing king, Charles IV, a pert, ugly child with an atrocious temper. She lived with her increasingly strange mother-in-law until the marriage could be consummated, and thereafter the children had come at regular intervals, nine in all, six girls and three boys. The last was born in 1806 and Dona Carlota reckoned she had done her duty to the dynasty. There had never been much love to lose between the two partners. Dom John's introspective timorousness, his passion for music and his preference for the low company of servants wilted before his wife's quick and wounding wit and Bourbon pride. He spent more and more time in the gilded chapel of his enormous palace at Mafra, built with Brazilian gold, while she worked off her abundant energy, dancing, hunting and shooting partridges from the saddle.

Dona Carlota was perhaps the ugliest royal personage that ever existed. She stood barely more than 4 feet 6 inches tall with bloodshot, malevolent eyes. She had a hooked nose and nutcracker chin and bluish lips that opened to reveal teeth like great bones, 'uneven like

Pan's flute'.[2] With immense diamonds in her ears or wreathed about her untidy hair, she resembled a doll, and when in hunting gear looked more like a gipsy than a princess. She had her admirers, who were seduced by the vigour of her irreverent mind or by fear of her wit, and in her time she counted Rear-Admiral Sir Sidney Smith, the hero of Acre, among them. Dom John, like Thackeray's King Valoroso XXIV, was 'very delicate in health and withal so fond of good dinners that it was supposed he could not live long'. In 1806, during one of his recurrent bouts of illness, Dona Carlota, anxious to promote the interests of her father, then Napoleon's ally, tried to have her husband certified as insane like his mother so that she could take over the throne on behalf of her son and rule as a pensioner of France. With the failure of that shoddy little adventure the unequal marriage foundered and the two spouses lived apart, dividing the affections of their two surviving sons.

The elder was Dom Pedro de Alcântara, born in 1798, who lived with his father and shared his father's love of music, and his good nature. He also shared some of his mother's passion for power and admiration and for constant activity. The other son was Dom Miguel, born in 1802, and he lived with mother. His was a childhood of unrestrained licence, so that he grew up a vindictive and often vicious child who inherited the ferocity of his mother's temper and a full measure of her Spanish pride. As a result of the events about to be narrated, Dom Pedro was to become the first Emperor of Brazil, and Pedro IV of Portugal. Dom Miguel lived to be the false angel of Portuguese legitimacy, a perpetual pretender to the throne and divider of homes and families.

It was only therefore a question of time before the strained and impotent kingdom attracted the attention of the overmighty emperor whom the Devil had placed on Louis XVI's old throne. Dom John had, along with the rest of monarchical Europe, dutifully declared war on republican France in 1793, but Portugal's position at the furthest point west of Europe gave her a certain immunity from republican anger. In 1801, however, Bonaparte, smarting from the loss of Egypt, decided to remember that unfriendly act. Spanish troops stiffened by French invaded the kingdom and Dom John was forced to detach himself from the war, pay an immense indemnity to his conquerors and close his ports to Britain's ships. By 1803, when war was resumed after the Peace of Amiens had collapsed, Dom John had grown a little courage, English if not Dutch, for this time his ancient ally offered to honour her treaty obligations and come to Portugal's assistance if she was attacked.

The French demanded that Dom John should close his ports to English ships. Dom John's ministers hummed and hawed. The minister of war and foreign affairs thought the offer should be declined. As former ambassador on his way to The Hague at the time of Louis XVI's execution, Antônio Araújo e Azevedo had been suspected of being a hostile agent and kicked his heels as a prisoner in the Temple. Rescued eventually by his diplomatic passport, the future minister had refused to allow the experience to cool his ardour for all things French. In his view, the old alliance with Britain had reduced Portugal to servitude, leaving her much the same shadow of independence as was enjoyed by so puissant a monarch as the King of Oudh. Professing, despite any evidence to the contrary, his complete faith in the benevolent intentions of the French emperor, he now argued for a policy of appeasement. It was one that appealed to the timid regent, but, like rulers before and after, he was to learn its limitations. For four years the French seemed to have forgotten about Portugal, but in 1807, with Austria and Prussia humbled, Russia an ally and Spain in bondage, Napoleon was ready to return to unfinished business in the west. On 12 August Dom John was given three weeks in which to round up all the English in his dominions, seize their possessions, stop their trade and put his fleet at the disposal of the French. The Council of State was appalled. The mood of England was now honed by war and bellicose. If the French walked into Portugal, the English would seize her colonies. Why should they not pretend to declare war on their old ally, and their old ally would in return protect the empire?

It was not really a serious proposition, and on 2 August there was a bolder suggestion. As Portugal could resist neither France nor England, let the colonies be saved! Dom John and all the court should leave instantly for Brazil. It was neither a new nor a particularly revolutionary proposal. It had been made twice already since the outbreak of the French wars and several times earlier in Portuguese history.[3] But it had never happened. Now the time seemed to have come for action.

One person in Lisbon heard of the proposal with undisguised enthusiasm. Percy Smythe, sixth Viscount Strangford in the peerage of Ireland, had first come to Portugal in 1802 as secretary to the British legation, and four years later, at an age when diplomats today have with luck reached the rank of first secretary, he was made minister plenipotentiary. His American mother and soldier-turned-parson father had endowed him with the brash confidence of the new world and the Brahminical pride of the old. The tasks of a legation secretary being generally undemanding, he had spent them in translating the lyrics of that poet laureate of the Portuguese discoveries, Luiz Camões, and this happy tribute to a land which most British diplomats treated as their backyard, endeared him to the court, if not to Lord Byron, who dismissed him as a Hibernian poetaster. It was, however, not poetry alone which warmed the 27-year-old minister plenipotentiary to the idea that the Prince of Brazil should make a voyage of discovery to his principality. His master in London, George Canning, also thought it was a good idea, and under the bustling eye of the imperious and red-haired envoy, the navy minister ordered unobtrusive preparations for withdrawal. But all that was decided was that if negotiations broke down with the French the nine-year-old Dom Pedro should sail at once for Brazil.

Araújo, meanwhile, treated the whole scheme as wild and impractical. Both the fury of France and the petulance of England could still be assuaged with tact and acquiescence. Indeed the threat alone of evacuation had already induced a more accommodating spirit in the dreadful emperor, for the ultimatum which arrived on 26 September was relatively mild. Dom John felt obliged to go through the formalities of declaring war on Britain, but he made no attempt to touch British goods and encouraged their owners to remove them from the warehouses while there was still time. On 27 October, however, his fate was decided. The delegates of France and Spain meeting at Fontainebleau agreed on the partition of Portugal. Five days before, quite unknown to them, Dom John's envoy in London had signed a secret convention with Britain. The Royal Navy would assist the evacuation of the Portuguese court to Brazil as long as the Portuguese navy and mercantile marine went too. Once he was safely across the Atlantic, Dom John would negotiate a new treaty of friendship and commerce with his old ally.[4]

Dom John at last began to move. On 9 November, influenced, it was rumoured, by a lucid moment in his mad mother's dementia, during which she announced that all or none of them should go to Brazil, the Council of State decided that the entire royal family, the court and the government should leave for Brazil if French troops crossed the frontier.[5] Lord Strangford surprisingly was not satisfied.

He had come to believe that the Prince of Brazil had no intention of leaving, for such an upheaval would be anathema to his torpid and irresolute soul and a journey across the Atlantic held horrors of a very special but unidentified kind. There seemed, moreover, to be few lengths to which the minister for war and foreign affairs was not prepared to go to placate the French. He even sent Napoleon a set of Brazilian diamonds with a request for the hand of one of Murat's daughters for the Infante Dom Pedro.[6] Then on 15 November, like the other side of a vice, a squadron of five ships of the line and 7000 men under the command of Rear-Admiral Sir Sidney Smith, sailed into the Tagus under flag of truce, with orders either to escort Dom John or his son to Brazil with the Portuguese fleet or to repeat Copenhagen and destroy it at anchor.

The seizure of that fleet was, in fact, the principal instruction to reach General Junot, waiting in Bayonne. Between 21 and 30 November, using every opportunity for speed and surprise, he was to march on Lisbon. 'No one' in Paris, he was told, 'believes that the Prince of Brazil will actually go to Brazil', and in this the French command and Lord Strangford were of like mind.[7] The diplomatic poetaster finally set off in a fishing smack on 18 November to join Smith in HMS *Hibernia*. It was not a distinguished exit for the high-spirited minister plenipotentiary, but he merely transferred his embassy to the admiral's state cabin, whence on 22 November he wrote a last appeal to Dom John to take his courage and his fleet in his hands and sail for Brazil. The moment of truth could not be long delayed, for he had certain information that Junot was already over the Portuguese border. Two days later the Paris newspaper, *Le Moniteur*, arrived in Lisbon with the announcement that the house of Braganza had ceased to rule.

Dom John's fragile solitude was now ceaselessly violated by councillors of state, who sat in continuous session for two days until, on 27 November, he was persuaded that further hopes of negotiations with the French were futile. The die was cast. The government would sail for South America. At once there was a wild scramble among the rich and titled for places in the ships. Cartloads of royal furniture, state papers and the apparatus of government trundled through the rain past sullen crowds gathered on the harbour side, whether in the hopes of joining the exodus or of preventing it no one quite knew. The mad queen threw a fit when her carriage reached the mole, and she had to be lifted prostrate into the waiting barge. Dona Carlota and her daughters went aboard, but Dom John, partly from a feeling that he should be the last to leave, partly from a persistent hope that there would be a last-minute reprieve, was still on shore. The imperious British envoy went back on shore to direct 'all his fears to a French army and all his hopes to a British fleet'.[8] The persistent young peer succeeded at last. On 28 November, Dom John allowed himself to be carried across the mud to his barge to save soiling his shoes, and by midday he was on board a man of war with his mother and his sons — his wife and daughters were to travel in another ship.[9] There Strangford came to congratulate him on his decision and to see that he kept to it. Ground between two irreconcilable foes, the Portuguese government had taken a bold step into an uncertain future. It was too late to turn back. At four o'clock in the morning of the 29th, the wind at last blew from the mainland, and just before noon Sir Sidney Smith welcomed 36 sail across the bar with a salute of 21 guns. They were just in time. A further two hours' delay and they would have stuck in the narrows with the death of the wind. When Junot led his ragged and footsore troops on to the heights behind Lisbon on the 30th he was galled to learn that the royal family, most of the ministers and councillors of state, 80 million cruzados, the Braganza library, the state archives and between 8000 and 10,000 courtiers, noblemen, soldiers and servants (the numbers varied because no one had time to take a count and a lot of people had decided to travel at the very last minute) were beyond his reach.

Dom John had placed himself under the protection of the British flag and Sir Sidney prophetically informed the Lords of the Admiralty that 'the scene impressed every beholder except the French army on the hills' (who in point of fact could not see them) 'with the most lively emotions of gratitude to providence that there yet existed a power in the world able ... to protect the oppressed, inclined to pardon the misguided and capable by its fostering care to found new empires and alliances from the wrecks of the old ones, destroyed by the ephemeral power of the day, on the lasting basis of mutual interest'.[10]

Between the present and the prophecy the voyage was to be an atrocious experience for the passengers, many of whom had never made a journey of more than a few miles. The squadron had been adequately prepared for a simple transatlantic sailing (Smith had to order only one ship to England as unfit for the crossing), but not for a hegira. In the *Principe Real*, which had already assisted at one royal evacuation when she rescued the Bourbons from Naples in 1798, there were 1400 passengers alone beside Dom John. There were no fewer than 1000 in each of the other battleships, far too many for the berths below or the supplies on board. Women, unable to undress in privacy, lived in their clothes. Headlice thrived so fiercely in the tropic airs that noblemen threw away their wigs. To make matters worse, the combined squadron was twice struck by storms and on the second occasion separated. Three Portuguese and three British ships reached Rio de Janeiro on 17 January 1808, with two royal aunts and two infantas. The prince, his wife and mother sailed into Salvador da Bahia five days later with the rest of the famished, parched and filthy court. The astonished ladies of the former colonial capital saw the naked polls of the *grandes dames* of Lisbon and wondered whether this was the new fashion from Europe. The governor and his pretty wife arranged a month of parties, galas and concerts to calm the royal nerves. On 7 March the royal squadron at last arrived in Rio de Janeiro. Dom John stepped ashore to three *feus de joie* from the loyal garrison and offered a Te Deum in the Carmelite church. He then thanked his faithful British friends and affectionate subjects for seeing him safely across the Atlantic. Three days later Queen Maria came ashore, the tears rolling down her cheeks, the first European monarch ever to set foot on American soil. She was never to see Portugal again.

On 1 February 1808, she was formally deposed in Lisbon.[11]

2· Brazilian Welcome

Jamas capital nenhuma Rio, empanará teu brilho, Igualará teu incanto.
(Rio, no capital shall ever dim your lustre or equal your fascination.) —

Manuel Bandeira (1886–1968)

'At last, at last we shall be going to a place fit for ladies and gentlemen to live in' —

Dona Carlota, when Queen of Portugal and Brazil,
on hearing that she was to return to Lisbon

Whatever the emotions in Dom John's phlegmatic breast on that steamy March day, few people have failed to be impressed by their first sight of the stupendous mountain backdrop to Rio de Janeiro. Its jagged profile reminded Smith's sailors of the old sea-dog, Samuel Hood, now President of the Greenwich Hospital, where some of them might be fortunate enough to end their days. The colossal Bay of Guanabara into which they now sailed had been so named from the Tamoio Indian word for the mouth of the sea, and when it was first sighted on 1 January 1502 by André Gonçalves and Amerigo Vespucci they had both agreed that it must be the estuary of a huge river to rival the Amazon. Three hundred years later it still seemed 'large enough to contain and sheltered enough to protect the navies of the whole world'.[1]

Clamped like a cluster of limpets to the narrow dip of land between the water and the mountains was the city of St Sebastian of the River of January. It had first been settled by Huguenots in a strange venture from France led by a renegade Knight of Malta, but in 1565 the Portuguese had overrun the heretical colony and rebaptized it. It had become the colonial capital only in 1763 and was still a small town of narrow streets and mean buildings, though it housed upwards of

60,000 souls. The coastline of the bay otherwise appeared to be covered by interminable forest, but was in fact neither interminable nor dense; the roads that led to the growing residential suburbs in the foothills to the east were, however, so narrow that there was barely room for two horsemen to pass. The city's most imposing structure was a huge, two-tiered aqueduct which resembled that in Lisbon, built between 1744 and 1750 to bring fresh water from the Tejuca forest to the fountains in the palace square.

This was to be Dom John's residence, formerly the house of his viceroy, 'more like a manufactory than the residence of a king'.[2] His loyal subjects had done what they could to make the approaches welcoming. Silk tapestries had been hung from the balconies and tropical flowers strewn in the streets while thousands of tapers burned on the public buildings for a week. But the flowers could not hide holes in the roads so large that horsemen had to ride on the pavements, nor the tapestries conceal 'dirty buildings, dismantled forts, decayed habitations and bare walls'.[3] And behind the flickering tapers the grim granitic stone houses with their immense shutters and the great bolted lower doors, behind which the people of Rio de Janeiro lived in almost oriental seclusion, did not promise much amusement. Everywhere finery lived in close proximity to filth. There were no elegant streets, just a grid of narrow alleys which housed the shops and artisans, and there was only one thoroughfare that ran straight from the palace to the custom house and on to the foot of the hill on which stood the baroque monastery of São Bento. The city centre was the palace square with its multiple fountains, and that was filled with black slaves drawing water for the family laundry, merchants smoking a cheroot while waiting for a cargo or being shaved while sitting on the steps by a mulatto barber dressed like Harlequin. The courtiers who came ashore with their monarch were not impressed by what they saw. Rio de Janeiro seemed scarcely worthy to be the capital of an empire.

The inhabitants of the city, known as *Cariocas*, from another Tamoio Indian word signifying either the stone houses the first settlers built or the catfish that inhabited the bay — no one is quite sure — had done little to embellish the savage marvels of their natural setting. The night was rendered hideous by the ox-drawn carts that trundled through the streets, their clumsy slug-wheels fixed so firmly on the end of each axle that they screamed and grated under their heavy loads like so many pigs being slaughtered. Dawn was heralded by the lusty cries of slaves taking the night-soil to the sea (but often only as far as the nearest hole in the road). By sunrise the streets were full of beggars and vendors, all begging and vending at the tops of their voices. Only when the sun was at its zenith did quiet descend on the city. The Europeans shut themselves behind their shutters that closed like a trap over their houses and left the streets to their slaves so that a stranger might suppose himself transported to Africa.

A diminutive mountain, the Morro do Castelo, or as the British called it, Flagstaff Hill, was the only eminence in the city and thus a desirable place for a house. But it masked the rest of the streets from the sea breezes, and the air trapped in those ill-paved ways, limned with offal and ordure, hung like a miasma inducing an often fatal lassitude. It was not surprising that the *morro* was levelled eventually to create an airstrip for the city airport of Santos-Dumont, called after the Brazilian aviator who first flew a power-driven tail-first biplane modelled on the box-kites he used to fly on the Rio beaches. 'A city deserted or reeking from the effects of an assault,' observed Lieutenant James Prior RN in 1813, 'could not exhibit much greater pictures of devastation.'[4]

None who had sailed with the first European monarch ever to set foot on American soil, therefore, was very surprised to see her come ashore in tears. But they were not tears of disappointment. She had recognized instantly the marks of her old enemy, the Devil, even in her new homeland. Without her special gift of recognizing the Enemy of Mankind, the royal librarian was inclined to agree with her. How were they to make their home among a people 'cursed for their insolence, thieving and other rascalities'?[5] Queen Maria I spent much of her remaining years weeping for the wickedness of the world in the Carmelite convent next to the palace, where she kept court among a few discreet middle-aged ladies. Part of her regime called for brisk exercise and from time to time her subjects would be surprised to meet their queen crowing and flapping her wings like a chicken. At other times she would peer into their faces and recognize the Devil, come to take her to hell. Dom John refused to sleep more than a few yards away from his demented mother, so he was happy enough to occupy the viceroy's manufactory. His wife, Dom Miguel and the infantas, however, took themselves off to a house on Flagstaff Hill, and only came to the former viceroy's palace for state occasions.

The viceroy had not been ready for an invasion of between 8000 and 10,000 people, particularly since most had employment near the court and expected to be housed for nothing in style and comfort, neither of which was characteristic of Brazilian homes. Yet householders proved surprisingly ready to move out of their homes to make way for the newcomers. Many of them, though, were to regret their loyal generosity, the more bitterly the grander the tenant. For a good few *Cariocas* it was not to be until Dom John went back to Lisbon that they were able to repossess their homes, from which many of the temporary residents had departed leaving neither rent nor thanks.

For Dom John had brought with him, not just the court but both the personnel and apparatus of administration so that the whole structure of the government of Portugal could be replicated with surprising speed as if it were still in Lisbon. Dom John resumed the practice of monarchy that he enjoyed best, the *beija-mão*, or kissing of hands, a ritual that preceded all business. And he was very happy to receive his Brazilian subjects at this ceremony; but that was as far as recognition went. With very few exceptions, the Lisbon caucus reassembled and treated their Brazilian hosts like strangers in their own land, refused to let them enter the Council of State and took little account of their presence in the machinery of government. Those whose source of income had been cut off by French bayonets resented particularly the wealth of the Brazilians with whom they had come to live, but that wealth was all they had to live on.

Business once resumed as normal, it had to be paid for. The main source of revenue, the taxes Portugal used to levy on colonial produce entering Portugal before being exported all over the world, could not be raised now that the court was in Brazil. The quint on gold and the royal monopolies in diamonds and Brazilwood were totally inadequate to support a government. The crown had to call into being a trade which could be taxed, and even before he reached Rio de Janeiro Dom John had recognized this fact with surprising clarity. Brazil was no longer a colony which under the eagle eye of the viceroy and captains-general had shipped all its produce to Portugal for the pride and profit of the *Reino*. The goods Portugal in Brazil wanted would now be imported from other countries, and if these were taxed the lost revenues from Brazil could be replaced.

The chief secretary of the custom-house at Salvador, a Brazilian himself, had originally gone to Coimbra to study for the priesthood, but after reading Adam Smith had strayed into more earthly theologies and was now an apostle of the Manchester School. Outside his office when Dom John arrived, the bay was jammed with foreign ships and the

Bahia warehouses were crammed with foreign goods, which had been diverted from Portugal to Brazil. Under the iron laws of navigation, goods for sale in Brazil must pass first through Portuguese ports, but there were no ports for them to pass through. The rules would need to be changed. The chief secretary wrote a paper for the newly arrived Prince of Brazil. Within a week Dom John had changed them.

Brazil could now trade direct with any ally or friendly nation she wished. That this meant, to all intents and purposes, Britain, then so be it. British goods had always been in high demand in Brazil, but unless smuggled in they had been outrageously expensive. Between middleman's profits and duty their price had often more than doubled. The royal edict now set the duty at 24 per cent on all dry goods. Suddenly British goods became cheap — even too cheap, for British supercargoes were intoxicated by their expectations from this brave new world. Napoleon's prohibitions on trade with Britain on the part of France, her allies and subjugated territories, promulgated at Berlin in 1806, lost their bite now that they could export to South America, where there were no competitors. By August 1808, more goods had arrived in Rio de Janeiro than there was labour to unload them or warehouse space in which to store them. Crates, boxes and barrels of hardware, earthenware, glass, clothing, saltfish, porter, paint, gum, resin, tar stood out in the rain in such profusion that many thought they were a free gift from a generous ally. Those that were not pilfered were auctioned for knock-down prices or exchanged for poor-quality hides, for tourmalines polished to look like emeralds or for gold dust mixed with filings from the very brass pots that had just been sold for a song. Some strange merchandise, stockpiled for the United States of America, also found its way to Brazil: thick blankets, warming-pans and ice skates, for a country where the temperature never fell below 20 degrees Celsius. Bought for next to nothing, they had their uses: the bed-warmers as scoops for sugar vats, the blankets as filters for gold-washing and the skates for beating into horseshoes!

British export houses that year went almost crazy and exported to Brazil goods worth nearly £3 million, greater than the declared value of all exports to North Europe. But they could not keep it up; the market was not as large as expected and, anyhow, British goods had never been in short supply. Lord Macartney, on his way to Peking in 1792 on the famously abortive mission during which that Irish grandee refused to kowtow to the Emperor of China, had found the shops in Rio as full of them as certain streets in Manchester.

Thirty years later the sphere for competition was overcrowded by competitors. And by goods. For the first fleet of merchantmen to come in 1808 overstocked the market and the second came to create a glut. But in faraway Britain the manufacturing houses thought they were on the threshold of a huge receiver of goods which would be paid for by fabled gold and diamonds, a land of resources no one had yet fully assessed, a new world to redress the balance of the old.

The impact of Britain on Brazil can be compared to the impact of the United States on Asian societies after the Second World War. A sudden appetite was created which it seemed only too easy to satisfy. The old humdrum colonial society looked dowdy and inefficient before the glittering array of consumer goods pouring in from Europe, and Brazil's own prophet of free trade, the 'Mancunian' chief secretary of the Salvador custom-house, now Dom John's regius professor of political economy, lectured the prince's subjects relentlessly on its benefits. Free trade was a source of power, competition a stimulus to industry. Brazilian wines, wools and silks could be as fine as the finest in Europe. 'A mighty commerce will grow and with it a merchant fleet to carry the immense produce of Brazil . . . until we reach a pitch of national prosperity far greater than we could ever reach under the old system.'[6] Rio de Janeiro in particular could become a new Venice, a second Genoa, emporium of the spice and China trades, a commercial Eldorado.

Well might the Portuguese merchants in the professor's native city ask how the British had conquered Asia if it was not by the domination of her markets, but the Brazilian planters, farmers and miners, as well as the growing population in the towns, were quite happy to buy imported goods cheap since it deprived the Portuguese middleman of his easy profits and thus of his relentless credit and social superiority. And so they gave a warm welcome to the outsiders who brought the whiff of a greater world than the mighty immensities of Brazil herself, and with it new fashions and new tastes. In the years between 1808 and 1815, when the European war finally ended, Brazil was to change more than she had in the previous two centuries. To many these changes were catastrophic. The Commercial Treaty of 1810, which gave Britain an overwhelmingly favoured nation status, virtually annihilated any hope of that professorial dream of a Brazilian mercantile marine. It destroyed her shipyards, ruined her merchants and dispatched her precious metals on the road for London. Even the counterfeit coins that circulated freely came from England. In 1862,

Richard Burton still found that Englishmen going to India lost their consciences at the Cape and wondered where they left that commodity when bound for the Brazils.

They certainly made themselves feel at home, as if in a new colony, and one of them climbed the Sugar Loaf Mountain to plant the Union Jack on its summit. Even for the complaisant court that was too much and it had to be removed by steeplejacks. Most of the British were traders or commission agents, and the colony's first newspaper, *A Gazeta do Rio de Janeiro*, was full of advertisements for English cane-grinding mills, furnaces, lightning-conductors, surgical instruments, carpenters' tools, carriages, boilers and ploughs. When, on 11 June 1809, Dom John, hankering after the light and airy buildings of the post-earthquake Lisbon he had left behind, ordered the great wooden shutters that made the town houses resemble prisons to be torn down, it was thought he had done it to please his ally. For he inaugurated an almost insatiable demand for glass and wrought-iron as new houses were built with high windows, iron verandas and graceful colonnades so that the suburbs of Rio de Janeiro began to resemble a tropical Tunbridge Wells.

In a relatively short space of time the thick mantles that shrouded the *Carioca* ladies in church were to be replaced by cashmeres and lace, the men took English scissors to their beards, ate with knives and forks made in Sheffield, put kerosene rather than whale-oil in their lamps, kept white mistresses instead of black or mulatta concubines, and drank like Englishmen. White bread replaced cakes of manioc flour, beds ousted hammocks, light English barouches proved smarter than slave-borne palanquins, light Yorkshire blue-cloth more comfortable than colonial frock-coats and breeches, the piano more civilized than the guitar. A new phrase entered the language, typifying the new preoccupation with appearances. Before the lofty gaze of the British merchants the new Brazilian bourgeois was only too ready to put glass in his windows, buy his daughters dresses from French dressmakers, order an English carriage for his wife and drink tea after dinner — *para Ingles ver*, 'for the English to see'.

3· Discovering Brazil

'Brazil is today the finest and most useful of all the conquests of the Kingdom of Portugal' —

Andre João Antonil SJ (João Antônio Andreoni),
Cultura e Opulência do Brasil (1711)

'I am convinced that the freedom of trade, regulated by moral laws, right-thinking and the common good, is the life-giving principle of social order and the most natural and secure measure for the prosperity of nations' —

José da Silva Lisboa (1808)

Rio de Janeiro was one thing, the rest of Brazil another, and the revolution that was being effected in the capital was a long time being felt in the rest of the country. Very few of the courtiers and gentlemen who came ashore with Dom John knew very much about Brazil and were only dimly, if at all, aware that the population of the colony (if the African slaves and indigenous Indians were included) had outstripped that of the motherland and that the colony had provided for many years now the lion's share of Portugal's exportable wealth. Indeed she had supported most of them in comfort and idleness for the best part of a century. The ignorance was not in every case unforgivable, for Brazil had been preserved in almost Japanese seclusion since the expulsion of the French and Dutch interlopers in the 16th and 17th centuries. No manufacturing industry had been allowed to develop more sophisticated than the weaving of coarse cloth. Everything the colony did not provide had to be imported from Portugal, no matter where it originated, and the import trade was handled exclusively by Portuguese factors. Foreigners were treated, as we have seen, with deep suspicion, and the few who managed to escape being corraled in the coastal towns described a country without newspapers or books, almost without roads, inhabited by ferocious, often cannibal Indians, dotted with occasional villages and crumbling plantation houses whose owners lived off the bare surplus of inefficient black labour, where endless rain or broiling sun marked the day and blood-sucking bats, buffalo gnats and termites the night.

This tropical nightmare was inhabited by a bewildering mixture of peoples. For two centuries now the creoles had been for the most part planters, ranchers and farmers, big and small (though they were not called creoles or *crioulos*, since that was a term applied to Brazilian-born blacks, both slave and free, but *mazombos*). The typical *mazombo* lived on the land, which was invariably worked by someone of a different colour, Indian or African, usually a slave. In the towns, *mazombos* and native-born Portuguese uneasily shared the business of government and trade. A Portuguese-born white was known as a *reinol*, since he had been born in the *Reino* or kingdom. From the outset of colonization the Portuguese had been anxious to encourage permanent settlement from the *Reino*, for settlers would fight to the death against interlopers, Spanish, French, Dutch and, most fiercely of all, the indigenous Indians into whose land they had blundered. But the human resources of the *Reino* were never adequate to populate, even thinly, the huge territory that had fallen to the lot of the tiny kingdom across the Atlantic. So the colonist, Brazilian and Portuguese-born, mated with Indian or African bondwomen to produce a race of half-breeds, and when Dom John arrived there were as many of them in the country as there were pure whites.

These men of Brazil formed a whole substratum of the semi-free. They were the stallholders and small-time businessmen who kept the urban services going, overseers, stockmen and cowboys on the growing estates, cultivators on their own account, muleteers, prospectors and hunters, thrusting deeper and deeper into the interior to find either land for themselves, Indians to sell as slaves or the fabled mines that would make them rich. They were variously known as *caboclos* — copper-coloured — or *mamelucos*, descendants of enslaved or domesticated Indians, and mulattos or *pardos*, half white, half black. But the largest proportion of the population of between two and three millions, about 40 per cent, were pure blacks fairly recently imported from Africa to work the land as slaves, a population that did not on the whole survive servitude and had constantly to be renewed. So many had been imported over the centuries that in 1808 nearly three-quarters of the people of Brazil, slave and free, were of African origin. None knew or could possibly tell how many Indians inhabited the vast tracts of still unexplored Brazil, but an informed guess put them at a quarter of a million.[1]

Brazil was really one enormous farm, pitted here and there by mines that had once produced untold wealth. The first product of the land to be exploited had been the *pau do bresel* or Brazilwood (*Guidalcina echinata*), used still for making violin bows but first garnered for the red dye it produced. It grew with such profusion that it gave the territory its name. But sugar had quickly become the main cash crop, the black, clayey *massapé* of the north-east proving ideal for the liquid gold for which Europe acquired an ever-sweetening tooth. By the end of the 17th century Brazil could have supplied all Europe's needs from one province alone. The sugar-mill (*engenho*) became the nucleus of colonization, an autocephalus community like the monastery in the Dark Ages, centre of economic life for everyone, free and unfree. The Big House or *Casa Grande*, surrounded by its ring of outhouses for the slave population that served its every need (the *senzala*), was also the farm, factory, market, bank, fortress and parish church of the locality. It was the home of the successful *mazombo*, and his fortune was measured in cases of sugar, each weighing between 650 and 700 pounds, and a big planter could send his daughter to the altar with as many as 3000 cases as her dowry. He ruled huge tracts of land where he was lord of the manor, judge and jury, patron of the church, tax-collector, senator in the provincial junta and captain-major of the local militia. This rural Pooh-Bah was absolute lord of his estate; most of the human beings on it were either black or members of his family to treat pretty well as he chose. Unassailable behind a great cloud of witnesses, small-time farmers, militia officers, priests and lawyers, he was beyond the range of coded justice. To the non-white he was God. The Indian who warned a choosey buyer not to handle his mangrove crabs so casually, 'for he belonged to the Amparo estate', knew that the owner of the estate required respect not only for himself but also for the crabs caught in his swamp.[2] The big planter was free with his protection and bought it with vassalage. The appearance of wealth and power were of little interest to him. He could live indefinitely through good times and bad on the produce of his land and labour.

And times had not always been good. Competition from the West Indies in the late 17th and 18th centuries had depressed the sugar market, but latterly the growing industrialization of northern Europe, the black rebellion in Santo Domingo (Haiti), which had cut off one of its principal suppliers, and the war in Europe had created a new demand for Brazil's sugar. For the past three decades prosperity had returned to the north-east. Moreover, Dom John's arrival in Salvador was marked by the occupation of the last French colony on the American continent when, in January 1809, troops from Pará, assisted by Captain Yeo in HMS *Tagus*, overran Cayenne. Though the occupation was in the name of King Louis XVIII and Portugal promised to return it at the end of the war, this other closely guarded botanical laager was plundered of the Cayenne cane, which was imported for the first time into Brazil. Originating from Tahiti and developed in Mauritius, Cayenne cane grew thicker, taller and faster than creole cane, which had been transplanted from Madeira, and could be cut not twice but thrice a year. Brazil once again became the foremost sugar producer in the world and a new golden age had dawned. It was to have only a brief life. Beet sugar, developed in continental Europe to beat the British blockade, and renewed competition from Cuba and the British West Indies were to bring it to an early end after the European war. To prove that God was a Brazilian, however, coffee was to save the country from ruin.

Only in 1727 had an enterprising smuggler been able to raise coffee trees in his Rio garden from beans smuggled from French Guiana. It was not until 1794, however, when the United States lost its supply from Haiti, that anyone thought it might be useful merchandise. Soon enterprising planters round Rio de Janeiro were planting coffee in all the space available to them. All they had to do was to keep the trees from choking weeds and the first fruits could be harvested in four to five years. A tree yielded on average 2 pounds of coffee a year and one slave could tend and harvest 3000 trees, collecting 32 pounds of beans a day. Selling higher and shipping lighter than other crops, coffee began to promise the huge profits which followed its intensive cultivation in the Southern Paraíba valley between Rio and São Paulo. By the middle of the 19th century a coffee planter's wealth was measured in trees, and the railway came to Brazil to shift the crop to the port of Rio de Janeiro. The riches earned in quenching the insatiable thirst for coffee of the United States and Europe sustained a patrician society in ostentatious elegance comparable to that of the cotton aristocracy of Louisiana. Coffee in Brazil is served as hot as hell, as black as night and as sweet as an angel; but despite the enormous quantities of sugar that are still added to thimblesful of coffee, the wealth and magnificence of the sugar plantocrat was to pale and decline before his southern compatriot. The fact that there was an awful lot of coffee in Brazil was to save Brazil from collapse more than once in her history.

Cotton, not coffee yet, was Brazil's second cash crop, produced in ever larger quantities to meet the rising demand from Portugal's textile industry. It grew best in the estuarine lands of São Luiz do Maranhão and in Pernambuco, which both had a climate not unlike that of Louisiana — and had the Brazilians taken more care of the quality of the staple they might have kept this market, for Pernambuco cotton was longer and silkier than that of North America. But King Cotton was to be easily overturned by sterner competition from the north. With his abdication, the revived economic prosperity of the north-east began to fade.

Brazil was also the world's leading producer of plug tobacco and snuff. The best was exported to Europe and the refuse was used to barter for slaves, Bahian snuff being in such demand from slavers on the Dahomey and Nigerian coasts that the air of Salvador was full of it. When Dom John and the court went ashore on that January morning in 1808, they were convulsed with sneezing. Sugar, cotton and snuff had between them built the glories of Salvador da Bahia, in its heyday a larger city than any in North America except Philadelphia, and with a bigger population than either Bristol or Liverpool. Even when Dom John arrived it was larger than Rio de Janeiro and still the busiest port of the colony. The smell of snuff was a blessing, for otherwise 'Cloacina [the goddess of sewers] seems almost publicly worshipped and so truly devout are her worshippers that the offerings are never removed except by the united influence of sun, rain and wind'.[3] The city had always been (and still claims to be) the traditional haunt of poets and prostitutes, with a rich religious life, pungent cuisine and the most celebrated brothels on the run to India. It was not for nothing that it was known as the City of Our Saviour in the Bay of All Saints and all Sinners!

Further north, a shanty town on the banks of a meandering river debouching on to a protecting reef which gave it its name, Recife was in terms of population the third city of Brazil, made, to a lesser extent than Bahia, by cotton and sugar. The Captaincy of Pernambuco, of which it was the capital, had once been Dutch and the memories of the local war which had ejected the Calvinist interlopers a century and a half earlier had made the Pernambucans proud and prickly. And poor. Yet in no other city of the colony did the culture of the old world persist more poignantly. Her streets at night were haunted by sad *modinhas* strummed on the guitar, Christians and Moors fought sea battles on balsa-wood rafts during Carnival and at the Passion her *tableaux vivants* were famous for the doyenne of the local prostitutes, a handsome mulatta who played the Magdalen.

Beyond the cotton and sugar plantations of the littoral stretched the badlands or *sertão*, dusty prairies where ranchers with huge herds of cattle were content to live very close to nature. And northwards of Pernambuco lay Maranhão, a huge tract of still largely uncharted land stretching from the forests of the Upper Amazon to Ceará on the equatorial coast. Once it had been ruled from Lisbon as a separate colony (and hence people used to refer to the Brazils in the plural), largely under the benign protection of the Society of Jesus, who had domesticated the more accessible Indians. The colony was suppressed in 1759 when the Jesuits were expelled from Portuguese territories and Maranhão was handed over to a trading company. The results were not a success. The Indians reverted to their old tribal habits and the state was eventually split into two provinces and subjected to the viceroy in Rio. It was not settlers' land, however, and the provinces of Maranhão and Pará were almost wholly run by short-term Portuguese immigrants from Europe who dragooned Indians to farm the cotton and exploit the forests. It was quicker to ship produce to Lisbon than to Rio and nearly as quick to ship to Liverpool, which during the war years took the bulk of the cotton crop.

Apart from the cotton hinterland, the rest was Amazonian jungle. The 18th-century Portuguese dictator, Pombal, had dreamed of harvesting the Amazon basin as if it were the Garden of Eden, but that ambition had wilted in the face of reality. The Indians who could have done it for the Jesuits had left their former settlements and were unwilling workers for a harder-hearted, ruthless trading company. Belém (Bethlehem) do Pará, at the mouth of the mighty river, was none the less able to act as an emporium for some of its products, and exported a great deal of cocoa, a little rice, and modest quantities of Maranhão cloves, annatto dye, saffron, balsam, vanilla and Brazil nuts. The Amazon's time was still half a century away, for the huge, equatorial forests were still largely impenetrable. Copper-coloured backwoodsmen, known as *caboclos*, had already learned to tap raw latex from the Amazonian fig and sheltered from the almost incessant rain under cotton capes thinly laid with a rubber coating, the first waterproofs in history. The Glaswegian, Charles Macintosh, succeeded only in 1823 in cementing two thicknesses of cloth together with india-rubber dissolved in naphtha, and patented the garment that bears his name.

Westward of the plantations of north-east Brazil, tropical forest or semi-desert *sertão* formed a barrier impassable to anyone without intrepid determination. That determination had been supplied originally by the demand for Indian slaves, but there was less demand for them now that Africans had replaced them. Largely as a result of the slave-raids, very few Indians were left in the drylands of Ceará and Piauí, so that the half-breed relics of those first hunting bands had settled down to rearing cattle. Addicted to cards, dice and women, for whom he had an insatiable appetite, the *sertanejo* was a true child of nature, wholly uninstructed except in the use of cowhide, which acquired in his hands a new versatility. From it were made his hammock, baskets, saddle-cloth, reins, breeches, tunic and water flask. Too poor for slaves, the cowpunchers (*vaqueiros*) both *mameluco* (half white and Indian) and *cafuso* (half Indian, half black) drove their thin but hardy herds across the dry scrub for pasturage, reducing the land each year further into a dustbowl, flagellated by God and the Devil alike. From time to time there strode from these deserts strange visionaries with a special remit from the Almighty, the most famous of whom was to be Antônio Conselheiro, who in 1896–7, with a band of devotees at Canúdos in the state of Bahia, renounced the impious rule of Rio de Janeiro and defied the might of the federal army.

For nearly two centuries most of the population of Brazil, except the Indians, were gathered round the seaports. The forbidding natural barriers to the interior had been breached by marauding parties, bringing in Indian slaves to work the land, but what had decisively drawn Brazilians into the interior was not a hunger for Indians or for land but the discovery of gold at the end of the 17th century. A constant stream of prospectors began to pour into what was later to be called the province of the Highland Mines (Minas Gerais). The Portuguese is not really susceptible to English translation: the word *geral* (plural *gerais*) means 'open' as opposed to 'enclosed'; the area was land open for mining: of gold principally but also of iron, lead, diamonds and other precious stones. The orientalist and traveller, Richard Burton, while serving as British Consul in Santos, called them the Highland Mines since the province was mountainous with mineral-bearing rock. Gold had a short but merry life, but the seams were virtually exhausted by the beginning of the 18th century, thus proving the wisdom of the Jesuit Father Antonil, who said in 1711 that sugar and tobacco were the true mines of Brazil.[4] Once they had finished with the entrails, men turned to the topsoil and found it good. The *vaqueiros* of the *sertão* drove their herds down to new pastures and by the end of the 18th century mule trains were being laden for Rio de Janeiro with guava jellies and the famous Minas cheeses.

The Highland Mines were still producing gold when Dom John arrived and fortune-hunters continued to invest their all in a couple of slaves in the hope of striking a rich new seam. What they found was hardly El Dorado. The great mines that had made fortunes a century earlier had flooded or subsided, though one of them, Morro Velho (the Old Mound), still works to this day. It was opened in 1725 by a Brazilian priest, Father Freitas, with a workforce of 70 black slaves who blasted tunnels into the side of a ravine. He was able to produce a quarter of a pound, Troy weight, of 19-carat gold a day. It remained productive throughout the ensuing century and in 1834 was bought by a retired English sea-captain. He in turn sold it to a company formed in a London pub, and the São João del Rey Mining Company was able to keep the golden legend alive in Brazil by producing in 15 years gold worth £11.25 million. Most gold otherwise was found by panning. It was certainly not the wealth that had created the temple-studded Rich City of Black Gold (Vila Rica do Ouro Preto) and made the Portuguese king the richest monarch on earth. Those days were gone for good. But more gold may have been found than the records showed. Since all gold was subject to strict laws about being handed into the government permutation office, there to be weighed, valued, taxed at 5 per cent and then cast into stamped ingots, smuggling had become the principal local occupation. As the most active smugglers were the soldiers employed to prevent the activity, gold in Minas Gerais was as rare as water in a desert. Travellers found the only currency was either copper coinage or wretched scraps of paper which were receipts for gold-dust turned into the permutation office and, though theoretically worth their face value in gold, exchanged for whatever they could fetch. The ingots had obeyed Gresham's Law and fled to the coast, where they sold at 10 per cent over par when used to buy slaves![5]

The royal quint on gold had in its time made the Portuguese monarch a modern Croesus. Brazilian diamonds had provided him with a second fortune. First discovered about the same time as gold in the Serra do Espinhaco (or Saddle-Back Mountains), and immediately monopolized by the crown, diamonds were now Dom John's main currency reserve. The royal collection, which had crossed the Atlantic with the court, was thought to be worth £3 million, and judicious selling in London was to help keep the government afloat. The finest diamonds were found in the *comarca* of Tejuco, which was preserved as crown territory, where the inhabitants hired their slaves to itinerant prospectors. They, in turn, would sit under an umbrella — for no white prospector would demean himself to look for stones himself — and watch them dig and pan and defecate (faeces were always examined in case stones had been swallowed surreptitiously). Occasionally a really big stone — say of $17^1/_2$ carats — was found, whereat the finder would be crowned with flowers and often rewarded with his liberty. But only two or three such stones were found in a year. In ten years the total value of diamonds found was barely 18,000 carats, and most of the population of the mining area lived near starvation, waiting for the find that would take them from rags to riches at a stroke. If prospectors were cheated by fortune, the crown was cheated by everybody. Diamonds were openly used as currency and seldom registered and the crown probably spent more on trying to preserve the diamond-mining area as a royal monopoly than the diamonds officially registered were actually worth. Rich Brazilians bought diamonds illegally and one young woman came to a palace ball in Rio wearing diamonds worth 6 million francs, arousing rather envy and rancour than admiration among the impoverished Portuguese who had no access to such treasures.[6]

Westward of the mining lands lay Goiás and Mato Grosso, still today *areas a conquistar*, huge tracts of sparsely inhabited land stretching to the River Paraguai and the head-waters of the Amazon. They had been incorporated as provinces in 1748 so that the unpeopled spaces could be settled before the Spaniards pushed over the swamplands of the Paraguai. The lure of gold had attracted a kind of settler and the tax-farmer drove them, mostly *mameluco* and *cafuzo* subsistence farmers, ever westwards, for a people with nothing to sell could not pay the tithe on their produce in cash. Packets of gold-dust adulterated with sand and ash formed the only currency there to be found, so that a cash economy could hardly survive. Travellers in a land of plenty could not buy even for good money the barest necessities of life.[7]

The spirit of the frontier, however, belonged, *par excellence*, to the natives of São Paulo, the heartland of the *bandeirantes* who had, during the early colonial time, thrust Brazil's borders deep into the heart of the continent. The *bandeiras*, roving gangs of *mamelucos* who had set out into the vast forests of the interior in search first of

Indian slaves, then of gold and latterly of land to farm, were now a national legend. They had also pretty well unpeopled the province, for the Indians they hunted had either died in servitude or fled deeper into Brazil to escape. The Paulista boasted an unrivalled skill in training horses and driving cattle. São Paulo itself was a rapidly growing rancher town (population about 25,000) with clean streets and brightly stuccoed houses; the mainly half-Indian Paulistas lived a frugal life not unlike that of their paternal ancestors in Tras os Montes or Upper Alentejo in Portugal. There were only the faintest premonitions of the magnificent time ahead when coffee and massive European immigration were to make the fortunes of the City of St Paul.

To the south stretched the plains of Paraná, Santa Catarina and Rio Grande do Sul do São Pedro, the last bordering on the Oriental Province of the Spanish Viceroyalty of the Plate, all three the home of huge herds of ungulates roaming almost wild. Forty thousand horses and mules were driven north yearly to São Paulo, Rio and Minas Gerais. Paraná's future capital, Curitiba, was a caravanserai for drovers of cattle on the hoof for the abattoirs of the capital. From Rio Grande came the jerked beef which was, next to manioc flour, the main constituent of the Brazilian diet, and the *gaúchos*, who roamed even further than their cattle, had but one education: to tame a horse, lasso a steer, geld a bull and bleed an ox. Not until the second half of the 19th century were these great tracts of temperate land able to fulfil their abundant promise, for they had to wait for the refugees from central and southern Europe willing to work the land with their own hands, something that up till then no European immigrant had been prepared to do.

4· First Steps, 1808–11

*'Este banco, sendo bem administrado como em Inglaterra, equivale
a ricas minas, e é Potosí de imensa riqueza'* (This bank, being well
governed as in England, is equal to rich mines, a Potosí of immense
wealth) —

Luiz Gonçalves dos Santos, *Memórias*, vol 1, p 276

*'Deep arts (have) been used to persuade the populace that England
favoured the views of the Princess of Brazil whose desire it was to be
proclaimed regent of Spanish America'* —

Vice-Admiral the Hon. Michael de Courcy to John Wilson
Croker, reporting the buzz in Buenos Aires, 17 July 1810

The Portuguese had by and large despoiled Brazil with an energy, even
madness, that was almost sublime. By the end of the 17th century the
indigenous population of the coastlands had been destroyed by slaughter,
slavery and disease, and the north-eastern provinces had become 'a huge
plantation for tropical produce' where the planter was king.[1] But the
Brazilian planters and farmers did not control the ports, and for the
rewards of their capital and labour they were dependent on another
race, a class apart. Between the *mazombo*, be he planter, rancher, farmer,
miner or local functionary, and the Portuguese-born governor and his
aides, the fiscal officers and the merchants, known contemptuously as
mascates or pedlars from the days of the itinerant shopmen who toured
the estates and villages like Donizetti's vendor of love philtres and
fashions, Dr Dulcamara, bad blood had brewed for over a century. It
was partly because the merchant made his fortune and then shipped it
and himself back to Portugal, partly from the usual suspicion that the wily
trader was a cheat. In political terms, if a generalization can be made (and
politicians deal in generalizations), the Brazilian belonged to the interior,
the Portuguese to the coast. In the five ports from north to south, São
Luiz do Maranhão, Belém do Pará, Recife, Salvador da Bahia, Rio de

Janeiro, an exclusive merchant class, constantly renewed — if not always *reinol* by birth, constantly *reinol* in sympathy — looked to Lisbon as its lodestar and to the court across the water for favours. It was rare for a Portuguese-born civil or military officer to show anything but tolerant contempt for his Brazilian colleague, while a Portuguese posted to the interior saw it as an exile little short of a living death.

From time to time racial tension had exploded into violence, and as late as 1789 a handful of *mazombo* malcontents had tried to declare the independence of Minas Gerais, inspired more by events in North America that by what was going on in Paris. The giant was beginning to stir, but a few rich planters and tax-farmers, unwilling to surrender power and influence to a Portuguese governor and his minions, did not constitute a national movement. *Mazombo* restlessness was confined to small and scattered cells of 'doctors of Coimbra', planters, priests, lawyers and poets who had been educated in Europe, usually at Coimbra University but sometimes at Montpellier and Heidelberg. The events of 1789 in Europe and the ever-present example of the United States of America did, however, prompt some to wonder whether the colony could not manage without the mother country; whether, in fact, so heavy a branch could long remain on so rotten a trunk.[2]

Brazil had overtaken Portugal not only in population (though a large proportion of that population was not free or only semi-free) but also in wealth. That wealth was what made Portugal prosperous in the latter years of the 18th century and without it her power would have been about as significant as that of the Duchy of Parma. The vigorous control that the *Reino* exercised over Brazil's trade, the burdensome system of taxes that benefited Portuguese rather than Brazilians, the high price of imported goods, whose mark-up represented the many Portuguese factors and shippers who handled them, all contributed to a perpetual rumble of grievance against rule from Lisbon. Had the Portuguese court succumbed like Spain's to France, the Brazilians would almost certainly have responded, like their Spanish neighbours, with a series of shifts leading inexorably to creole independence in two or more separate republics, north and south. Though the 1789 conspiracy had been betrayed with shameful ease, liberals and malcontents continued to meet, more circumspectly, in small groups at one of the plantation houses or in a shuttered and bolted town house, where they bound themselves by the high-principled oaths and rituals of Illuminist or Masonic brotherhoods to improve the lot of mankind. Their activities were usually known to the local governor, who felt disinclined to do anything about it. To him a lot of it was just hot air.

For in recent years the colonial government had grown more confident and more efficient. From the 1750s, when the Marquis de Pombal had overhauled the Portuguese state, expelled the Jesuits and tightened the control of Lisbon over the colony, moving the capital from the disaffected and patriarchal north-east to the emerging capitalist farming states of the south, colonial rule had been inexorably consolidated. The captains-general of the provinces destroyed native manufactories and came down hard on smuggling, both of which incurred a loss of trade and revenue to the metropolitan power. They had driven tracks — they could hardly be called roads — into the interior to facilitate commerce and policing. The Brazilians had felt both the gall and the benefit of it all. For all that, the social and racial gap between the *reinol* governors and the *mazombo* governed was never extreme. Even the patriarchal lords of the *engenhos* sent their children to Portugal to be educated, married wives from the *Reino* and kept close ties with the ancient homeland. They depended on the Portuguese to sell their produce abroad, and to bring them slaves to keep their estates going. Brazilians, too, held many of the judicial and administrative offices in the colony and were willing king's men. But if the colony were not really on the brink of rebellion, like so many of its Spanish American neighbours, it had none the less begun to feel a sense of nationhood. Now, suddenly, the colony had become the metropolitan power and open to the world.

Open in the first place, as we have seen, to the English. On 22 July 1808, Lord Strangford arrived in Rio, newly accredited to the Portuguese court in Brazil, charged to see that the secret convention signed in London on 22 October 1807 was honoured. The poet-ambassador had already informed his masters that, with the successful evacuation of the court from Lisbon, 'he had entitled England to establish with the Brazils the relations of sovereign and subject, and to require obedience as the price of protection'.[3] A British naval squadron was to be stationed in Brazilian waters. Resident British merchants were to enjoy the same privileges of extra-territoriality as in Portugal, where since 1654 all civil and commercial cases to which any one of them was a party were heard by a special judge appointed for this purpose. Brazilian ports, too, were to be used for the entrepot trade to Spanish America, a favourable trade agreement was to be signed and the Portuguese were to be persuaded to abolish the traffic in slaves from Africa. It was a formidable shopping list.

With the exception of the last, Strangford was to achieve them all. A treaty of commerce and navigation was agreed in Rio on 9 March 1809, and this fixed the duty on British dry goods at 1 per cent lower than the 16 per cent which was charged on British merchandise to Portugal itself, newly liberated following the Convention of Cintra. Indeed the British trading with Brazil were to pay a lower rate of duty on their imports than the Portuguese themselves, who only achieved parity of treatment in 1810.

The British envoy was aided and abetted in all this by Dom John's new chief minister, appointed to replace Araújo de Azevedo, whose French sympathies could not be tolerated by the paladin from Penshurst. Dom Rodrigo de Souza Coutinho had been a former secretary of state for the navy and overseas territories (1796–1801) and treasury minister until relieved of office as a result of French pressure on the Regent in 1803, and he had been one of the party for evacuation to Brazil. On his father's side he was descended from Alfonso III, Conqueror of Algarve (1248–79), and on his mother's from the 17th-century *bandeirante*, Mathia Barbosa da Silva. At his baptism in 1755, the almighty minister, Pombal, had stood as sponsor and Dom Rodrigo was, in many ways, a carbon copy of his godfather. Both had a devotion to the power of fact that would have pleased Mr Gradgrind, and both had brothers who were in their time captain-general of the Amazonian province of Pará. As secretary for the navy and overseas territories he had fiercely championed the policy of active colonial rule. Brazilians were constant guests at his Lisbon house. He commissioned a survey of the mineral resources of the Highland Mines, he encouraged the development of iron foundries, he purchased gins and looms from Manchester to assist the birth of a native textile industry and he encouraged the growing of hemp for ships' ropes in Rio de Janeiro. He lectured the sons of Brazilian planters at Coimbra University on modernizing their estates. He gave cash prizes for useful discoveries and printed Brazilian treatises on his private press. He appointed Brazilians to positions in the *Reino* itself, the most important of whom was the mineralogist, José Bonifácio de Andrada e Silva, Brazil's future first chief minister, as intendant-general of mines. Now that he was actually in Brazil, his 'English' energy could work freely on creating the wealth he had dreamed of from afar.

Like Pombal before him, Dom Rodrigo admired the pragmatic oligarchy that ruled in London where his brother, Domingos, was ambassador and had negotiated the secret convention of 22 October 1807. Though, like his godfather, he found the British overbearing and continuously demanding, he never wavered from his conviction that the fate of Portugal was indissolubly linked to that of Great Britain. His insatiable appetite for detail now ranged over every department of state to create a worthy ally for that indomitable power. Legislative decrees poured from his pen. He dictated that the new capital should be managed in the image of the old, and Rio de Janeiro was given a whole set of institutions that replicated those left behind in Lisbon. The principal legal tribunals, the royal press, the police intendancy and the exchequer were all established between April and May 1808. A Junta for the Commerce, Agriculture, Manufactures and Navigation of the River Doce was charged on 23 August to advise on the development of lands in Espirito Santo still being troubled by Indians. He tore up the old colonial exclusions. Foreign industrialists were by a decree of 1 April permitted to establish industries and to import their materials free of duty. In November they were allowed to own land, regardless of their religious beliefs. Taxes were raised, the coinage reformed and an issue bank was founded. For a short time smuggling as the national occupation almost came to an end. The magic bank was going to make money much easier to earn.

The fate of this bank was instructive. The brain-child of Silva Lisboa, it opened on 12 October 1808 with 1200 shares each worth a *conto*. Its income was to come from commissions on the selling of gold and silver, discounting bills and the sale of crown monopoly goods: dyewood, diamonds and marble. In a rash moment, Silva Lisboa likened it to a rich new mine, and like a rich mine it was plundered to meet the new and unfamiliar needs of government. So many ministers drew on it without warning that Dom John had to bribe new share purchasers with honours in order to replenish its stock. In few of the years after 1815 were the revenues equal to more than 6 per cent of the note issue, and paper money circulated at a greater discount every year. It was suppressed eventually just short of its 21st birthday, having lived as it died with more unredeemed bills than cash in its vaults. (Bankers who lent so prodigally to Brazil in the 1980s would have done well to study its early demise.)[4]

Dom Rodrigo and his regius professor of economics, José da Silva Lisboa, could have claimed, had they lived to do so, to be the founders of independent Brazil. But while the *mazombo* professor may have had some dim idea of the future he was helping to create, neither the minister with his fussy preoccupation with reform, nor Dom John, with his kindly feelings towards his new home, had any idea beyond showing that the Portuguese government in Brazil was in full exercise of its powers and that *El Rei Junot* commanded no authority outside the area of French-occupied Portugal. The commercial policies were to produce revenue, not to create a self-sufficient colonial economy. The provincial governors ruled their provinces as if the court were still in Lisbon. Taxation, justice and military control were administered in traditional colonial style with only minor, often more oppressive adaptations. Where the throne was, there was the seat of government, and Brazil at large became as much a colony of Rio de Janeiro as it had been of Lisbon. But another phenomenon was also observable. As Portugal itself was first partly and then wholly liberated by Wellington's army, she ceased to be the metropolitan power and became one of Dom John's overseas dominions. The longer the regent stayed in Brazil, the more unlikely it became that the institutional life of the former colony could ever revert to what it had been before the arrival of the court, subservient to the colonizing power across the Atlantic.

Dom Rodrigo, created Conde de Linhares in May 1808, was determined to show who was in charge. The two other pillars of his ministry were the former viceroy, the Conde de Aguiar, and the new secretary for the Navy and Overseas Territories, the Conde de Anadia, likened to three watches 'all out of time. Linhares very fast, Aguiar going more slowly every day while Anadia had stopped.'[5] In fact Anadia died at the end of 1809, leaving Aguiar to compensate himself for the shadow of power by translating Alexander Pope's *Essay on Man* into Portuguese verse. (The New World passion for Pope, the poet of rational enlightenment, was also being met in the Spanish-speaking world in Quito by José Joaquín de Olmedo, the author of an epic poem on the victories of Bolívar.) The Brazilians, however, only heard the ticking of the first watch. That restless ticking was now to start on an adventure that nearly destroyed the new kingdom Linhares was trying so busily to create.

In the restless probing of frontiers that had, in the middle of the 18th century, provoked the ruthless suppression of the semi-independent Reductions of the Society of Jesus in Paraguay and in southern Brazil, the eastern bank of the River Uruguay had been disputed land between Portugal and Spain. Control of the riverine trade of the fabulous Silver

River, the Rio de la Plata, was a prize not lightly to be surrendered to
one side or the other. With Spain under the heel of a conqueror and
a Spanish infanta as the wife of the Portuguese regent safe in Brazil,
Dom Rodrigo saw another chance to promote Portugal's interests in
that area. On 13 March 1808, darkly hinting at 'commercial ruin and
fatal catastrophe' if it were refused, he offered the *cabildo* in Buenos
Aires Portuguese protection against a French invasion.[6] In the years
after Trafalgar and Copenhagen, however, this was only the rattling
of bones. The Spanish captain-general, a French loyalist soldier, the
Conde de Liniers, rejected the offer disdainfully. Having seen off
the English invasions of 1806-7, when Sir Home Popham had led
a disastrous filibuster to secure the mouth of the Plate as a British
entrepot port for South America — which their free access to Rio de
Janeiro now gave them — the Argentines had nothing to fear from the
French! Dom Rodrigo, smarting at the snub, resolved on a display of
force; he would occupy the eastern province, known to history as the
Banda Oriental, now Uruguay, as a precaution against any French
landing. He was encouraged in this disastrous venture by Sir Sidney
Smith, who arrived on 17 May that year to command the British
squadron at Rio and who offered not only to cover the expedition
from the sea but to lead the Portuguese troops into battle himself.[7]

On his arrival on 22 July, Lord Strangford was appalled at this
evidence of the admiral's indiscretion. He was spared the embarrassment
of vetoing it by the news that Charles IV of Spain had been cynically
dethroned by Napoleon, who had nominated his brother, Joseph, as
King of Spain in his place. At once Spain had risen in the name
of Charles's son, Ferdinand VII, Dom John's brother-in-law. First
Montevideo, then Buenos Aires declared for the new king. That
did not mean, however, that the two *cabildos* were ready to join in
common action. The Governor of Montevideo believed that the
French captain-general across the river was a secret Napoleonic
partisan; Liniers was for his part convinced that the governor was
in league with the Portuguese. On the evidence of that belief he
deposed him, whereupon the *cabildo* of Montevideo reinstated him.
The British, with their customary impartiality, supplied both ports
freely with 'a source of supplies by which they were virtually enabled
to meet the expenses and exigencies of civil war'.[8]

From such a witch's brew no witch could decently stay away. Dona
Carlota Joaquina, bored by her husband and hating Rio de Janeiro, was
delighted to find a cause to which she could apply her abundant skill for

mischief. This was nothing less than the preservation of her brother's empire. And in this noble task she enrolled an unexpected ally. Between the diminutive, ugly, 33-year-old daughter of Spain and the 44-year-old hero of Acre there was a sudden and powerful attraction, not unlike that which had caused his name to be associated with another unattractive princess, as the lover of Caroline of Brunswick, Princess of Wales. If she became with his help her brother's regent in the Plate, the French could never find a foothold there and the estuary would be open to British trade. Sir Sidney, who spoke enough Portuguese to talk to Dom John and more Spanish to conspire with Dona Carlota, was soon up to his eyes in an intrigue from which he would, if it were successful, emerge as Duke of Montevideo.

The susceptible admiral was the largest but not the only fly to tangle in Dona Carlota's web. The liberals of Buenos Aires began to dream of a constitutional monarchy on the banks of the Plate, a bulwark of ordered progress and liberal principles against the tide of republican anarchy. Sir Sidney Smith stood guarantor for the Spanish infanta. No such dream, however, disturbed Dona Carlota's sleep; there was no place in her conception of Bourbon monarchy for liberal principles. But Lord Strangford, now the representative of a power once more in alliance with the legitimate government of Spain, could allow no adventures likely to disturb the peace and integrity of Spain's colonial possessions.[9] He was convinced that Dom Rodrigo intended to use any excuse to occupy the Banda Oriental and it was his duty to stop him.

Dona Carlota recognized her enemy. She used Smith shamelessly to urge her husband to let her go to Buenos Aires to protect her brother's interests as his vicereine, who, the admiral pronounced naively, 'had the experience, perspicuity of genius and liberality of sentiments' to reconcile all parties.[10] What neither understood was that the Spanish colonies had accepted the Supreme Junta in Seville as the true government of Spain and everything Dona Carlota did and said smacked of a Portuguese takeover. When her agent was arrested in Buenos Aires carrying proposals for her proclamation as regent and for the calling of a Cortes, she stood uncomfortably exposed in a plot to overturn that junta's authority.

Dom John would have been only too happy to get rid of his virago wife, but though Dona Carlota swore that she would sail for the Plate even under the guns of Rio's forts, she sat by her packed trunks and raged in vain. Lord Strangford's veto was too strong for her. Her ally,

Sir Sidney Smith, was recalled in May 1809, at Dom John's request, ventriloquized by the all-powerful envoy, and when the representative of the junta in Seville arrived in Rio in August, Strangford and the prince quickly agreed that the Princess of Brazil should be allowed neither to press her claims to a regency of the Plate nor to set foot on Spanish American soil.

Events took a decisive turn in May 1810. An open *cabildo* in Buenos Aires deposed Liniers and swore fealty to Ferdinand VII but not to the Supreme Junta. Emissaries were sent to Paraguay and to Montevideo to urge a creole alliance for independence. Revolution in Spanish America had begun. Dona Carlota, with a backward look at Isabella of Castile, of whom legend said that she had pledged her jewels to finance Columbus, offered hers as collateral for a loan to Montevideo, which had declared its loyalty to Seville. The new viceroy arrived in February 1811, charged to bring Buenos Aires to heel, but his loyal Spanish garrison was pinned to Montevideo by local farmers, led by a former cattle rustler turned guerrilla captain, José Artigas. On 25 May the viceroy, hoping for Brazilian intervention against the rebels, invited Dona Carlota to join him, provided she first recognized the sovereignty of the Spanish General Cortes. Strangford marched straight into Dom John's box at the opera and said she could not accept. Great Britain had offered to mediate between Spain and her rebellious colonies. Dona Carlota in fury informed the Spanish nation through its junta in Cádiz that her husband intended to annex the Banda Oriental.

The viceroy, who did not much care who saved him as long as he was saved, now asked formally for Portuguese help. On 19 July 1811, the Captain-General of Rio Grande do Sul, Dom Diogo de Souza, protesting that he had no vicereine in his baggage, advanced on Montevideo from two directions. At once the two warring ports closed ranks and made common cause against the invader. It was just what Strangford had wanted to avoid. Not only was British trade with the Plate at risk, but civil war could only impede the greater object of defeating Napoleon. Dona Carlota, for her part, trumpeted to anyone prepared to listen that England had already resolved on the independence of the Spanish colonies, which was why she had been prevented from going to the defence of her brother's realm.[11]

Seventeen years later, countless thousands had died in this forlorn venture to carry Brazil's southern borders to the banks of the River Plate, and the new empire had been brought to the brink of political and economic collapse. The mirage that had inspired it, a Brazil from the Amazon to the Plate, proved as great an illusion as the hope that Portugal in Brazil could have a foreign policy independent of that of Great Britain. Only disarray and civil war among the creole population of the Viceroyalty of the Plate allowed the venture to go on for so long. But all the time it did so, Brazil slipped more and more into client status towards her overmighty ally whose Treaty of Alliance and Friendship had bound the country to it with hoops of Sheffield steel.

5· Brazil Observed, 1811–16

'Aqui não tem nada' (There is nothing here) —
a Brazilian proverb, describing the interior

*'It is never very pleasant to submit to the insolence of men in office,
but to the Brazilians . . . it is nearly intolerable, but the prospect of
wild forests tenanted by beautiful birds, monkeys and alligators will
make any naturalist lick the dust from the feet of a Brazilian'* —
Charles Darwin, Diary (1832)

If Byron had a poor opinion of Strangford's occasional verse, he had
a profound contempt for all the works of Robert Southey. Childe
Harold, however, was on his grand tour when the first volume of
a three-volume *History of Brazil* appeared in 1810, and he was
not called upon to read it. Southey had spent a year in Lisbon
in 1800–1 to recover his health, and he there had at his disposal
the surprisingly comprehensive library of his uncle, chaplain to the
Anglican community in Lisbon, with whom he lodged. He had really
hoped to write a monumental history of Portugal, but in the event the
only sections of this great work to be written were the three volumes
on Brazil, from her discovery down to his own time. The architecture
of such a work was, however, too vast to bear the superstructure of a
greater history of Portugal, enclosing it like an envelope, and though
by 1822 he claimed that he had completed it up to the death of King
Sebastian in 1557, nothing more was written and nothing published.
The *History of Brazil* was a stupendous work enough.

Despite Southey's very correct Protestant attitude to the Church
of Rome and to the superstition of the Mass, the volumes as they
appeared became increasingly a panegyric to the work of the Jesuits.
Their failing struggle to protect the wretched autochthon from the
ravages of Western man became in Southey's hands almost an epic
worthy of Gibbon or Macaulay. Southey thought he had by this

work, the third volume of which appeared in 1819, hard upon his triumphant *The Life of Lord Nelson*, established his claim to be the Herodotus of the New World,[1] but he was an indifferent stylist, and in his haste to complete the work, translated great chunks of turgid Portuguese into turgid English. But on 7 May 1809 he wrote to Walter Savage Landor that 'of all the new states which are arising in the world I think Brazil is likely to be the greatest'.[2] He held out no such hopes for the United States of America.

The future poet laureate had a lively correspondent in Brazil, an Englishman who under the new rules about foreigners owning property had bought a sugar mill on the island of Itamaracá, near Recife. Henry Koster — Henrique Costa to his familiars — was a tough and seasoned traveller, like George Borrow. He had learned Portuguese and was the first foreigner to penetrate and write about the badlands of the north-east, the *sertão*. His *Travels in Brazil* were dedicated to Southey and appeared in 1816. At about the same time that Koster arrived in Recife, the English mineralogist, John Mawe, had made his way from the Plate, looking for a fortune in the wake of Home Popham's disastrous expedition of 1806–7. His hopes dashed in the south, he turned north with a letter of introduction from Dom Domingos de Souza Coutinho in London, and was hired as a consultant to report on the wealth remaining in the Highland Mines. He, like Koster, was a 'first', the first foreigner to visit the mining region with a government commission. Though the Portuguese-language weekly in London accused him of being a smuggler like all the rest, Mawe held to the end that he had really been hired to teach the farmers of Minas Gerais how to make butter. Certainly, in his opinion, cattle farming was likely to be more profitable than goldmining, a point of view he reiterated in his *Travels to the Interior of Brazil*, which appeared in 1821.

The Brazilian Japan was now well on the way to being revealed to a curious world. And the lure of quick profits was not the sole attraction. For years the huge continent had tantalized Europeans whose scepticism about the Munchausen-like narratives of Admiral Byron, the poet's grandfather, was slowly being enlightened by the marvels described by the dourly scientific Humboldt, whose 34-volume account of Spanish America was just beginning to appear. Humboldt had never managed to get to Brazil. Indeed the very same Dom Rodrigo who was now welcoming foreigners had given orders for him to be deported as an undesirable alien if ever he crossed the frontier.

One foreign-born scientist, Wilhelm Sieher, had managed to explore the Amazon basin before 1808, but he had not written anything and was really a collector, a former resident of Portugal in royal service and therefore privileged. To the encyclopedic German-speaking world that Humboldt represented, Brazil was still a closed book, a world within a world, populated by birds, beasts and insects enough to make the world gasp, not to speak of Indians who knew less of the great world than the Caribs who had greeted Columbus. The first explorer to reach the newly opened country was the Hessian baron, Gregor von Langsdorff (1774–1852), who had also been domiciled in Lisbon since early manhood. But in 1803–7 he had taken part in a Russian expedition that had circumnavigated the globe, and the dedication of his botanical findings to the tsar earned him his appointment as Russian consul-general in Rio de Janeiro, where he supplemented his income by growing coffee. His prime duty was to ensure the regular dispatch to St Petersburg of skins, mineral samples and insects. He employed for this purpose two professional collectors, the Frankfurt-born Georg-Wilhelm Freyreiss, and the Prussian Friedrich Sellow, with both of whom he travelled extensively.

A second Hessian baron, also in the employ of the King of Portugal in the Intendancy of Mines and Metals for the *Reino*, arrived in 1810. Wilhelm Ludwig von Eschwege was summoned to carry out John Mawe's recommendations for the revitalization of the extractive industries of Minas Gerais. He spent eleven years in the province, but the childhood sweetheart he married in his forty-sixth year had no desire to make her permanent home at a lead mine on the banks of the Abaete river, and he returned to Portugal, where he published his first work, a geognostic portrait of Brazil. These 'Portuguese' Germans were to travel Brazil extensively until they could be followed by other, sometimes more generously financed, sometimes more gifted, scientists when the European war was over.

The merchants and explorers who descended on Brazil in the first decades of the 19th century all lived on the threshold of the romantic age. They felt the lure of the unknown continent with its legend of El Dorado, an undiscovered Eden where the innocent and uncorrupted Indian lived among vast forests, where mighty rivers protected the secrets of fabled wealth and lost civilizations. Charles Darwin was overwhelmed by what he saw at Salvador da Bahia on

1 March 1832: 'nothing more nor less than a view in the Arabian Nights, with the advantage of reality'.[3] Fact was stranger then fiction, truth almost too rich to tell. Even humble commercial travellers were afflicted by the same illusion that here, at last, was a land in which man was diminished by nature. That nature with which the Portuguese had for three centuries lived at variance now needed to be tamed in the interests of national survival.

To the Europeans who began to see the colony unveiled it was a daunting prospect. As there were no roads outside the towns more dignified than mule tracks, the principal thoroughfares were the rivers, so that a traveller to the interior had to have a firm purpose and a hard seat. Once out of the town it was 'goodbye to the ease and comfort of European life'.[4] His only resource was the mulatto muleteer (or *tropeiro*) who accompanied him and whose reputation for honesty and reliability was high. This was just as well since most Brazilians, like the viceroy who had greeted Captain Cook, 'could not believe that a European would put up with the discomforts of travelling for love of science', so that he was met as often as not by suspicion and hostility.[5] Bivouacking with the mule trains in the open air was often preferable to staying at the occasional inn, which was usually a vermin-ridden barn. Whatever the traveller might have to say about the stupendous beauties of nature, the fantastic range of bird and butterfly life, the unlimited possibilities for development, he had no good word to say for the *carapato* tick that bored into the flesh, for the cloud of mosquitoes that followed him like a canopy or for the rain that fell for days on end and then dripped for more from the dense overhanging foliage.

Benighted travellers could count on hospitality at the Big House, but not on beds, clean linen or hot water. They might dine with their host in the company of old hounds and black toddlers who were fed from the table and fought among the crumbs. Tolerance of filth among finery was bred from years of isolation from advancing civilization elsewhere, protected by a limitless supply of domestic slaves. To symbolize his mandarin aloofness from manual labour, the planter grew his thumb and forefinger nails to prodigious lengths and filed them to a point, either to separate the fibres from the tobacco leaf when he rolled a cheroot or to strum a guitar. His women lived in almost oriental seclusion, addicted to cards and gossip, bone idle and despotic. Frequently pregnant, like many of her slave women on the estate from the same attentions, the planter's wife often slouched round the house 'in a single petticoat over a chemise so loose as to be almost transparent', exposing her fat, obscurely tawny flesh (of which dirt appeared to be a component part), her hair knotted on the top of her head and loaded with 'a profusion of pomatum and powdered tapioca'.[6] She very seldom appeared before strangers. Surrounded by coconut palms, jackfruit trees and tamarinds, a Portuguese from Angola, Goa or Macao could feel at home among the pictured tiles and whitewashed walls, the plates of mango and couscous, the spiced foods, the tea from Chinese porcelain, the Indian fabrics, the cashmeres and all the perfumes of the East. Only the great unpeopled spaces would remind him that he was now in the Far West.

The intrusion of the outside world on the closed life of the planters and farmers was not wholly unwelcome. They had never been much interested in the instruments of Portuguese rule when it was exercised from distant Portugal. They resented the royal inspectors who checked that they did not mix sand with sugar, that their cotton was clean and their tobacco properly cured. They despised the merchants who sold them short and charged them dear, and because these were Portuguese, like their king, they had correspondingly little respect for the monarch whose phantom power was exercised through governors and officers from over the water. Now the phantom lived among them, the fount of favour and repository of power. The *mazombo* could not let the *mascate* enjoy all the benefits of the monarch's presence. Up till now the Brazilian planter had preferred to live on his estate, but now he saw the advantages of a town house if he wanted to walk where power was or if he had a suit to prosper. Dom John's addiction to the *beija- mão* or ceremony of kissing of the royal hand, meant that anyone who could afford the uniform might approach him with any request under the sun. He had a good memory for faces and liked to see suppliants regularly, like the Portuguese who attended every *beija-mão* for a year in case the Prince noticed his absence and his suit suffered.[7] For many the *beija-mão* was the only real instrument of government. Dom John otherwise appeared but briefly in public, and then usually only at the Chapel Royal for a sung mass or at the Opera.

The Brazilian aristocracy of land, too, became immediately interested in titles. On 13 May 1808, Dom John had affirmed the survival of the Portuguese monarchy by resuscitating the ancient Order of the Turret and the Sword, first created by Alfonso the African in the 15th century. He and his heirs were to be the grand masters to the end of the Bragantine line, and on 17 November, the 74th birthday of his mad mother, he made Lord Strangford and Sir

Sidney Smith its first honorary Grand Crosses, the sea captains of the escorting British squadron its first *comendadores*. From among the faithful *fidalguia* he created six new counts with Portuguese titles, among them Dom Rodrigo, to show that despite the French he was still ruler of the *Reino*. He soon found that these titles gave a lot of not always innocent pleasure, particularly when the newly ennobled were persuaded to buy shares in the Bank of Brazil or to make handsome contributions towards the expenses of government. He shrewdly realized that he was buying more than just temporary relief. From the 12th century, when Portugal under the house of Aviz achieved nationhood, the nobility had comprised only 16 *marquesados*, 26 *condados*, 8 *viscondados* and 4 *baronados*. By 1815 Dom John had created a further 28 *marqueses*, 18 *condes*, 16 *viscondes* and 21 barons. On 26 October 1826 the journal *Aurora* calculated that by the year 2555 'when our nobility (now composed of gipsies, slave-traders, counterfeiters and pedlars of bad money) will have reached the same antiquity as the Portuguese nobility of 1808, we shall have no less than 2,385 *marqueses*, 710 *condes*, 1,421 *viscondes* and 1,813 barons'. Before he left Brazil, Dom John had additionally been the fount of 4000 knighthoods, commanderies and Grand Crosses of the Order of Christ and over 2000 of the Orders of São Bento de Aviz and São Tiago.[8] There were also the titles of *conselheiro* (carrying more prestige but little more significance than 'By Appointment to Her Majesty the Queen'), given even to goldsmiths who advised the palace on its gilt furniture. In the scramble for honours there was 'no species of tyranny which was not put into active force nor any degradation which was not cheerfully submitted to . . . The gratification of their hopes was in every instance accompanied by an instant change in their standard of living.'[9]

A new urban class, too, was to be born of the union of the children of Brazilian minor government officers, tax-collectors and custom-house officials and of Portuguese functionaries, traders, merchants and carpetbaggers who flocked into the colony on Dom John's coat tails. The newly-weds set up in business as moneylenders, conveyancers and traders in slaves, and their children were to become the brokers in coffee and sugar, the bankers and commission agents of the young empire. In three generations a new city aristocrat, 'a gold chain about his neck, silk hat, tiled mansion, luxurious carriage, eating imported delicacies', had emerged to compete for power with the old plantocracy.[10]

In the short run, however, the regent's freedom with honours helped the crown to purchase the loyalty of the Brazilian-born *senadores da câmara*, the privileged members of the local governor's councils; it flattered the old plantocracy and gave respectability to men whose grandparents had indulged in the most infamous trade in history. It bound *mazombo* to *mascate*, creole to *reinol*, in a common commitment to stability and resistance to change. Despite the old wealth of the Portuguese merchants and the new wealth of the Brazilian bourgeoisie, despite, too, the debts and mortgages with which the planters were encumbered, power was not to leave their hands for over half a century. Self-sufficient on their sugar, cotton, and later coffee plantations and protected by their unpaid labour force (of which a replacement supply did not dry up until 1850) they survived the post-war depression better than the merchants and bankers. They preserved their right to be the ruling class of the new empire that was to be born from the old colony. Only in the late 19th century was that political dominance successfully challenged by the new industrial entrepreneurs, the coffee barons of São Paulo and their brokers in Rio de Janeiro. Before that the old Portuguese titles had given way to an almanac of names that even the Brontë children, composing their Legends of Angria, could not have dreamed of, as *mazombo* planters became counts, viscounts and barons of Rio Seco, Cairú, Abaete, Baependi, Barbacena, Iguapé, Itanhaem, Jequitininhona and Jundiaí.

Were those precocious children, far away in the gaunt parsonage at Haworth, thinking of Brazil as they wrote their adolescent novels? Was the saturnine and sultry Angrian, by name Zamorna, who made his first appearance from that wind-swept Yorkshire village in 1834, a portrait inspired by the book of a fellow Irish clergyman which the perpetual curate of Haworth may well have bought? The Reverend Robert Walsh produced his *Notes of Brazil* in 1830. The Angrian capital, Adrianopolis, is a city in the tropics (believed to be West Africa since the children had definitely read Mungo Park), but it reads very like the Rio de Janeiro described by Walsh. Charlotte's Byronic hero, Zamorna, had a remarkable living prototype in the person of Dom John's eldest son, Dom Pedro I, Emperor of Brazil; and the main square in Adrianopolis, Saldanha Park, bore a close resemblance to the Campo Sant'Ana, the principal open square of the capital where most of the great events of the day were celebrated. Zamorna's palace, a tropical Versailles, reads very like the country farm which Dom John turned into a royal residence.

It lay where the Bico de Papagaio, the Parrot's Beak, known to English sailors as Lord Hood's nose, rushed down to the waters of the bay. The former viceroy's palace, 'that miserable abode of royalty', was on the steaming waterfront hemmed in by hills and as hot as a punchbowl.[11] Dom John preferred to spend the day (he always slept within call of his mother in her convent while she was alive) in the fresher airs of St Christopher (São Cristovão). The palace that grew on the slope was approached (and still is) through a replica of the archway at Syon House on the banks of the Thames, erected by the Duke of Northumberland's master-builder. It soon became the usual set of ceremonial rooms, looking down on a landscaped view, with endless back stairs where the courtiers who could not stomach Dom John's constant table of boiled chicken, smoked sausage and rice, set up their own stoves and filled the corridors with the smells of cooking. The court, while the palace was building, took over a former Jesuit house at Santa Cruz and lived a crude and comfortless existence like the inmates of a British public school. Visitors were unduly conscious of hundreds of unmade beds and processions of slaves emptying chamberpots into the nearest stream. As the estate was also used for the compulsory pasturage (at a fee which contributed to the household expenses) of cattle that had hoofed it from the southern *campos* and needed fattening for the abattoir, it resembled a huge livestock market. Dom John also had a hunting lodge on a near-by island chiefly remarkable for a Russian bear, a gift from the tsar, which roamed freely where the international airport now receives Aeroflot. These royal abodes were a far cry from the gilded splendours of Mafra and Queluz, but Dom John was happy enough with them, and when he was offered, by a French architect, a palace like the one he had built for Jerome Bonaparte at Wilhemshöhe, near Kassel in Germany, the prince was in no hurry to accept.[12]

Dom John was to stay in Brazil longer than anyone expected when he finally decided in 1807 that he should go there. The news of Masséna's headlong retreat from before the lines of Torres Vedras was greeted with rapture by the Portuguese court, which immediately rejoiced at the prospect of an early return. General Wellesley was elevated from Count of Vimiero to Marquis of Torres Vedras, and the sun shone again on the fortunes of Portugal. But Dom John was in no hurry to go back to Lisbon. He liked the warm, luxurious climate, the distance from danger, the gentle and cheerful black slaves, the absence of crisis. He was content to leave foreign policy to the 29-year-old Lord Strangford, whose piercing blue eyes and glacial calm had an almost hypnotic effect on him, and the governance of the realm to Dom Rodrigo, Count of Linhares, while he escaped to his music.

There had been an opera house in Rio de Janeiro since 1776, but it was far too poky to please so fastidious a monarch, who ordered it to be rebuilt as a replica of São Carlos in Lisbon and financed by a public lottery. A resident castrato, Signor Faschiotti, and his wife were the stars, and Madame Sabini, *la seconda soprano*, was as fat as the *primo tenore*, Signor Capanica, was thin. A French ballet master, Maître Lacombe, and a pair of Parisian dancers, Monsieur and Madame Toussaint, presided over a corps of Venuses 'not exactly of our European tint'.[13] Dom John did not think much of the opera on arrival, but he was astonished by the *Te Deum* that greeted him in the cathedral. Its composer and maestro were a mulatto deacon, José Maurício Nunes Garcia, whom he instantly appointed inspector of music. When the Faschiotti, Capanica and Sabini sang Pergolesi, Gluck and José Maurício at the Capela Real, Dom John felt that the patriarchal church in Lisbon could have done no better.

The ascendancy of José Maurício was soon to be challenged by Dom John's former musical favourite, Marcos Antônio Portugal. The prolific composer of operas, known in Europe as 'Il Portogallo', had not followed his master across the Atlantic but stayed to greet the French, from whom he had higher expectations. Disappointed by their barbarous flight from Lisbon, he took sail penitently for Rio, where Dom John instantly forgave him and appointed him *mestre de capela*. Il Portogallo was appalled to discover a more talented composer already *in situ* whom he recognized as a rival to be destroyed. There was nothing he was not prepared to do to win the favour of his complaisant master, even writing operas for the slaves to perform at Santa Cruz. He was able to prevent José Maurício from becoming director of the Royal Opera but he failed to climb 'up the ladder of do re mi to become Baron Tuning Fork'.[14]

For a sterner rival appeared as soon as the war was over, when Talleyrand, perhaps the first diplomat to understand the importance of cultural diplomacy, sent Dom John a court composer at his own expense. This was Sigismund Neukomm, Haydn's favourite pupil and a friend of Cherubini. He had been the tsar's musical director and then joined Talleyrand's household, from which he organized the music at the Congress of Vienna. Now he became music tutor to the

Infante Dom Pedro and his sister, Maria Isabel. He supervised the first South American performance of Haydn's *Creation* and Mozart's Requiem Mass under the baton, not of Il Portogallo, but of José Maurício. The venom and hatred of the snubbed maestro was now totally dedicated to the fall of the Austrian intruder, but Neukomm, who was to dazzle the Birmingham Festival in 1834 and for a brief and tantalizing moment seemed about to join the immortals, was only, in fact, toppled into a musical limbo by the meteoric appearance of Felix Mendelssohn. His most interesting remains are an arrangement of *modinhas* improvised by another mulatto, the illiterate Joaquim Manoel, the first time that folk music from the new world was heard in the drawing rooms of the old.[15] José Maurício, Marcos Portugal and Sigismund Neukomm all had a hand in the musical formation of the heir to the throne, Dom Pedro, who played the clarinet in the orchestra for Il Portogallo's slave operas and who conducted his own slave band when emperor. His reputation was more royal than real, but he did compose two national anthems: the first in a few minutes between 5.30 and 9.00 on the day he proclaimed Brazilian independence, and which remained the National Hymn until his own abdication; the second for Portugal, composed in 1833 and only abandoned with the monarchy in 1910.

Dona Carlota was interested neither in music nor in Brazil and she nourished for Lord Strangford some of the feelings that Il Portogallo had for the mulatto inspector of music. When he refused to dismount on her appearance in the streets, but merely doffed his hat, she ordered the cadets of her escort to unhorse him on the next occasion at the point of the sword. As a dry run they threatened the newly arrived envoy from the United States, Thomas Sumter Jr, who coolly drew his pistols and offered to shoot the first man to lay hands on the representative of a friendly power. Dom John, shocked at this incident, wisely changed the protocol and only required foreign envoys to bare their heads at the approach of royalty. And with kindly forethought he also decreed that slaves carrying loads on their heads need only stand still and not put their loads down, after which they were often unable to get them up again.[16]

Apart from these personal unpleasantnesses, little disturbed Dom John's serenity in Rio de Janeiro. The only cloud, the size of a man's hand, hung over the south. Dom Rodrigo could not bring himself to abandon his Uruguayan adventure without trying one more throw. Though Dom John formally promised to disengage from the Banda

Oriental, Diogo de Souza's orders were to prevent reprisals against Brazilian territory by keeping a military presence in the Spanish province.[17] But before he could shake the dice, Dom Rodrigo was dead, on 26 January 1812, so suddenly that he never received the last rites of the Church.

He was only 56 and in full vigour, too vigorous perhaps for the unfamiliar tropics. Seldom idle, his head buzzed with plans, his office with decrees, so that Dona Carlota dubbed him Dr Bedlam ('Dr Barafunda'). His ambition was to be a great, even unforgettable, reformer like his godfather, Pombal, but he was so busy issuing orders and constructing systems that he did not realize that some of them were contradictory and that many existed only on paper. He fussed over detail, like uniforms and regimental organization, and his curriculum for the Military Academy was so complete that if adequately taught every Brazilian officer would have been a polymath. He had the Portuguese love of paper to a fault, but he did manage to make distances, Indians and disease in Brazil all seem less formidable. Formerly the traffic from the interior had crossed thousands of miles by a complicated conjunction of rivers. By 1812 it came to the capital by newly cut mule tracks. His Junta for the Navigation of the Rio Doce had tamed the horrendous Botocudo tribe, and his military hospital in Rio had sent the first Brazilian-trained doctors into the outback. He died the day after Dom John decreed the establishment of a national laboratory. By his insistence on the development of Brazil's natural resources, he set her economy for the next 150 years. His southern adventure nearly cost Brazil her throne and unity, but the damage he did to the old colonial fabric by reproducing the apparatus of government within the colony was a positive stimulus to the Brazilians to master their own land. He deserved but does not have a monument in Rio de Janeiro, but he has given his name to a road-head in Espirito Santo, in Botocudo country.

There was no one really to replace him. His brother, Domingos, preferred to stay in London. Dom John selected another of the councillors of state who had supported the flight to Brazil, José Almeida de Castro, but though he feared that the 'entire toleration of the Protestant religion was all that was wanted to render Brazil an English colony', he did not live long enough to act on his fears.[18] He died on 18 January 1813, debauched, according to the liverish royal librarian, by daily intercourse with adolescent catamites. Strangford went to the opera in gala dress to celebrate.[19] José Almeida was replaced by the third person of the orological trinity, the Marques, formerly Conde, de Aguiar. 'Crushed like a toad under the foot of the bull,' he was more interested in poetry than the affairs or spoils of office, so that when he too died in that month fatal for secretaries of state, January 1817, his widow had scarcely enough money to bury him.[20] The translator of Camões had no time for the translator of Pope. 'The ignorance of the individuals composing this court,' Strangford wrote to Castlereagh on 20 February 1814, 'is such that scarcely one among them . . . is capable of writing an ordinary letter.'[21] Certainly he had never succeeded in persuading anyone to give attention to the one remaining item of his list of objectives — the abolition of the slave-trade with Africa.

6· Black Gold

'Brazil has the body of America and the soul of Africa' —
Antônio Vieira, 1608-97

'The Africans . . . bear the mark of the royal crown on their breasts
which denotes that they have undergone the ceremony of baptism
and likewise that the King's duty has been paid on them' —
Henry Koster, *Travels in Brazil* (1816)

George Canning, as British secretary of state, had refused to let
Dom John relegate the abolition of the slave-trade to a secret
codicil of the draft Treaty of Commerce and Alliance which he
ratified on 30 February 1809, so that in 1810 the Portuguese had
found themselves publicly committed to abolish the traffic with all
ports not in Portuguese hands. Lord Strangford never wavered in
his conviction that the complete abolition of the trade was all that
was needed to bring Portugal into line with civilized nations, but he
would have found very few Brazilians to agree with him. For, almost
to a man, from the *mazombo* planter to the free mulatto artisan, from
the *mameluco* overseer to the *cafuzo* prospector, they believed that the
wealth and prosperity of the country depended on the *braços* or arms of
the black slave. Nothing was to cloud relations with the indispensable
ally more than Britain's insistence that her help and protection could
only be secured by an undertaking to cut off the traffic in slaves from
Africa. An enormous expenditure of political and moral energy was
to be spent by successive Portuguese and Brazilian governments in
averting that evil day. For when William Wilberforce called Brazil
'the very child and champion of the slave-trade, nay, the slave-trade
personified', he spoke nothing less than the truth.

Sugar had been at the bottom of it. The crop's cultivation required
strong and persistent labour, and the native Indian, robust enough
before the cruelties of nature, wilted and died from the effects of

organized labour. Furthermore he was not to be enslaved, only to be put to work 'voluntarily', unless he was a condemned criminal. Altogether Indians were unreliable. A very satisfactory substitute could, however, be had from Africa, and after the Dutch had been expelled from Pernambuco in 1654 profits from the sale of sugar soon became big enough to start capitalizing that regular trade in human beings which was to provide most of Brazil's manual labour for 200 years. When the sugar boom began to decline, the discovery of gold kept the demand for *braços* steady, and when gold ran out in turn, the black revolution in Haiti restored the demand for sugar from Brazilian plantations. By the end of the 18th century they could not import slaves fast enough, and by 1800 various estimates believed that up to half the entire population of the colony lived and worked in bondage. Just how many this represented is impossible to calculate, since such censuses as there were did not distinguish slave from free among the black and half-black population and no one can be quite sure what the total population of the colony was. But it could mean that there were nearly a million slaves in Brazil. Slaves certainly greatly outnumbered free men, white, black and mulatto, in Maranhão, Pernambuco, Bahia and Minas Gerais, and there was scarcely a family north and west of Rio de Janeiro that did not own at least one as a domestic.[1]

The British had abolished their own trade in 1807 and expected their obedient ally to follow at once. But Dom John knew that so radical an action in a state totally unprepared for it was unthinkable. He had to acknowledge in the treaty 'the disadvantage of introducing and continuously renewing a foreign and factitious population', but he was able to confine immediate action to banning the trade in slaves from all African ports north of the equator since they were not in Portuguese hands and so part of the Portuguese empire. But both he and his son were able to keep the trade going within the Portuguese empire for another 40 years, so that the object for which Lord Strangford strove in vain was only accomplished in 1850.

There was no part of the Brazilian economy which did not depend on slaves, for no one who was not a slave would labour in the fields, in the mines or in the house, not even former slaves who had acquired freedom. Whites would rather be beggars, thieves, even soldiers, than do any manual work. Agricultural science as such was unknown and there had barely been any change in farming practice for 300 years. Slash and burn was the method used to open new land, which, once exhausted, was abandoned. Land was, after all, not in short supply.

The large estates were mainly under-farmed and in 1817 the most
sophisticated rural instrument one British visitor observed in use was
a water-driven pestle for grinding manioc flour. Even this he thought
was derived from the Indians.[2] Farmers had no need for labour-saving
devices. It was not only cheaper, but also morally acceptable, to buy
more slaves.

The authority for that surprising opinion was none other than
the founder of the most advanced school of learning in the colony,
the seminary at Olinda, near Recife — advanced because, from its
inception in 1800, it boasted chairs in physics, chemistry, mineralogy,
botany and drawing in order to form 'generations of priests and
explorers who at the same time would undertake the cure of souls and
open up the vegetable and mineral wealth of their parishes'.[3] Bishop
Azeredo Coutinho published his *Analyse sur la Justice du Commerce des
Esclaves de la Côte d'Afrique* in 1798. An English translation followed in
1807, a Portuguese edition the following year. It was by way of being
a bestseller, and its purpose was to refute the arguments of the British
abolitionists, about whose secret motives the good bishop was gravely
suspicious. In his view, life on the plantations under Christian masters
was preferable to pagan darkness in Africa. Even if it were not — and
he had to admit that there were owners who abused their slaves
despite the humane laws that governed their treatment — many slaves
had been sold by their (legitimate) native governments as convicted
malefactors and rebels and had forfeited any right to civil liberty in
their own lands. Bishop Azeredo could not defend the enslavement of
innocent members of such miscreant families, the wives and children;
he could only encourage those enslaved to labour diligently for their
redemption and commend them to the good nature of their owners.[4]
His optimistic faith in that good nature was sadly misplaced.

Nearly three centuries of the brutalizing and licentious effects of
slavery upon the free population, only loosely if at all fettered by
Christian precept, had largely bred indifference to a slave's lot. He
was, after all, only a 'piece' (*peça*) of property with much the same
rights as a horse or a cow and with as limited a working life. He
was cheaper to replace than to preserve. By the end of the 18th
century, a plantation slave did well to survive seven years and a miner
was worked out in 12.[5] In 1817, slave-owners in Pernambuco who
preferred Brazilian-born slaves (*crioulos*) found it almost impossible
to buy them.[6] Only when new slaves were no longer imported did a
slave's working life extend to something like 20 to 30 years.[7]

The prelude to this life, the journey across the middle passage in a *tumbeiro* or floating hearse (the familiar nickname for a slaver), had no parallel in any of the circles of Dante's Hell. In 1829, the Reverend Robert Walsh boarded the *Veloz*, suspected of shipping slaves from the, by then, illegal Costa da Mina, mainly Nigeria and Dahomey. The Royal Navy regulars who intercepted her thought she was a better slaver than most, but even she carried 336 men and 226 women crammed below decks so closely that they sat between each others' legs, unable to change their position by day or by night. The space between decks was divided into two compartments both 3 feet 3 inches high; the men were squashed into an area 40 feet by 21, the women into 16 feet by 18. The men had some 23 inches within which to move, even for excretion; the women, many of them pregnant, had 13. When the holds were cleared, small children were found lying up against the sides in a state of torpor, more dead than alive. On other slavers, the men were often fettered by neck and ankle to a shelf only 18 inches high, not even the width of their shoulders, and here they lay for the 35 to 50 days it took to cross the Atlantic. There was drinking water on board the *Veloz*. Another slaver shipped from Bahia with kegs of salt water for ballast and forgot to change it for fresh on the homeward journey. Not a slave survived that voyage. Even on the *Veloz* 55 had already died and been thrown overboard, and six more had typhus fever.[8] In the latter days of the trade, cruisers searching for illegal slavers averred that if you had not already identified one from its train of waiting sharks, you could smell it from several miles to leeward.

The legal freight was five slaves for every two tons for slavers up to 201 tons; thereafter it was one slave for every additional ton. Few freighters observed the rules. Cargoes were often one tenth male, one fifth women from ages 18 to 25, and the rest were children of both sexes from 7 to 15.[9] These were the survivors. How many had been shipped from the port of origin it was often impossible to tell. When the trade became illegal, conditions worsened still further. The heat, rising to 120 degrees Fahrenheit in the hold, the unfamiliar diet of salt beef and black beans, induced dysentery, and lack of water drove cargoes mad. Men strangled their neighbours, women put out each others' eyes. The shrieks of the dying could sound like a riot, whereupon the crew would open the hatches and fire indiscriminately into the hold. A sober estimate put the loss of life on a *tumbeiro* at between a quarter and a third of the cargo, even though healthy slaves had been shipped in the first place. As these illegal slaves fetched correspondingly higher prices, slavers were over-crammed with men, women and children in the expectation that the survivors would fetch sufficiently high prices to compensate for the dead.

Before 1831, when the traffic in slaves was declared illegal with any port anywhere in the world, the sale of newly arrived slaves was a daily feature of life in the ports of Brazil. They were usually sold quickly as lots to the local dealer. At times of great demand, particularly after 1831, the new arrivals rarely observed quarantine. This wise health regulation — considering what slaves had been exposed to from the moment of their consignment to the slave-trader in their native Africa — meant that shippers could not turn their ships round quickly to fetch new cargoes. The dealer, who 'dealt out human beings to their customers with as much sensibility and sang-froid as they would British goods', then exposed them, naked or semi-naked, in his barracoon, their limbs glistening from the oil rubbed on their skin to remove the white scurf which covered them as a result of the unspeakable crossing and the salt diet.[10] Often the newly arrived slave was pathetically anxious to be bought and would bare his teeth in a smile so that potential buyers could judge his age, and flex his muscles to show that he was fit. An intending purchaser examined 'the mere animal capability without the remotest inquiry into the moral quality as if he were buying a dog or a mule'.[11] Slaves were sold as separate 'pieces': a *peça da India* was a black man in his prime, between 15 and 25 years old. Three black women, aged 5 to 15 or 25 to 35, counted as two 'pieces', and two males under 8 or over 35 counted as one. Slaves over 45 were valued separately and children at the breast were sold with their mothers at no extra charge. In the first decade of the 19th century, a 'piece' in good working condition might cost the equivalent of between £20 and £40, not a great deal more than an ox or a horse. In the 1820s this price had risen to £70. In 1819 a skilled and experienced slave — not a new arrival — could cost up to £200.[12]

After 1831, when all imported slaves were illegal, selling became clandestine. Cargoes were landed at night or in deserted creeks, sold in rapid auctions, and assimilated to resident slaves before they could be identified. Slave-running became so prevalent that the market was over-supplied and the price of a 'piece' fell below that he could fetch before the trade was abolished. Yet, despite the almost universal tolerance of slavery, slave-dealing was never considered socially acceptable. Many of the dealers were gipsies who had been deported to Brazil in droves during the 18th century in periodic clean-up operations. They had quickly found farming uncongenial and become tinkers and muleteers. It was a short step from dealing in horseflesh to dealing in human beings, and the French artist Debret has immortalized two overfed gipsy women taking their alfresco breakfast in the courtyard of a large house in Rio, crowded with slaves waiting for sale, undeterred by a savage whipping taking place only a few yards from them.[13]

Most of the African-born slaves were required for the plantations. Domestic and town slaves were usually *crioulos*, Brazilian-born, requiring less supervision. Chained neck to neck like Jacob Varley's cash-boxes, the newly sold slaves were marched, often over great distances, to their plantation. There they were put in charge of an experienced slave who instructed them, pretty perfunctorily, in the Portuguese language, Christian doctrine and their job. As baptized slaves tended to hold pagans in great contempt, the catechumen was eager enough to pass an elementary examination in his new faith from a priest more often than not deprived of his faculties for disciplinary offences but allowed to earn a stipend as a catechist. Slaves already baptized, like those from Angola and Mozambique, were confirmed. As instruction seldom went beyond the sketchiest account of Christianity, tribal animism and fetishism survived to form the basis of the syncretism which today forms the religious conviction of the greater part of the Brazilian population.[14]

The role of the church in the slave system was equivocal at best, for it had corrupted itself by owning slaves. Henry Koster, no friend of priests, thought that the church's belief that making good Christians of slaves was a greater good than the evil of slavery lined it up on the side of generosity and mercy. The plantation chaplain could sometimes persuade a reluctant owner to accept redemption money when it was offered, and to patronize the Christian marriage of his slaves, after which, on the north-eastern plantations particularly, he might feel a seigneurial obligation not to sell them apart.[15] To the up and coming coffee planter in the Southern Paraíba valley, such sentimentality was simply not business-like. 'A conscientious confessor should instil in the slave love for work and blind obedience to his masters and those who controlled him.'[16]

By and large church-owned slaves were *crioulos* and as a result better treated; the Benedictines and Carmelites allowed no savage punishments on their estates. But the church did not generally manumit its slaves; the religious preferred to evade judgement on the trade by not buying new slaves. So many were the by-blows of white owners that the slaves of the Benedictines were known as 'white slaves'. Even so, the order did not proceed to a general emancipation until 1873, followed by the Franciscans in 1877.[17] For urban slaves, the church was less helpful than the black religious brotherhoods, which, in cities like Salvador, could be a powerful agency in the redemption of slaves, each redeemed member working for the redemption of another slave. Well organized and often rich, the fraternities could from time to time enforce customary law on the treatment of slaves and appeal to the authorities with a collective strength individual slaves could never command.[18]

By law (and custom) slaves were to observe religious holidays which, with Sundays, might amount to some 100 days a year, the 30 major feasts comparing well to the four permitted in the British West Indies.[19] Very few slaves, however, enjoyed such opportunities for leisure. Indeed, during seed-time and harvest, the plantation chaplain, if there were one, might just be influential enough to secure them an hour off on Sunday for mass. Plantation slaves could in such spare time as they were allowed work their own allotments or tend their own animals, growing food to supplement their basic diet of manioc flour, jerked beef and black beans, or to sell towards their redemption money. A skilled slave in a sugar-mill, however, could expect little free time, for he was too valuable a 'piece', and frugal though he might be he could never earn enough money to buy his freedom, even were his owner to accept his indemnity. By law, if a slave could offer his owner either his purchase price or his current market price, whichever was the higher, he must be freed. But the law could not be enforced. If a slave found another buyer, he could legally insist on being bought, but there were few people ready either to value or to buy a discontented slave and so both annoy a fellow white and purchase a pack of trouble.[20]

In the patriarchal north-east, where there was more feeling for ancestral land and duties, owners were known to behave almost humanely, even sentimentally, towards their slaves.[21] Faithful domestics and concubines might be freed at the end of their useful lives, and a newly born love-child might be redeemed at the font. But freedom could never be taken for final. It could be revoked for an act of 'ingratitude' and 'uppity niggers' were no more tolerated in Brazil than in the United States of America. Conditions were usually harsher for the slaves of newly arrived Europeans in search of a quick fortune, especially from mining. The harshest conditions of all were to be experienced on the coffee plantations of the south, where none of the patriarchal conventions applied. A slave was a unit of productive work, not a human being; even love-children were treated like any other slave, white half-brothers treating their father's by-blows with particular ferocity, often selling them out of sight to other owners. Slaves who were married in slavery could be sold away from their spouses and their children away from both. Only in 1869, two years before the Law of Free Birth, was it made actually illegal to sell a child under 15 away from its mother. To be fair, in so far as it is possible to be fair to a system so palpably unfair, no slave society gave slaves any right to the company of their wives or children, who were 'pieces' like their husbands or fathers. The church tried to encourage Christian marriage among slaves, but, as the Founder had foreseen, Christian precept usually lost in the confrontation with mammon.[22]

From early colonial times, there had always been a place for the freed slave. Farmers and planters needed some kind of tied labour between a white immigrant and a black or Indian slave, able to carry out essential tasks for which a slave could not be used. These included clearing Indians from the land, overseeing slaves, tracking down runaways and stock-raising, for which slaves could not be trusted with guns, horses, whips and lassos. The *bandeirantes*, too, had opened up the interior with freed men, usually mulattos, often their own offspring, and to their number had been added the *pretos da ganha* or *escravos da rua*, slaves who were hired out for contract work by their owners. Some of these, like the Rio custom-house porters who were all owned by custom-house officials and did very well at the dockside (which is one reason why their owners objected to the introduction of an English crane), were able to pocket enough tips and commissions to join a confraternity, save up their purchase price and redeem themselves.[23] Some, not a great number, had been freed for good service by generous owners. These occasional manumissions, however, could not account for all the free blacks and half-blacks in the colony, estimated at equal in number to the whites. Most of these were probably the offspring of slaves who had escaped into the anonymity of the towns and acquired freedom because no one could establish any claim to them as slaves.

Between them the black and half-black freedmen provided most of the technical skills in the colony. Many of them had bought slaves of their own and set up as masons, tailors, cobblers, leeches, laundrymen, barbers, bakers and cooks. The capital's first newspaper employed black typesetters and printers. The girls apprenticed themselves to French dressmakers as cutters and stitchers and to Italian pastrycooks as cake-makers and then set up in business on their own. In the north and north-east, mulattos formed a growing proportion of the free urban population, providing the larger part of the rank-and-file militia and penetrating the professions, including the church.[24] A successful mulatto was white. In 1813, Henry Koster asked his servant if the captain-major of the local militia was not a mulatto. 'He was,' came the answer, 'but he isn't now. How can the *capitão-mor* be a mulatto man?'[25] It was often difficult to know when a man was not white, and impolitic to ask, for somewhere in most *mazombo* ancestry there was a slave or Indian woman. The rich took their wives from Portugal more as a symbol of status and exclusive breeding, for mulatta wives were acceptable, often beautiful and usually fecund. Only the *fidalgos*, or well-born, found it hard to acknowledge mulatta wives, like Fernando Delgado, Governor of Goiás, who took his own life on recall to Portugal because his mulatta mistress would only accompany him as his lawful wife and the wretched man could not bring himself either to leave or to marry her.[26] For a non-white, whiteness was the dream. Rich mulattos offered handsome dowries with their daughters, both attractive to newly arrived Portuguese, and liberals like Brazil's first chief minister, José Bonifácio de Andrada, looked forward to a time when the black population was wholly bleached by miscegenation. The birth-rate among slaves was low and at any one time there were probably four times as many male as female slaves so that an unrenewed population must surely die out in time.[27] Why did it not happen?

7· The Trade Ends

'*Portugal and Spain, England and France, Wellington, Bonaparte and the Prince may all go headlong to the shades provided their darling traffic — the subject of their waking and sleeping dreams — be but permitted to remain*' —

Lieutenant James Prior, RN, 1813

'*The moment has not come for us to abandon the importation of slaves, for though it is an evil, it is a lesser evil than not importing them*' —

Brigadier Raimundo José Cunha Matos, member for Goiás on the Commissão de Diplomacia, June 1827

The mulatization of Brazil did not happen as José Bonifácio had hoped. The low birth-rate among slaves provided the strongest incentive to continue the importation of slaves by hook or by crook. For most owners were convinced that if they did not, the slave population would die out in 20 years. Given this conviction, it was strange that no concerted effort was made to encourage owners to breed slaves, but this did not start to happen until the supply of new slaves began to dry up. A major deterrent to such a practice was the fearsome example of Haiti, ravaged from 1791 to 1820, first by a slave rebellion, then by civil war between creole blacks and mulattos. While Brazilian slaves were predominantly new arrivals from different African ports and belonged to a wide variety of kinships, tribes and language groups, the chances of a rebellious combination were slim. This might not be true if the slave-force were predominantly Brazilian-born. Most of the plantation slaves came from the sub-equatorial areas of the Lower Congo and Angola, the slave-ports of Cabinda, Santo Antônio do Zaire, São Paulo de Luanda and São Felipe de Benguela. Others came from Mozambique, but they were the least prized, being small and often so homesick that they died. In the 1820s they were sold in lots of one or two hundred on generous credit terms to poorer planters in the north and north-east. In four years most of them were dead.[1]

The slaves most prized for hard work and endurance were the West Africans from the Costa da Mina, of whom there had been a steady importation into Salvador since the 1770s, paid for by snuff and the sweet Bahian shag which was so popular with Nigerian and Dahomean middlemen. These slaves were known from their place of origin. The most numerous were the Yoruba-speaking Nagôs from Lagos and the coastal area (*Nagô* being the name they gave their local tongue). From Dahomey came the Gegês, and from the Hausa-speaking areas of the north, the Malês, mostly Muslims. Most of them were casualties of Muslim jihads or tribal wars. Some could read Arabic and a few of the Malês were mullahs. As normally not one in a thousand slaves could read or write, this was a portentous distinction.[2] Christianity sat very lightly on the pagan and animist Nagôs, and among the Muslims in Salvador active cells inspired a contempt for their pagan and Christian fellow-slaves and a religious hatred of their masters. The Nigerians were the least submissive but most productive slaves, and they were frequently used as *pretos da ganha* or contract workers. In 1809 the Governor of Bahia was worried about the 8000 or so of warrior stock who had been shipped to Salvador in the previous five years, victims of the great Fulani jihad of 1804. This concentration of slaves of the same tribe, language and religion did, in 1807, 1814 and 1816, lead to trouble which required repressive action by the militia, and as late as 1835 the cavalry had to fight a pitched battle against a well-armed, aggressively led cohort of Nagô slaves who planned to seize the arsenal, master the city and escape to Africa by sea.[3]

They were too ambitious, for these risings and the numerous affrays between bands of slaves and the militia never seriously challenged the forces of repression. But memories were long and Brazilians had not forgotten the famous Republic of Palmares, which survived nearly 60 years in the Pernambuco *mato*, where an organized society of runaway slaves only succumbed in 1694, after a three-year siege and a three-week bombardment by regular troops. None of the *quilombos* or runaway havens, which, as the century progressed, drew nearer to every major city, enjoyed so fearsome a reputation. By 1820, however, one did not have to walk very far out of Rio de Janeiro to meet gangs of runaway slaves rather as travellers met banditti in the Roman *campagna*. Few travellers reported any trouble. A resolute act of defiance usually frightened off these generally timid creatures, and that redoubtable Scots widow, Maria Graham, who first came to Brazil as the wife of a sea-captain and later as governess of the heiress to the Portuguese crown, frightened off her runaway burglar with a kitchen knife.[4] The expense of rounding up runaway slaves and the increasing reluctance of the militia to do it were used as a further argument for maintaining the slave-trade, but walkers in the hills round the capital frequently met the bush-captain or *capitão do mato*, himself a free black or a mulatto, and his gang of slaves combing the hillsides for runaways.

Brazilian owners, especially in the towns, took constant pains to keep their slaves under lock and key and most houses resembled domestic fortresses as a result. One owner in Rio de Janeiro insisted that his slaves pace up and down the corridors all night so that they could not slip away unnoticed. Escape was in fact not too difficult, especially as in the towns a slave could merge into a relatively large and amorphous body of free blacks, many of whom had been free for generations, and in the interior there was a lot of bush or forest into which to escape. One runaway stayed away undetected for so long that he managed to buy six slaves of his own and put them out to contract labour. Recognized in an evil moment by his former owner, he offered him four of his slaves in return for liberty, but his master successfully claimed possession not only of his former slave but of the other six as well.[5]

Once recovered, a slave could only expect savage punishment. First he was publicly whipped; then he was fitted with an iron collar or *gancho* with two steel prongs designed both to identify a slave who had run away and to impede flight if he ever tried again. Repeated runaways could be shackled with chains to an iron ball, light enough to enable them to go about their business but too heavy for rapid movement. Even small children might be chained to blocks of wood weighing five to six pounds. Nobody walking about the towns could go far without noticing the agents of discipline, for such police services as there were largely existed to recapture runaway or punish refractory slaves.

The Reverend Robert Walsh 'never walked through the streets of Rio [in 1828] but some house did not present to me the semblance of a bridewell, with the moans and cries of the sufferers and the sounds of whips and scourges within announced to me that a corporal punishment was being inflicted'.[6] No household was without its *palmatória*, a wooden paddle-bat bored with holes to strike the upturned palm. Even the mild and constipated librarian who had been so catty about Almeida de Castro was sure that his slave, excellent though he was, and a loyal servant, needed a few blows with it from time to time, just to keep him up to the mark and to encourage the others.[7] In every town square the *pelourinho* or whipping-post had been worn smooth by the writhing of flogged slaves. The calaboose was open day and night to receive slaves for punishment at their owners' request. Fifty to a hundred lashes were normal for attempted escape from servitude, for robbery or for assault, and the fee went to provide civic amenities like the public promenade built along Rio's sea front in the 1780s. Back and buttocks bared, the offender was tied to the pillar and the *carrasco* or public flogger, often a slave himself, laid it on with a whip made from seven or eight strips of dried leather. A skilful *carrasco* drew blood at the third stroke, and as the lash grew soggy with blood it was replaced. The raw stripes were then disinfected with a mixture of vinegar and pepper which caused further pain. Flogged women might be further bled to calm their nerves! It was not unknown for slaves to die under the lash and they sometimes died as a consequence, often from tetanus infection. The usual medical cause was given as cerebral congestion.

Though a decree of 1813 confined the flogging of slaves to the calaboose in order to restrain the sadism of owners, it was regularly flouted, as Robert Walsh could hear as he walked about. He also knew of a slave who was solemnly flogged to death by his owner in a cellar — by permission of the police intendant — for striking his master.[8] On the plantations, moreover, owners were unrestrained by the vigilance, however inefficient, of the law. Slaves could be subject to the *novena* or *trezena*, hideous parodies of religious observance, when they were flogged daily over 9 or 13 days, after which the wounds were washed with urine or the weals were teased by a sharp blade to ensure that they were tender for the next beating.[9] On one coffee plantation near Rio de Janeiro an ingenious overseer invented a water-driven flogging machine to save his time and energy.[10]

Slaves were often hired for murder and assault. The real perpetrators rarely suffered from implication in their agents' guilt, but any slave apprehended and convicted was consigned to the chain-gang without indemnity to the owner. In 1829, the government tried to secure the summary execution of slaves who murdered their masters, but a slave once dead had no economic value and if hell could be continued on this earth, why give the criminal a blessed relief by executing him? It was not until 1835 that resistance was overcome and capital punishment allowed.[11] Often a slave could face no more and tried to take his own life. He might eat earth, considered by most owners to be a form of attempted suicide, though it was often eaten as an antidote to the bitter cassava root (*Manihot utilissima*), which contains prussic acid and which he may have eaten untreated. The penalty for this, and for greed or drunkenness, was to have a tin mask clamped to the lower face so that the wearer could only eat or drink under surveillance. But the human frame could become inured to physical maltreatment. What slaves feared most was solitary confinement without food or light on their free days. Essential furniture in every town and country house were the stocks in the cellar: the *tronco simples* for legs only, the *tronco duplo* for hands and feet and the *tronco de pau comprido*, which could take six offenders at a time.[12]

Did the Brazilians treat their slaves more humanely than the North Americans or the British and French planters in the West Indies? There is a persistent legend that they did, and the reasons given were variously the lenity of the Portuguese character, the enervating climate, even the protective efforts of law and church.[13] But the law was such a 'hodge-podge of *alvarás, cartas de lei, cartas regias, provisões* and *decretos*, edicts and instruments promulgated by successive monarchs of the Braganza dynasty', that it was so much mumbo-jumbo to the wretched, the illiterate and the helpless.[14] A slave before law and church had the right to marry, to seek another master, to own property and to purchase his own freedom. But the law was unenforceable if the owner was determined to deny all or any of these rights to his slaves. Indeed the police might give a double dose of punishment to any slave who quoted the law at them.[15] British and American visitors who made comparisons unflattering to conditions further north were often abolitionists who wanted any stick with which to beat the inhuman institution they detested under their own flag.[16] They would comment favourably on the comparatively large number of free blacks and mulattos in Brazil, and assume that this was the result of a generally benign regime and a constant practice of manumission.

Such an assumption goes against the evidence. Because Brazilians could often escape undetected, and because all Brazilians feared another Palmares republic, this time on a much larger scale reproducing the horrors of Haiti, some owners may have been persuaded to reduce the risk by what for them passed as gentle treatment. But the large number of runaways suggests that treatment was seldom less than harsh and it was probably they who explained why in the 1860s, when 90 per cent of the black population of the United States of America was still in servitude, half Brazil's may have been free.[17] When the Golden Law of 1888 finally abolished the institution of slavery, it was calculated that there were three free blacks to every slave. Because of the low birth-rate among slaves, that could not have been the result of the 1871 Law of Free Birth, which freed any child born to a slave at birth. Though it is probably true that most slaves died in slavery of overwork, poor diet and ill-treatment, an increasing number found the courage of desperation and disappeared into the crowd.

The Golden Law was accompanied by a holocaust of slave records, and this has thrown historians back on to those accounts of life at the turn of the century for their principal evidence on how well or badly Brazilian owners treated their slaves. Conditions varied between town and country, between the north and the south, between provinces and between decades. The slaves likely to have been best off were the town-house domestics, who were often reasonably well-fed and clothed for the sake of appearances, like the 'completest burlesque of an equipage' observed in Salvador — a sedan chair loaded with gilded cupids and carried by two robust, bare-footed slaves in light-blue jackets, short pantaloons and petticoats like a waterman's, deeply vandyked with red and pink.[18] Some slaves enjoyed remarkable freedom of movement; one visitor was astonished to see black girls walking unescorted through the streets of the mining town of São João d'El Rei carrying gold ingots on their heads.[19] No one watching the blacks, both slave and free, dressed up to the nines on Sundays in the Campo Sant'Ana in Rio or in the streets of Salvador, would have recognized the subjects of an anti-slavery tract, with their pink, yellow and blue calico waistcoats, matching sashes, gold chains and seals without watches, cocked hats, snuffboxes and yellow canes, aping the social graces of their white masters and dancing with ever increasing abandon to raucous music.[20] Slaves on the sugar plantations of Bahia were worked hard, but they lived with their families on the older estates during an era of agricultural decline so that their servitude was often 'characterized by a gradual and continuous growth of intimate personal relations between master and slave which tended to humanize the institution and undermine its formal character'.[21] On the older estates, most whites had been suckled by a black *mucama* or mammy, had played as a child with a *pajem*, a slave of the same age and sex on whom every frustration of bad temper and caprice could be worked off without recrimination, and had had their first sexual encounter, if an adolescent boy, in the *senzala* or slave quarters. The poorer the estate, the fewer the amenities, the brusquer the relation between master and slave and the worse the conditions. To 'sleep like a slave in a sugar-mill' is a Brazilian way of describing the repose of sheer exhaustion.

The worst treated were undoubtedly the slaves in the mines and on the burgeoning coffee estates on the southern Paraíba river. Here the coffee boom represented 'the transition from the patriarchal to the individual economy, with the slave less a member of the family than a mere worker, a money-making machine'.[22] The Brazilian equivalent of selling a slave down the river was to sell him to the coffee plantations of São Paulo, the mines of Minas Gerais or the distilleries of Maranhão and Pará, where a slave could be worked out in a year in pursuit of a quick profit. To the new coffee capitalist, the slaves merely formed a 'link in the chain of animated beings between ourselves and the various species of brute animals', an uncompromising enemy to be restrained and kept working to schedule by fear of punishment, by vigilance and by discipline.[23]

By a combination of torpor and licence, punctuated by sudden and extreme brutality, the Brazilians in the north and north-east had kept their slaves divided and repressed. Charles Darwin, coming ashore from the *Beagle* in 1833, hoped that cheerful, good-natured, stout-hearted and obstinate as they were, the day would come when Brazil's slaves would assert their own rights and forget to avenge their wrongs.[24] There seemed at the time little chance of it, since all Brazilians had grown up so convinced that slavery was part of the natural order that abolition was a distant dream. Abolition in the United States actually spelled its death-knell, but Brazil only followed suit 20 years later. Its final collapse, however, also spelled the ruin of the empire born of independence from Portugal, for by a black irony the slave-owning plantocrats and coffee barons, who had supported the constitutional monarchy and espoused the politics of conservative gradualism throughout the greater part of the century, ended by leaguing themselves with republicans and emancipationists to dethrone the emperor who had liberated their slaves. They could not forgive the monarch, no matter what their sentiments of loyalty, who dared to destroy an institution as old as Brazil herself. The true child of emancipation was the Brazilian republic.

Brazil's British allies, however, could see no reason why the trade should not be stopped and stretched the fabric of protection and friendship to the point of rupture. The 1810 treaty had cut off the valuable Nigerian and Dahomey trade. Unable and unwilling to understand the niceties of Portugal's claims to ports on the Costa da Mina, which, if they could be proved, would have restored them to Portuguese 'ownership' and thus legalized the trade, the British instructed their cruisers to seize any ships suspected of carrying slaves from the Bight of Benin. By 1813 they had seized so many that there was a dramatic shortage of slaves for sale in Salvador, provoking the merchants of that city and of Recife to publish a protest in London. By the end of the war, after Bonaparte had made a bid for British sympathy during the Hundred Days by abolishing the French trade, only Spain and Portugal of the major slave-trading countries had not yet joined the ban. Dom John succumbed enough to Lord Castlereagh's pressure to ratify the Vienna Convention of 20 January 1815, which condemned though it did not abolish the trade, in return for which Britain acknowledged a contingent possibility of wrongful sequestration of Portuguese slavers by expunging all claims for damages in an indemnity of £300,000. On 22 January, in return for a moratorium on Dom John's remaining debts to the British crown (worth another £300,000), Portuguese subjects were once again forbidden to ship slaves from any ports north of the equator. Portugal also put her name to the 18-power declaration of 8 February that the trade must be suppressed as soon as possible.

It was not worth the ink with which it was written. Traders from Salvador could get such good prices for slaves from the Costa da Mina that it paid them to beat the ban. The fabrication of flags, the falsification of log-books and ships' papers became such a minor industry that the British insisted on an additional convention in 1817, strictly defining the latitudes south of which the trade was still legal, and establishing their rights of search. Adjudication was made the responsibility of two mixed commissions, in Freetown and Rio de Janeiro, and once again Portugal undertook to abolish the trade completely. Spain ended her trade in 1820, but Portugal was able to hang on until Brazilian independence. Thereafter abolition was to be the price of Britain's recognition of the new empire.

As the pressure grew to abolish the trade, so conditions on the middle passage became the queen of horrors. The constant promises to abolish the trade encouraged traders to disregard cargo limits before the axe fell. Between 1800 and 1850, when shipments finally ceased, 1,600,000 slaves were imported into Brazil.[25] Between 1813 and 1817, 40,000 of them came from the prohibited Costa da Mina, but the numbers from Angola and Benguela progressively increased. When, on 28 November 1826, the imperial government agreed to end the trade within three years, conditions became the most frightful in the history of the trade. Slavers became more ruthless and efficient. They bought vessels in North America and shipped under US flags to escape inspection; they packed far more slaves into a cargo than could be expected to survive the journey; they were even known to throw whole cargoes to the sharks to lighten the load and escape pursuit.[26] Cases brought before the mixed commissions in Rio de Janeiro were endlessly prolonged and inconclusive. Even when a slaver was condemned and his cargo declared free, it had usually been sold into the interior long before and disappeared without trace. No matter what preventive action was taken, if 99 doors were closed and one remained open, the whole slave-trade of Africa would rush to it. In 1814 the US minister in Rio calculated that if only two out of five cargoes reached Brazil, the slavers still incurred no loss on their outlay since the sale of those that were disembarked made a profit of between 60 and 120 per cent.[27] Sir Thomas Buxton, on whom had fallen the mantle of William Wilberforce, told his countrymen in 1837 that 'no illicit trade can be suppressed when the profit exceeds 30 per cent'.[28] But inexorably the vice of political pressure and naval action closed, and at last, in 1850–51, the Brazilian government took the firm and consistent action against slavers that had been urged for 43 years. The transatlantic trade came to an end.

Between 1808 and 1850 Brazil imported three times as many slaves as the United States, yet in 1871 her registered slave population was only 1,540,829. At the beginning of the century, the two great slave-owning nations may have had a slave population each of between one and one and a half million. By the time of the American Civil War, America's slave population had grown to four million, by some half million a decade. By the same period, Brazil's population should have reached three million by natural reproduction. Yet it was little larger than it had been in the 18th century, despite the fact that over a million slaves had been imported since the arrival of the court from Lisbon.[29] In those statistics probably lies the answer to the question about how well Brazil treated her slave population. Slaves died at work; only those who could escape undetected had any chance of living to a reasonably old age, poor but free. Few Brazilian slaves were more than a generation away from their African origins.[30]

At least one of the founding fathers of independent Brazil, José Bonifácio, believed that Brazil would never be properly independent or constitutional, never have a proper army or navy, until she had a population of free people. 'Without individual liberty you can have neither civilization nor solid wealth; you cannot have self-respect, power or authority among nations.'[31] In 1823 he proposed a plan for the gradual elimination of slavery. First he would declare mulatto children free from birth (the Law of Free Birth only entered the statute book on 28 September 1871). Then he would create a fund to redeem all slaves of mixed blood. The pure black population, deprived of new arrivals from Africa, would then die out. But even he could not bring himself to advocate outright abolition. Such a measure, so calculated to offend his countrymen, could only bring down the new empire in ruins before a revolutionary and oppressive republic. A new source of labour must be found. European colonists, poor, wretched but industrious, must be encouraged to find a new home in Brazil. 'The population we want,' he told the British chargé d'affaires in April 1823, 'is a white one.'[32] His contemporaries were openly contemptuous of his ideas. 'The author of creation has given Brazil a climate for Africans to work in.'[33] Since most immigrants came to Brazil in the expectation of buying slaves to look after their every need, if there were no slaves to buy, then there would be no immigrants. Even as late as 1859, the Austrian minister in Rio saw no point in beating about the bush. 'In a country based on slavery, the immigrant is just a substitute for coloured labour and treated accordingly.'[34]

The first experiment in government-sponsored immigration was not a success. In 1818 Dom John imposed a tax on newly imported slaves and decreed that half the proceeds should be spent on European colonization. The first beneficiaries were to be Swiss peasants from the canton of Fribourg, who were assigned a patch of virgin land some 90 miles inland from Rio over the Organ Pipe mountains (Serra dos Orgãos) and called Cantagalo. It was not suitable either for sugar or coffee, but could have been converted into good farming land, and the first 100 families, all Roman Catholics, were installed at public expense and presented with the tools to clear the land. They should have been skilled peasants, but they turned out to be either former soldiers who brought fowling pieces instead of tools, hoping to shoot rather than dig for the pot, or the usual village ne'er-do-wells who were sent abroad to improve themselves. For two years they were kept going by royal bounty, but the more improvident drifted off to the coffee plantations or to domestic service and the remainder struggled so half-heartedly with the inhospitable soil that the colony of New Fribourg (Nova Friburgo) was a warning to all Britons not to leave Britain for the doubtful prospects of Brazil.[35] Tess Durbeyfield's husband, Angel Clare, did not heed it.

The Cantagalo experiment was a failure, not only because the settlers were ill-chosen but also because the planters wanted cheap labour not rival farmers. 'Colonization for Brazil means getting hold of a class of labourers who will live in captivity and whose contracts will make them dependent on their employers, to whom they will always be in debt for their outward passage.'[36] The Swiss also went to the wrong place. They should have gone to the slaveless south, the campos of Paraná and Rio Grande where the war with the *gaúchos* of the Banda Oriental had like another gold rush unpeopled the land. Young men had vanished to escape enlistment, and vast tracts of farming land lay untilled and untended. In due course that was where the eventual immigrants were to go. But while there were slaves to be had no one wanted white immigrant, expensive and probably truculent labour. Apart from doing all the work in the fields, the mines and the docks, slaves bore the lady of the house to mass, the militiaman's rifle and parasol to parade, night-soil to the sea, gold dust to the smelting house, the mail to the interior, specimens to the collector, Maria Graham's easel and stool to the sketching site, criminals to the gallows, and beggars to their graves. Even the quality of the harlots was judged from the size and splendour of their retinue of slaves.[37] That they should not be available for these tasks was as unthinkable to the subjects of Dom John in 1808 as it was to an Athenian living in the age of Pericles.

8· Staying On, 1814–17

'"Nach Brasilien" klang die Losung, Nach dem Paradies im Westen. Wo mit gold'nen Pomeranzen Sich die faulen Tiere maesten.' (To Brazil, that is where we must go, to the Western Paradise, where lazy beasts gorge themselves on golden oranges.) —

a popular refrain in Germany among would-be emigrants in the 19th century

'Count Metternich is still with me, and continues to reassure me that I have a brilliant future before me.' —

Dona Carolina Josefa Leopoldina, Princess of Brazil and Arch-Duchess of Austria, to her father, the Emperor Francis I, Poggio Imperiale, 24 July 1817

Napoleon Bonaparte abdicated in June 1814, and the Atlantic became safe enough once more for the court to attempt another oceanic passage. But even as in 1807 Lord Strangford had had great difficulty in turning Dom John's eyes towards Brazil, so now he was to experience as much trouble persuading him to return to Lisbon. Dom John had become quite comfortable where he was. He had grown very fond of his tropical home and liked the rough colonial loyalty of his Brazilian subjects. Why should he hurry to change them for the stiff-necked Portuguese? Dom John's principal closet adviser, since the Marques de Aguiar was hopelessly at sea with affairs of state, was now none other than the principal opponent of the hegira to Brazil in the first place. Dom Antônio de Araújo e Azevedo, elevated to Conde da Barca, was firm in his counsel that the regent should be in no hurry to leave Brazil. It was important first to discover how stable conditions were in the *Reino*, which had been fought over repeatedly by Napoleonic and Wellingtonian armies. Constitutionally suspicious of the British, he also wondered why they were so anxious to see the regent return. When Lord Strangford offered Dom John the services of any British admiral he chose (except Sir Sidney Smith) to escort him home, the regent obediently ordered his battle squadron to prepare for an Atlantic crossing and recalled his sailors from service in British ships. But he was up to his old tricks. Everyone believed that the royal family would sail for Lisbon on 17 December. Admiral Sir John Poo Beresford, brother of the British commander-in-chief in Portugal, arrived at the end of September with two ships of the line and a frigate. Dom John complained that he had not asked for an escort. After that, the departure seemed about as imminent as the second coming of King Sebastian.[1] Though extensive works on the Ajuda palace were reported in Lisbon, equally extensive work could be observed at both São Cristovão and Santa Cruz outside Rio de Janeiro.

Sir John Poo's brother, Sir William Beresford, was in addition to being commander-in-chief of the joint British and Portuguese armies also Dom John's regent in Lisbon. He wanted above all to hand his charge over either to the regent or to his son, since the kingdom desperately needed a focal point round which to rally a disaffected people and a mutinous army. Dom John had always said that he only needed to know what the British government wanted 'for him instantly and implicitly to adopt it'.[2] Dom Antônio, however, was resolved that he should not go back to become the tool and mouthpiece of the British commander-in-chief. No government likes to be helpless before the magnanimity of another friendly but infinitely more powerful nation, and even the normally insensitive Strangford had noticed the strength of anti-British feeling among all classes in Brazil. The colony's commercial dependency on Britain was one irritant; the truce which the envoy had forced upon the Portuguese in the Banda Oriental on 26 May 1812 was another. But neither irritation compared to that caused by Britain's insistence on stopping the traffic in slaves. In 1811, during the furious naval activity that had made British sea-power almost as hated as Bonaparte's armies of occupation, her cruisers had seized 17 out of 32 slavers trading from Salvador. Five trading houses failed, and at one point it was feared that the city might make common cause against Rio de Janeiro and Britain and, like Buenos Aires, declare independence.

With this rising tide of hostility, Lord Strangford's time in Brazil came to an end. He had been minister to the Portuguese court since 1806, and over nine years the frosty air of superiority which came naturally to the descendant of Sir Philip Sidney had helped to preserve Dom John as the puppet monarch he had been in Portugal. Lord Strangford's transfer (for which he had asked) arrived in the middle of a ding-dong battle he was waging with the government over the publication in Rio of British parliamentary debates on the slave-trade, which were considered an incitement to Brazilian slaves to rebel. He sailed with Sir Poo Beresford in the ship sent to escort Dom John to Lisbon. He declined the customary gift for parting envoys of 12 bars of gold, presuming to think that 'he had done more for His Royal Highness than any other foreign minister resident at the court', and that the affections of a friend were reward enough. He failed to return two valuable books to the Braganza library so that he did not leave Brazil empty-handed.[3]

With Strangford gone, the affairs of Portugal called on increasingly deaf ears in Rio. Marshal Beresford and his officers ruled Portugal as a military junta on behalf of the absent monarch, resented by the merchants of Oporto and Lisbon alike, who had hoped to recover from the destruction of the war by the restoration of their monopoly of imperial trade. That hope was frustrated by Britain's control of the Brazilian market and her influence over both regents. Beresford, convinced that Dom John's presence in Lisbon could alone safeguard Portugal's economic and political recovery and Britain's hegemony, came himself to Brazil in September 1815, to persuade him to return. With the marshal also came 5000 Peninsular veterans who were instantly formed into a regiment of King's Own Volunteers (Voluntários Reais d'El Rei) and sent to Santa Caterina. There they were to await the first opportunity 'to kill with a blow the infernal revolutionary hydra in Buenos Aires'.[4] Wellington was bitterly to regret their absence from the field of Waterloo! Beresford in the meantime, who suffered dreadfully in the Rio summer, sweated in vain. For Castlereagh had proposed that Dom John should formally end the slave-trade before he returned to Lisbon, and as that was like waiting for the Greek kalends, Beresford, unable to endure idleness or the heat any longer, returned to Portugal in June 1816 to resume his thankless task as regent of an absentee regent.

The 1812 armistice had not brought peace to the Plate. Buenos Aires changed its governments like top-coats. A mission had been dispatched to Europe to look for a constitutional monarch, while in the Banda, José Artigas, now Chief of the Orientals and Protector of the Free People, not only refused to recognize the government(s) across the estuary, but also planned to recover the area of the former Jesuit missions, occupied by the Portuguese for the last 60 years, and to revolutionize the *gaúchos* of Rio Grande do Sul.

As soon as Beresford was off the premises, the court's eyes followed the *voluntários* southwards. Strangford had gone and in the long-winded presence of the British chargé d'affaires, Henry Chamberlain, the shadow of the Court of St James had shortened. Moreover, the chimera that Strangford had constantly scotched reappeared when an official agent from Buenos Aires repeated a formula that seemed irresistible to Portuguese ears. Why should there not be a Latin American empire with a Braganza enthroned on the banks of the Plate?[5] It was a fancy bred from fear of Spanish revanchism. The writ of Buenos Aires no longer ran in the Banda. Old Spain seemed determined to recover her control of New Spain and the Holy Alliance in Europe seemed ready to help her. Artigas's brand of patriotic revolt was anathema to both the creole establishment in Buenos Aires and the Portuguese government in Rio de Janeiro. It was also likely to make Spanish intervention more probable. Portuguese protection from Spanish invasion in return for the Banda Oriental? The deal had a deceptive simplicity, and despite Chamberlain's protest that as no Portuguese territory was under threat there was no cause for the Portuguese to go to war again, Portuguese troops, reinforced by their Peninsular veterans and led by Carlos Federico Lecor, who had earned his epaulettes in the Peninsular campaign, entered the Banda without a declaration of hostilities. Within four months he had been welcomed with open arms into Montevideo.

But he could not subdue the rebellious province, and soon Lecor was himself invested in Montevideo while Uruguayan privateers attacked Portuguese shipping in the sea-lanes to the Plate and even in the mouth of the Tagus. Castlereagh in London viewed this turn of fortunes with a jaundiced eye. British trade was being choked by Lecor's floating custom-houses stationed off ports he could not control, and the secretary of state was profoundly unimpressed by Dom John's proposal to offer the Banda to Ferdinand VII of Spain as a wedding present with his daughter Maria Isabel. It was no better a proposal than that the Argentines had earlier made for the rebellious provinces to be united under a descendant of the Inca kings married to a Braganza princess.[6] The Spanish government, moreover, had asked the great powers to mediate in South America, and if Dom John persisted in molesting Spanish territory, Britain's undertaking to protect Portuguese territory from foreign attack could be forfeited. The Conde da Barca reaffirmed Dom John's unalterable resolve to secure a reliable frontier on the Plate. What King Ferdinand thought in Madrid was a matter of indifference to Rio since he could do nothing to preserve his own possessions from anarchy. Artigas, 'the rebel of rebels and criminal of criminals', must be crushed. It would be extraordinary if Spain would rather that her provinces were in rebellion than pacified by Portuguese arms.[7]

When in 1817 the Marques de Aguiar died, it was inevitable that the francophile Araújo e Azevedo should replace him. Araújo's return to the Ministry of Foreign Affairs at the age of 63 was not solely because he was the only man suitable and experienced enough for the post. It was also inspired by the return of Bourbon France to the community of nations as a great and friendly power. No one was more anxious to lighten the heavy hand of Britain on the affairs of Portugal in Brazil than this disciple of French rationalism and light. Diplomatic relations had been restored on 22 July 1814, and Talleyrand had appointed an *émigré* colonel in Portuguese service, Jean-Baptiste Maler, as consul-general in Rio. The dispatch of a formal embassy was delayed by Napoleon's last adventure, but Talleyrand assiduously cultivated the Portuguese envoy at Vienna. His sharp eye had noticed that Articles 15, 16 and 17 of the Treaty of Vienna had referred by a slip of the pen to Dom John as Prince Regent of the Kingdom of Portugal and Brazil. Indeed, why should not Brazil become a kingdom in its own right? Much trouble might have been saved in Spanish America if a similar device had been adopted. The idea seized Dom John's ceremonial fancy and on 10 December 1815 he declared Brazil a co-equal kingdom with Portugal. Her own coat of arms — a crowned and golden armillary sphere on a blue ground — was granted on 13 May 1816.

Mad Queen Maria died at long last on 20 March 1816, in her 83rd year. Dom John was bowed with a genuine grief. Though he had been regent for 24 years, he never once usurped her royal position. All the ceremonial events took place on her birthday not his, and now she was dead he refused to be acclaimed king for a year. This was not, contrary to gossip, because the royal theologians could not assure him earlier that his mother's soul had left purgatory, but because the kings of Portugal were not crowned, an event that could only require a small gathering, but acclaimed, and as no Portuguese king had ever been acclaimed anywhere but on Portuguese soil, it would take time to assemble the dignitaries for the ceremony. In the event, his acclamation was delayed, partly by his son's wedding, partly by revolts in both Brazil and Portugal, until 6 February 1818, on which occasion the courtiers, without a backward glance to Montezuma or Atahualpa, also acclaimed him as 'the first king of the New World, the first to live there ... the first to enrich her, the first to found a new monarchy, a new kingdom, a new empire'.[8] His son Dom Pedro had already been elevated to the style of Prince Royal of the United Kingdom on 9 January 1817. That all these new events needed his presence was also a very good reason for delaying any return to Lisbon.

Meanwhile, on 30 May 1816, an embassy of Napoleonic magnificence had come to Rio de Janeiro, headed by the Duc de Luxembourg, a premier peer of France, as ambassador extraordinary accredited to the new United Kingdom. The British had never sent anything like it. The duke's objectives were to secure the return of Guiana unconditionally — Dom John had rather hoped to use it as a bait for a marriage between one of his daughters and the Duc de Berri — and to secure trading privileges like those enjoyed by the British. He succeeded in the first but not the second. He also visited his sister, the widow of the one member of the Portuguese nobility, the Duque de Cadaval, who had died on the voyage to Brazil in 1807. Perhaps more significantly still, his embassy brought cultural gifts. It was possibly the first time that cultural diplomacy, in the meaning that has been given to that phrase, was seen in practice. For in his train came the complete staff and equipment for a school of fine art to be established in Rio with the collaboration of the French government. Among the team was Jean-Baptiste Debret, history painter and student of David, who was, over his stay of 15 years, to achieve immortality as the greatest *descubridor* with the brush of the new United Kingdom. The school, later academy, had a chequered and undistinguished history, its founding team of French artists being exposed to the venom and jealousy of Portuguese colleagues, so that one by one they gave up. But Debret became virtually court painter, charged with the designs for the splendid fetes with which the Braganzas celebrated their family revels. And all the time he turned off the brilliant water-colour sketches that have immortalized the epoch in his *Voyage Pittoresque et Historique au Brésil* (published in Paris in three volumes in 1834). The originals can still be seen in a villa high in the Tijuca forest overlooking Rio de Janeiro, a peep-show of the daily life of a city which Charles Darwin likened to 'the gayest scenery of the opera house or the great theatres'.[9]

Also in Luxembourg's train were Sigismund Neukomm, the personal cultural envoy sent by Talleyrand, and Auguste de Saint-Hilaire, who came privately. Saint-Hilaire had marched with Junot into Lisbon in 1807 to plunder the museums, but finding the prints of a *Flora Fluminensis*, the work of a Brazilian Franciscan, Fra José Mariano da Conceição Velloso (1741–1811), he decided then and there that he must visit this botanical Eden. Between 1816 and 1821 he travelled throughout central and southern Brazil, and a nine-volume *Voyages dans l'Intérieur du Brésil* began to appear in Paris in 1830. 'So many new plants at every turn!' he exclaimed. 'I nearly accused nature of being too prodigal.'[10] In his own view, his masterwork was the *Flora Brasiliae Meridionalis*, and when he succeeded to Lamarck's chair in Paris, he was the 'father' of two new floral families, *Paronychia*, the genus of whitlow-wort, and *Tamaricaceae*, of tamarisks and other xerophyte plants.

The example, even challenge, of Bourbon France stimulated more traditional allies. Now was the time for a royal match. The Portuguese ambassador in Paris, the Marques de Marialva, took a proposal to Vienna that Dom Pedro, the prince royal, should marry an Austrian archduchess and that his sister, Maria Isabel, should marry the emperor's heir. Metternich, anxious to bind all royal houses together in a common cause against revolution and republicanism, could not persuade the Archduke Ferdinand that he was in a marrying mood, but Napoleon's sister-in-law, the plain and dutiful Archduchess Leopoldina, was ready to do her dynastic duty. Marialva, in his role as wooer, promised an early return of the intended groom to Europe, but even without that prospect Leopoldina was enthusiastic. A keen amateur naturalist (her father once jokingly remarked that had she not married he would have made her director of the Vienna Natural History Museum), she was excited by the prospect of living in Brazil and would have preferred as a betrothal present a cabinet of specimens to the portrait of her betrothed set in diamonds.[11]

The wedding had to be postponed by the death of Queen Maria, but on 13 May 1817 Dom Pedro and Dona Leopoldina were married in Vienna by proxy. Nothing was allowed to suggest that times had changed since 1708 when Dom John V had married Marie-Ann of Austria. Marialva made a gorgeous entry on 17 February. On 1 June he gave a splendid reception for the Emperor and Empress and

2000 other guests at a cost of 7 million florins. The newly married princess was escorted by both Metternich and Marialva to the court of her cousin Leopold at Florence, where she was instructed in the grandeurs and miseries of dynastic marriage by her sister, Napoleon's separated second wife, Marie-Louise, Duchess of Parma. There she stayed until a Portuguese squadron came to fetch her, longer than she expected because the escort was delayed first by the desertion of the Algarve sailors, specially signed-on to crew the *Dom João VI*, then by two sudden and unexpected revolts, first in Recife, then in Lisbon. When the news of the Recife rising reached Vienna, the British ambassador, hoping to use fears for her safety to secure the return to Europe of at least the heir to the throne, suggested that the princess royal should not sail. The emperor, unwilling to annoy his daughter's new father-in-law, replied that she was now a Portuguese subject and should leave for Brazil at once. Leopoldina declared with spirit that if her husband was in danger, her place was at his side. Her new subjects were to have other occasions on which to applaud the spirit of their new princess.[12]

To mark the wedding of his nature-loving daughter, the emperor decided to send the largest scientific expedition yet mounted to her adopted land. It was led by Professor Mikan, a botanist teaching at the Charles University in Prague. He was accompanied by another botanist and mineralogist, Johann Emmanuel Pohl, the zoologist Johann Natterer, of the Imperial Zoological Gardens, the flower-painter Johann Buchberger, the horticulturist Heinrich Wilhelm Schott, gardener imperial at the Belvedere Palace, and Crown Prince Ferdinand's chief huntsman and taxidermist, Domenik Socher. The Austrians went about their mission with method. Their industry was immense. Pohl was to write a two-volume work on the province of Goiás and to contribute to the classification of Brazil's inexhaustible flora with *Plantarum Brasiliae* (published in Vienna, 1827–31). Natterer was on the trail for 19 years, collecting and annotating, only returning to Vienna in 1835 when the Austrian government refused to fund him any longer. Despite prolonged ill-health and the deaths of Buchberger and Socher, the expedition continued to send home specimens until the Vienna museum was bursting at the seams. When Pohl returned in 1821 with an Indian Botocudo couple, complete with forest hut and domestic utensils, the emperor inaugurated the Brazil museum in which the Indian couple provided a daily tableau vivant and seven rooms were given over to rock samples alone. During the 1848 revolution, Natterer's collection and notes went up in flames, a tragic holocaust of an endeavour that deserved to rank high in the annals of scientific exploration.

Mikan's expedition had its own artist, Tomas Ender, who was attached to it at the personal expense of Prince Metternich. Worn out after 11 months in Brazil, where he spent 'night and day reproducing this entirely new world so that I was at last prostrate from physical and mental exhaustion', Ender's industry was for a sick man prodigious. He returned to Vienna with 527 water-colours of Rio de Janeiro and São Paulo.[13] They were added to the Brazilian museum in Vienna and saved from destruction in 1848 because Ender, appointed professor at the Academy of Fine Arts, had taken his collection with him. Yet, however admirable the sheer energy of Natterer, Pohl and Ender, everything the Austrian expedition was to do would eventually be outshone by the work of two Bavarian scientists attached to the expedition at the last moment.

Dona Leopoldina's grandfather, the King of Bavaria, had no wish to be left out, and the emperor graciously consented that Johann Baptist von Spix and Karl Friedrich Philip von Martius should join the expedition. Spix was curator of the Munich Museum; Martius, though not yet 23, already had a reputation throughout Europe as a botanist, though he was, as yet, only an assistant to the director of the Botanical Gardens. They both had the widest possible brief. They were to observe the native and animal life, to study the botanical families peculiar to Brazil, to comment on the soil and its cultivation and to give an opinion on Indian native medicine. They were to make geological observations, chart the variations of the magnetic needle, record electrical phenomena, test the phosphorescence and salinity of the sea, take meteorological readings, investigate the tides and study the electricity of fishes. They were also to collect materials on the social history of Brazil for university classes. Above all, they were to collect. On one expedition their specimens were packed in the pinewood boxes in which English china had arrived, protected by cowhide and carried by 30 mules.[14]

The first volume of their *Travels in Brazil* appeared in 1823 and was acclaimed by both Goethe and Humboldt. They had travelled further than their Austrian colleagues, and further than the Russian consul-general, Langsdorff. From Rio on 16 July 1817, they had set off through São Paulo and Minas Gerais, down the São Francisco river, over the Bahian and Pernambucan *sertão* into Piauí and Maranhão, on to Belém, whence they shipped 80 different animals for the Munich zoo, of which 57 arrived alive, and hundreds of plant specimens to the botanical gardens. Spix died in Munich before the second volume was written, but from their joint observations Martius went on to build his gigantic *oeuvre*: dissertations on the vegetable kingdom of Brazil, on the natural history of palms, on making cassava bread, on Indian maladies and their cures, on Amazonian cryptogams. He produced an atlas showing in detail for the first time the whole course of the Amazon river. He finished, with expert assistance, Spix's work on the mammals, birds and amphibians of Brazil. His *magnum opus* was the mighty *Flora Brasiliensis*, in Latin, 20,753 pages long, with 3,811 plates and 6,246 drawings, 37 volumes in folio, describing 2,253 species and 22,767 variations, 5,887 of them for the first time. It was launched in 1840 under the patronage of the Emperors Ferdinand I of Austria and Pedro II of Brazil and of King Ludwig of Bavaria. It was completed only in 1906. Martius died in 1868, a few years after completing a glossary of the different tongues and dialects spoken by the Indians, honoured by countless universities but secure in his proudest title of 'intellectual conquistador of Brazil'. He gave his name to the babaçu palm (*Orbignya martiana*) and so christened a tree almost as versatile as himself, for babaçu palm oil was used as food and fuel, its nuts were made into buttons, its leaves into fibre and its flowers into beer. He is commemorated in Brazil by the von Martius rapids on the River Xingu, at the extreme north point of the last natural preserve of the Brazilian Indian, the Xingu National Park.

The Austrian and Bavarian missions were also to spur the Russian consul-general into action. With personal finance from the tsar, Baron Langsdorff arranged to lead the deepest penetration of Latin America yet made by a naturalist. For this he assembled an international team. It consisted of a Russian naval officer, Nestor Rubtsov, commissioned to observe the movements of the magnetic needle and the night sky in the southern hemisphere, two Germans, the botanist Ludwig Riedel and the zoologist Christian Hasse, and two French nature painters, Hercule Florence and Adrien Taunay. With Langsdorff in the lead, they set off from Santos in September 1825, along the rivers Tietê, Taquari and Paraguai, reaching Cuiabá in January 1827. From then on misfortune dogged them. Hasse had already dropped out to marry a farmer's daughter he met on the journey. Taunay was drowned in the River Guaporé. Langsdorff himself fell ill, and as the expedition dragged its weary way to Belém do Pará, the smell of death was on it.

Foul water and mosquitoes took their toll in due course. Rubtsov died soon after his return to Russia, and Langsdorff, though he lingered until 1823, covered in academic honours, never recovered the full use of his mind. Lost in Mato Grosso were all his notes on the Indians, most of Taunay's drawings and his own sketches of 50 new species of fish. Only his collection of 1,600 species of butterfly survived, and Langsdorff never produced his great work to take its place alongside Spix and Martius, Pohl and Eschwege. Almost his sole printed work was an essay intended to promote emigration to Brazil, where, he rhapsodized enticingly, 'the richest and happiest imagination can only give a poor idea of the extent of the treasures and magnificence of nature'.[15]

Langsdorff had first contracted as his nature painter Johann Moritz Rugendas, a native of Augsburg, but the two men quarrelled and Rugendas struck off on his own. His *Voyage Pittoresque dans le Brésil* (Paris, 1835) was a *succès-fou* with a public now avid for accounts of life in the tropics, of alligators, serpents, cannibal Indians and brutal slave-owners. Rugendas and Debret have left the most vivid memories of life in a tropic where it was either perpetual carnival or perpetual misery. Moreover, they had depicted Indians at work and play. After the horrors of nearly twenty years of European war, the citizens of that continent were avid for more details about those innocent and fragile inhabitants who had never known the doubtful benefits of civilization, the untamed Indian.

9· Indians

'The primitive inhabitants of America lost no opportunity to amuse themselves while the more recent arrivals, the Europeans, were addicted to sadness, and oppressed this poor people in all manner of ways, envying them the little happiness that they were permitted to enjoy' —

Baron von Eschwege, *Brasilien, die Neue Welt*, vol 1, p 86

'The Indian who crosses a forest wafts about him the fragrance of a thousand plants, his hair is scented with aromas, his breath is fresh and pure' —

D. Gavet and P. Boucher, *Jakaréouassu* (Paris, 1830)

Dom John had arrived just as the Indians were back on the warpath. The Kaingáng were successfully fighting off the Paulista *bandeiras* who were moving into the Campos de Guarapava where the modern states of Paraná and São Paulo join. And the Aimoré, a horrendous tribe known as Botocudos from the way they distended the underlip and earlobes with plugs (*botoques*) of the floss silk tree, were on the rampage in the valleys of the Rio Doce. Dom Rodrigo de Souza Coutinho ordered them to be pacified, if not by blandishments, then by force. He established a Junta for the Conquest and Civilization of the Indians and for the Navigation of the Rio Doce in Vila Rica do Ouro Preto, the chief town of Minas Gerais, charged with 'settling' the turbid Indians to peaceful pursuits. He recruited six companies of special scouts from among local volunteers to out-Indian the Indian in his forest lair, men hardy enough to survive jungle warfare in bare feet and *gibão d'armas*, an arrow-proof vest of plaited cotton.[1] They were to round up the fractious Indians into settlements where they were to be bound to the land. Each company was required to take with it two priests to ensure that the new sons of Christ were treated with Christian propriety, but 'the waters of baptism, for many the way to redemption, for many more unfortunates meant years of captivity'.[2] The rule that allowed armed prisoners to be reduced to servitude and kept in chains until tamed, meant that the forest Indian, who was seldom abroad without his weapons, indispensable for his livelihood, was too often assumed to be on the warpath, and any harmless and pacific tribe whose lips and ears were artificially extended could be taken for a Botocudo and enslaved. It did not help that the Botocudos, also known as Bugres, were believed without substance to be both anthropophagous and sodomitical.[3]

None of this was new to the Indian. Over the centuries the Indian had been confronted by the white man or, even worse, the half-white man, in search either of gold, for which he needed diggers, or of virgin land upon which he needed labour to start scratching for a living. He would not live like the Indians he encountered, hunting and fishing and gathering the fruits of the forest. He was a civilized Christian who proposed to create a land like the one he had left or which he felt he ought to recreate for his father's sake, in which the Indian could either elect to live as a virtual slave or be hunted like an animal. The early *bandeirantes* had carried their manhunts as far as Mato Grosso and had even invaded the Jesuit missions as early as the first quarter of the 17th century. The need to settle the vast colony before interloping Spaniards got there first meant that for the work-shy Portuguese settler a source of labour had to be found. If the Indian could be persuaded to become a Christian and dwell in a superior civilization, the wishes of the government in Lisbon could be met; if at the same time he could be made to work the land, that would satisfy the settler on the spot.

Unfortunately most of those Indians who voluntarily or otherwise accepted superior civilization found that was just what it was not. A servitude no different from slavery, an incomprehensible set of religious rituals and duties and the constricting necessity of clothing, wholly unsuitable for their way of life, were also accompanied by exposure to maladies against which they had no natural immunity and from which they died in thousands. Only the Jesuits had achieved any success with settling the naturally religious Guarani in the celebrated reductions of the Paraguai basin; but that success had been achieved with the imposition of a system that virtually denied the Indians in their care the exercise of free choice. Elsewhere the missionary orders were less independent and were, moreover, contaminated by the ignoble ambitions of the secular powers with whom they had to live. For all tribes of Indians, civilization meant the encroachment on their traditional and historic living space by a set of ruthless raiders who even to this day have failed to realize that a tropical forest cannot readily be converted into farm land. The brutality, moreover, with which the 'savage' was treated by his 'civilized' European fellow-citizen and by his semi-civilized half-brother, the *mameluco*, rendered wholly ineffectual such efforts as were made by well-intentioned administrators in Lisbon to see that the Indians were brought to civilization by peaceful and not by violent means.

The Jesuits had taught their Guarani Indian colonists to defend themselves, and as a result their settlements had been overrun by colonial armies directed by settlers who wanted the Indian lands for themselves. In the great Amazonian estuary lands of the Captaincy-General of Pará, the Jesuits and other missionaries had had rather less success in bringing the Indians into Christian settlements. The tribes were less tractable, the forest more dense. Though every attempt at settlement did violence to the Indian's nature, it was the logical result of the decision from the onset of colonization to treat the Indian as an equal citizen with rights to Christian freedom and development. This freedom and development was interpreted by every informed and well-intentioned person at that time as bringing the stone-age savage as quickly as possible into the state of civilization which his white 'brother' enjoyed. With the expulsion of the Jesuits, however, the belief that this was what the autochthon was being assisted by his white neighbour to achieve was held in Lisbon only. The crown's intentions towards the Indian had always been of the best. Decrees of 1596, 1605, 1609, 1611, 1735 and 1742 repeated that Indians, baptized and pagan, were free men. Pope Benedict XV had pronounced that anyone who enslaved an Indian without judicial authority could be excommunicated. In 1755 Pombal, accusing the Jesuits of having infringed the liberty of the Indians in their charge, once again insisted, in more than usually flamboyant prose, that the Brazilian Indian was the equal of any other free Brazilian. To ensure that this would be so, he replaced the Society in the Amazonian provinces by a trading company, and hedged it round with a formidable barrage of instructions about its duties towards and care for the Indians in its territories.

These were to be gathered (by kindness and consideration for their own eternal good) into settlements under a Portuguese director, where they were to be afforded every opportunity to develop into good colonists. Yet one clause in those instructions undid all the good of the others, for a director was permitted to keep for his own part a sixth part of the produce of the settlement. Thus these experiments in civilization quickly became a source of cheap labour for the enrichment of the director, and Pombal's instructions were as a result breached in nearly every other respect. Far from dignity and freedom, the Indian in his villages lived a life of squalor and neglect, debauched by drink and idleness and reduced by disease to sexual sterility.[4] Those who could escaped into the forests, those who remained lived lives little better than black slaves. The former missions in the south on the Paraguay border, where the Guarani still cultivated maté as a cash crop, had given way to military settlements and the villages had been turned into fortresses, the inhabitants impressed into a frontier militia to dispute the territory with the Spaniards, against whom they acquired an enviable reputation for cutting out herds of cattle from under the noses of armed patrols and for slaughtering pickets.[5] 'Acculturated' Indians were indeed used to do a lot of colonial dirty work, to lure unacculturated tribes into settlements, to betray their hideouts and to deceive them by promises that were instantly repudiated. The chiefs of acculturated tribes enjoyed the nominal rank of *capitão-mor* and sometimes led bands of tribesman into police action, like the Indians who helped to pacify Recife after the 1817 rebellion. The Indian was no longer a brand to be plucked from the burning. He had become the common timber of colonization.

Even before the court left Portugal, Dom Rodrigo, in his capacity as secretary for overseas territories, had realized that his former patron's plans had gone wrong. In 1798 his brother, Francisco de Souza Coutinho, Captain-General of Pará, recommended the abolition of the corrupt settlement directors and their replacement by an earthly trinity of village headman (usually an Indian), the local judge and a chaplain. Once again the crown insisted that the Indian was a free citizen and his instruction and conversion were made a charge on the royal treasury.[6] The sad truth was that laws made in Europe were ignored on the frontiers of colonial Brazil and the situation was little improved when the seat of government moved to Rio de Janeiro. On the forest fringe, far from authority's regular remit, the natives continued to be exploited as unpaid labour, and the funds from government for their development were embezzled by the venal successors of Pombal's venal directors. Saint-Hilaire saw a Kayapó settlement in Goiás run by the military. The colonel in charge lived in the city. His deputy, with one dragoon and 15 infantrymen, was responsible for the local security and 'pacification' of the Indians. The troopers had not received their pay for months and, being for the most part mulattos and used to contumely and contempt they were not averse to living off their wards. 'Can anyone think it anything but absurd to expect soldiers to behave like missionaries?' asked the French botanist. The Indians disliked the settlement and had fled to the *mato*. 'One Jesuit could lead many thousands but 17 soldiers have difficulty in keeping 200 Kayapós together, with no advantage either to the state or to themselves!'[7]

The hatred between the rough frontiersman and the Indian was perpetual and endemic and the forest Indian was doomed by every government's resolve, whether colonial or imperial, to 'descend' Indians from savagery to civilization. Whether the *bandeiras* sent to bring them in did so by persuasion and cajolery or by brute force was immaterial; indeed, with the removal of the capital to Rio de Janeiro, closer to the influence of the big *mazombo* landowners, the government was ever quicker to resort to pacification by force. Dom Rodrigo's declaration of war on the Kaingáng and the Botocudo and his resolve to open up the interior by a network of roads were all results of this influence; and that war was not declared over until 1831. When, in 1813, the road from Belmonte on the Bahian coast to the Falls of Jequitininhona was completed, a distance of some 200 miles, the government proclaimed the pacification of the Botocudos.[8] The boast was premature. The Aimoré continued to molest farms and villages in sporadic attempts to hold back the tide of destruction, until in 1824 the imperial government was persuaded to abandon the policy of continuous warfare by a remarkable Frenchman, Guy Marlière, a Napoleonic deserter to Portuguese service who came to Brazil with Dom John. By dint of personality and his successful way with Indians, whom he genuinely liked, he rose to be director-general of all Indians in Minas Gerais. At the time of his death in 1836, the Doce valley had been pacified, the Botocudo and neighbouring tribes had been settled in conditions which preserved to some extent their own way of life and a profitable barter trade in ipecacuanha had been developed for the enrichment of the crown.

But after his death the remorseless antipathy between white and red man resumed, and three years later the thirteen settlements over which he had presided were all gone, as settlers poured into the Doce Valley and expropriated the territory reserved for the Indians they found there.[9] Farmers encroaching on Indian lands were never prevented from doing so by the authorities because the encroaching frontiersman could always provoke violent resistance, after which he asked for and invariably received 'protection' from the local militia. It little mattered whether the tribe was pacified or hostile. A settled tribe, like the Coroado, molested travellers on the roads of Minas Gerais, because they were the worse for drink. The armed companies of the Junta for the Conquest and Civilization of the Indians were then permitted to put into action the lethal skills they had so assiduously acquired and set about their slaughter. The Aimoré faced extinction as surely by their violent resistance to 'civilization' as the Kayapó and Coroado Indians by their acceptance of it. What police action began, hard labour, *cachaça*, measles and influenza completed.

Neither Pombal's directorate nor Dom Rodrigo's junta made any effort to repeat the Jesuit attempt to create an Indian civic personality under platonic conditions. 'Civilization' now meant keeping the savage under surveillance, instructing him in the Christian faith and introducing him to productive farming. Even so enlightened an operator as Marlière accepted that this was his task, only he discharged it with love, not, as was usual, with indifference and harshness. It was a hopeless undertaking. The white man thought the Indian lazy and unambitious, failing to recognize his amazing industry at hunting and fishing, or his ambition to preserve a way of life in which he had lived in equilibrium for centuries. The civilization gap between the white man and the red was not just of centuries but of aeons. Even so intelligent and thoughtful a man as José Bonifácio, Brazil's first chief minister, believed that the Indian must be persuaded to achieve the happiness of the greatest number by settling down to productive work with the same aspirations as the rest of the nation. As chief minister of independent Brazil, he put a motion before the Constituent Assembly on 18 June 1823, urging seriously that those charged with the conversion of the Indian should be equipped with 'an electric machine . . . on which to do curious and exciting experiments with matches and inflammable gas', in order to catch their attention and bring them to associate with civilized people.[10]

That assembly did call publicly for justice to be done to Indian land-claims and for peaceful commerce and intermarriage, and in this respect its members were as worthy as their colonial predecessors. They were also as ineffectual. Since it had no more time to give to the protection of the red man than was consumed in framing high-sounding legislation, it allowed terror and pacification to go hand in hand as the situation seemed to demand. In the dawn of anthropological science, it was too much to expect that the rough-hewn, often illiterate frontiersman should see the Indians as anything but livestock to be exploited or as squatters to be evicted from land he wished to farm. 'Condemned to a kind of perpetual childhood,' Saint-Hilaire observed in 1819, 'the Indians are frequently abandoned to the mercies of our barbarous superiority. Entire nations have disappeared before the men of our race. Like children the Indians need honest and vigilant teachers animated by Christian sentiments, continuously preoccupied with their happiness.'[11] His words are, alas, no less true today than 170 years ago.

It was hard for the missionaries to understand that the Indian had no interest in Christianity, which at best seemed to be only white man's magic and at worst the reason why so many of them had been reduced to slavery. Drink gave the Indian more spirit than did Christianity. More often than not baptism was a useless solemnity; but as white man's magic it might be powerful against an enemy, so that families presented themselves for the sacrament repeatedly to different priests, both for the aura it gave and for the customary gifts that went with it. Johann Emmanuel Pohl met baptized Indians who were wholly ignorant of the Lord's Prayer and who so liked the marriage ceremonies that they asked for them to be repeated so that the two spouses could receive their presents again.[12] To the *roceiro*, hacking out a farm from the wilderness, the crown's solicitude for the Indian's status as a free Christian meant that he had to be paid for labour that he could otherwise be enslaved to do. Drink was used to lure Indians into settlements, to entrap them into debt, make them drunk and disorderly so that they could be punished with hard labour and to lure them back when they ran away. Colonization 'turned the drunkenness of the Indian into a permanent state . . . Had it not been for miscegenation . . . the Indian strain would have been condemned to extinction.'[13]

The true forest Indian has not yet vanished from Brazil, but his survival is increasingly unlikely. The pure Amerindian has proved fatally susceptible to the diseases and delights of civilization. The naked innocence, too, of the Indian woman was irresistible from the start to the Portuguese male, and Indian women were as eagerly 'descended' for concubinage as their men for slavery. Arnaud Pallière, visiting Rio in the 1820s, was surprised to find that his Brazilian mistress shaved her pudenda because her Portuguese husband liked her without pubic hair, like an Indian girl.[14] The mixed breeds, *mamelucos* and *caboclos*, often indistinguishable from free mulattos, were of a tougher strain, more resistant to European diseases. They were also the pure Indian's most unremitting foe, haunting the fringes of the towns as freelance fishermen, ferrymen, *tropeiros*, guides and huntsmen, readily enrolling in armed bands bound for the forests on a 'civilizing mission' to 'descend' Indians.

The settled Indians gave such an impression of melancholic misanthropy that the naturalists and anthropologists who flocked to Brazil at the end of the European wars spared them little more than a passing glance. Their quarry was his forest cousin, whose savage inaccessibility was a lure purer than gold. Travellers penetrating the interior would often meet a family on the move, headed by a naked hunter, bow and arrow in hand, clad only in a head-piece of skins and a sheath of tightly sewn leaves for his penis, followed by his sons and women, wholly naked but for a girdle of spun bark, carrying the children and the old people on their shoulders and their pots and skins in baskets slung on each side by a thong across the forehead. Sometimes this sad procession trekked for months before their leader stopped and they built a cluster of palm-leaf huts, scorched the *mato* and planted manioc. Those who had come to study the noble savage in his forest haunts soon found that there was little noble about him but his patient and unlimited capacity for movement, his best, indeed his only real protection against the thraldom of civilization and his surest expression of that dislike for monotonous labour which had made him so much less desirable as a hand than an African slave. Spix and Martius were saddened by the grim wretchedness of the dominant tribe they visited in the region of Vila Nova in Rio Negro, the Mundurukú, 'for it seemed that they provide for even the simplest necessities of life in the manner of animals'.[15] Yet to their minds the Amazonian Indian had a higher level of culture than their southern cousins, closer to 'civilization'.

The two Bavarians set about classifying the Indians they met, and von Martius has a claim to be called the father of Brazilian ethnography. His work was so unusually thorough that for years it inhibited disagreement. Its main achievement was to establish eight separate linguistic groups, which enabled him to trace the migration patterns of the various tribes. He sketched their features and ornaments minutely, dwelling with loving detail on the Miranhas,

who distended the sides of their nostrils until they could be hung
from their earlobes, the Araná, who wore a reed through their noses,
the Munduruku, whose skill in plaiting birds' feathers rivalled that
of the lace weavers in the cloisters of Madeira, and the Maxuruna,
who spitted their ears, cheeks and lips with quills and thorns. He
transcribed their songs in the triple clef. He described their long
arrows tipped with bamboo or iron so that they drew a thick trail of
blood; their skill with the bow, especially that of small children, who
as soon as they could stand were taught to shoot at monkeys' heads
for popinjays and were considered to be beyond a parent's care when
they could shoot straight. He admired their legendary hunting skills,
their unerring aim. Another of Martius's countrymen actually claimed
to have seen an Indian repeatedly split an orange on the ground with
arrows shot vertically into the air from a distance of five paces.[16]

Against the ounce or Brazilian tiger and the alligator they had
perfected the blowpipe and poisoned dart. They could spear fish in
deep water, making the correct adjustment for refraction. They were
unaffected by the insects which drove Europeans mad. All tribes, if
they did not mutilate their features, painted their depilated bodies
with annatto and madder dyes and wore necklaces, often their only
clothing, of berries and anteater teeth. They brewed their own beer
from the manioc root, less potent than white man's liquor, and their
great delight was to dance their strange and lugubrious rounds 'like
regret for a lost paradise'.[17] They enacted strange ceremonies, such
as the depilation of a two-year-old female Tukuna child which
Martius witnessed at Tabatinga where Brazil meets the Colombian
and Peruvian borders. The men all wore animal masks made of bark
and the child was carried round in a bacchanal for three days and
nights; during these ceremonies the child being celebrated sometimes
died.[18] The Amazonian Mura had an insatiable thirst for *cachaça*
and their favourite sport was to thrash one another in a duel with
staves and then to stuff their nostrils with *paricá*, the leaf of *Cohaba
piptadenia*, which induced a state of insensibility often so complete
that the wretched savage never emerged from it alive.[19] By precise
and mordant observation, Martius destroyed the myth held only in
Europe that the Brazilian Indian lived in a kind of Rousseauan natural
paradise.

Considering the visible effects that civilization had had on the
Indian, the visitors showed an unexpected desire to expose some
of them to an experience they had observed to be fatal. The Prince

Maximilian von Wied-Neuwied, a disciple of the great ethnologist, Blumenbach (1752–1840), came to Brazil in 1831, resolved to make a study of the Aimoré or Botocudos. These studies were carried out with the help of a faithful Botocudo servant, Guack, who returned with him to Germany and whose portrait hangs in the castle of Neuwied. Saint-Hilaire also had a Botocudo servant who died of measles shortly after opting to return to his tribe rather than go to France. Martius bought six young men, two girls and three little boys from an Amazonian Indian who traded in captives from forest hutments. The eldest girls reached Munich and the others, 'all otherwise destined to die from fever', were distributed among his Portuguese acquaintances.[20] The Botocudo couple whom Pohl took to Vienna became the main attraction of the Brazilian Museum.

As Europe became passionately interested in the autochthon, that hunted and dispossessed creature became for a short time the symbol of Brazilian national aspirations. Indianism became for the *mazombo* almost a badge of authenticity. Portuguese names were exchanged for Indian. It became socially distinguished to boast some Indian blood in one's veins. When Brazil became a co-equal kingdom with Portugal, the exalted chronicler of the event warbled that 'Indian Brazil put aside her head-dress and plumes . . . and received from the munificent hand of Dom John a crown of diamonds and the royal cloak of purple to cover her ancient nakedness'.[21] On the birthday of Dona Leopoldina in 1818, Lacombe, the French *maître de ballet* in Rio, put all his 200 dancers for the gala performance into Indian undress. But the interest was superficial, even nominal. When a deputy suggested to the Constituent Assembly that Tupi might replace Portuguese as the official language of the empire, there were no aids to learning the language in existence and virtually no literate people who knew a single word of the language that was common to most of the Indians of the coastal and Amazon regions. The Indian as a myth was one thing; the Indian as squatter on coveted land was another. Despite Indian party games in Rio, the pressure on the untamed, footloose native was relentless.

The methods of oppression have not changed much over the past century and a half. The destruction of the Indian's environment drives him to forest retreats which in turn disappear before the tractor, the bullock and the plough, or to national parks. When he resists, his enemy kills him by any means to hand: physical assault, poison, lethal injections, infected clothing, booby-traps and terror.

The methods may not have changed, but the weapons have become more precise and the ubiquity of the white man enormously increased by the aeroplane. It has been obvious to all who have studied them that the Indian and European cannot be governed by the same laws. Saint-Hilaire's judgement of 1819 has been repeated by the Vilas Boas brothers who founded the Xingu National Park in the present century. The great French botanist could only hope that his own long and dolorous journey into the inhospitable interior and his many pages of detailed notes would enable his 'weak voice to be heard by a Brazilian who combined power with a love of good'.[22] Anthropologists are still waiting for that to happen.

10· Rebellion, 1817

'Here we need bayonets' —
Louis-François de Tollenare, 16 March 1817

*'Our Father in heaven created all men equal. The spirit of darkness
breathed a hellish vapour into the souls of the wicked who bound the
arms of their brethren, armed themselves with scourges and called
them Absolute Principles'* —
The dean of the cathedral in Recife, blessing the
new flag of the Pernambuco republic, 21 March 1817

The event that had delayed the arrival of Dona Leopoldina and the
acclamation of Dom John VI was an outbreak of insurrection in that
traditionally volatile province, Pernambuco. It looked, to an easily
frightened court, like an outbreak of the dreaded contagion from
Buenos Aires, revolutionary fever contracted in the Plate and carried
to Brazil by the 'doctors of Coimbra'. There had been insurrectional
conspiracies in Brazil before, but they had all been mild and relatively
short-lived affairs, and the colony had been only faintly disturbed
by tiny echoes of the greater revolutions in North America and in
France. The most celebrated had been the *Inconfidência* of Ouro
Preto in 1789. Since then, two Jacobin plots had been aborted in
1794 and 1798, one in Rio, the other in Salvador; the second was
known as the Tailors' Sedition from the two mulatto tailors who were
hanged for advocating the extinction of monopolies, the opening of
the ports to international commerce, the suppression of the religious
orders, the abolition of slavery and the establishment of a free republic
of black, brown, red and white.[1] These brave but futile gestures
of defiance lacked any form of organization or public support, and
any movement that advocated the abolition of slavery was bound to
receive short shrift from most of the people it was attempting to
revolutionize.

The spirit of revolutionary France, and to a lesser extent of the United States, remained lively among the younger clergy and planters' sons who had studied in Europe and who expounded the contents of their forbidden books in local *academias*, the more freely and more openly the further they were from the colonial or provincial capitals. The members of these learned societies were political innocents, but they gave their secret societies grand names and grander ideals, like the Areópago de Itambé, founded in 1798 by the botanist, Frei Arruda Câmara, doctor of Coimbra and Montpellier, protégé of Dom Rodrigo de Souza Coutinho. By the study of books, mostly French, this secularized Carmelite friar hoped to inculcate in his fellow-members liberal sentiments in harmony with nature and human dignity, to inspire in them hatred of despotism and to prepare for a republic in Pernambuco. The *Areópago* was dissolved in 1801 when three members, all brothers from a notable planter family, were suspected of plotting another *Inconfidência*. Its dissolution was followed by the rapid growth of other societies. The Academia de Suassena sought 'to cultivate, propagate and tend the roots of the occult science of liberty'.[2] The Oficina de Iguaraçu met under the presidency of the local *capitão-mor* of militia. The Academia do Paraíso of Recife gathered in the library of a hospice for the infirm and old. Members affiliated themselves either to the Orient or to the Occident Patriotic Lodges of Pernambuco, their aims a just society and the amelioration of the human condition. 'Academicians' taught at the seminary of Olinda, which was, as a result, accused of being a nursery of republicanism.[3]

A society of *Illuministas*, calling themselves the Cavaleiros da Luz ('Knights of the Light'), had been formed in Salvador in 1797, but the first masonic lodge in the colony was founded by a Frenchman in Niteroi, across the bay from Rio de Janeiro, in 1801 and affiliated to the French Grand Orient. Others proliferated, with fine names like Virtue and Reason Lodge (Salvador, 1802), Constancy, Emancipation and Philanthropy Lodge (Rio de Janeiro, 1803). Indeed, the great rallying-cry uttered by Dom Pedro when he declared the independence of Brazil, 'Independence or Death', was the name of a masonic lodge in São Paulo. The original members of these lodges were mainly Portuguese merchants and civil servants, and they followed the ceremony of the Lusitanian Grand Orient. Brazilians founded their own lodges, the first also in Niteroi (just out of reach of the capital across the water) in 1812. Its grand master was a young man whose name was to be famous in Brazilian annals, for he was none other than the younger brother of the Patriarch of Independence. Carlos Antônio de Andrada e Silva, born like José Bonifácio in Santos, was a lawyer, doctor of Coimbra naturally, and an intrepid and emotional talker. In a very short time there were exclusively Brazilian lodges in most big towns and in many country areas too, and nearly all influential *mazombos* were members of some lodge or other, meeting in the country, often in the *Casa Grande* itself. Brazilian masons were rather anti-Portuguese than anti-monarchical, so that the heady mixture of Illuminist and republican ideas was certainly too strong for most members, many of whom were planters and farmers, who nominally commanded the militia and were surrounded by an ocean of unfree blacks for whom the doctrines of liberty were not intended.

When Carlos Antônio de Andrada was transferred to Olinda as *ouvidor*, or district judge, he looked for the most likely lodge to give him the platform he could not be without and joined the Academia do Paraíso in Recife. There he lectured its members on the inadequacies of the Portuguese governor, Caetano Pinto de Miranda Montenegro. That genial dignitary, however, made it his business to be well-informed about the meetings, especially the dinners, which were held in the seemingly innocuous surroundings of an old people's home. Cakes made of manioc flour instead of bread were served, *aguardente* instead of wine, to emphasize that these were Brazilian occasions. In addition, excited toasts were given to any Brazilian-born wife who murdered her Portuguese-born husband in the cause of liberty.[4] Caetano Pinto was inclined to treat these horrendous libations as harmless, but one day a black officer from the Henriques regiment of free blacks struck a Portuguese officer for allegedly insulting Brazil, and this could not be overlooked. The governor assembled all the regular and militia officers, both *reinol* and *mazombo*, and dressed then down equally. The *mazombos* felt that the rebuke should not have been directed to them and that night, 5/6 March 1817, a handful of disaffected 'academicians' started to plot the expulsion of the Portuguese from the province of Pernambuco, like the Dutch before them. The rising was to be on Easter Sunday. But the governor's intelligence was too good and the following day he ordered their arrest.[5]

All but one of the ringleaders were rounded up, but that one, a militia veteran of over 60, José de Barros Lima, killed the officer sent to arrest him. As blood could only be paid in blood, the conspirators decided on an immediate insurrection. Their plans were not properly laid, but anti-Portuguese feeling had been simmering for so long that within a few minutes the streets were full of rioters and the governor prudently shut himself in the fortress of Brum at the harbour mouth. The rebels, half a regiment of artillery and a mixed brigade of white and mulatto militiamen, about 800 in all, rescued their arrested leaders and emptied the gaols at the same time, adding to the confusion in the streets. But they did secure the bridges connecting the island of Santo Antônio to mainland Recife, and so commanded the town. Caetano Pinto in Brum was sitting on all the live ammunition in the city, but the loyal troops who could have used it, not having been paid for 12 weeks, had all surrendered to the rebels on the distant promise that their needs would be the first call on the local treasury. By dawn on 7 March, all Recife was in rebel hands. The governor parleyed for a safe passage to Rio, which he was granted on the 12th. A revolutionary junta, calling itself a provisional government, declared Pernambuco a republic.

Believing that Bonapartes were born of bayonets, this junta in all its inexperience proceeded to send home the armed patriots who flocked into Recife to advance the cause of independence. It would not do to be seen as dependent on a disorderly rabble. Like so many revolutionaries before and after them, they were proposing a new order in which virtue would triumph. Agents were accordingly dispatched into the interior to reassure the planters and enlist their support. Before they had done so, however, they turned their energies to the forms rather than substance of revolution, and played at being Paris 1793.

Offices were distributed among the ringleaders. Religious affairs went to the professor of drawing at the Olinda seminary, Padre João Ribeiro Pessoa, who, 'nurtured on ancient and modern philosophers . . . only breathed for liberty'. A cotton factor, Domingos José Martins, the founder of the Pernambuco Occident Lodge, took commerce. He had once lived in England and sworn there a pact of friendship between the republics of their dreams with the Venezuelan revolutionary, Francisco de Miranda. Martins saw himself as the Robespierre of Brazil. His colleague, the *juiz de fora* or district magistrate of Recife, Luiz de Mendonça, wanted to be its Mirabeau. He now headed the justice department, but though a conspirator in name he was a conformist by nature and hoped to find a formula which would allow the republic to profess its loyalty to *El-Rei*. There were two other members of the

junta, which was modelled consciously on the French Directory of
1795. They were Militia-Captain Domingos Teotônio Jorge, who had
accepted the surrender of the loyal troops, and Militia-Colonel Correia
de Araújo. Both were ardent masons and Jorge had earlier travelled to
Niteroi with Martins to establish links with the lodges there. All of
them had a bookish knowledge of how revolutionaries should behave,
and as the first act of revolutionaries was to produce a constitution,
Ribeiro went off to consult his friend the resident French cotton
merchant, Louis-François de Tollenare. From this impeccable source
he hoped in vain to find a model which would promise universal
citizenship without extending it to most of the population, the slaves.
For Ribeiro, more sensible than most of his colleagues, put very little
trust in the conversion of semi-literate planters, unamenable to any
law they did not administer themselves, to the principles of republican
government.

'The first constitution made in Brazil by Brazilians' was the work of
another Carmelite, Frei Caneca do Divin Amor. Not surprisingly, it
was a document full of uncertainties. A Constituent Assembly was to
be called as soon as the neighbouring *comarcas*, or counties, had also
declared for independence. Until it met to produce a new code, the
public laws must prevail, unless they conflicted with the new freedoms
of conscience, opinion and the press. On 9 March a Council of Five
was co-opted to assist in the processes of government, but none
of them, even the 'walking academy', Carlos Antônio de Andrada,
had any experience of governing. All, however, knew with a deadly
clarity that if the republic were not to be brutally destroyed by its
own supporters, liberal measures must be very carefully expounded.
On their estates, as Padre Ribeiro had feared, the planters regarded
any talk of liberty as applicable only to themselves and their equals
and viewed popular sovereignty as providing the back door to a black
Napoleon. The good padre emphasized that the republic had no
intention of emancipating the slaves. The provisional government
would only take measures to reduce the evils of slavery, but it would
not end the institution by decree.

An early gesture was to send an emissary to the great sister
republic in the north. The ambassador was another merchant, Antônio
Gonçalves da Cruz, founder of the Patriotic Lodge of Pernambuco,
whose house had been converted into a 'chapel for baptized masons',
dedicated with portraits of the saints of the American and French
revolutions. He was to offer President Monroe free trade with

Pernambuco, 'in memory of your brilliant revolution which we are trying to imitate', in return for military supplies.[6] In Recife itself, honorific titles were abolished. White and mulatto citizens were addressed as 'Patriot' and the salutation 'Your Honour' was declared non-revolutionary. A new flag was designed for what was now to be called the Equatorial Republic. Horizontal bands of white with a red cross represented Santa Cruz, the first name with which the colony had been christened; a rainbow signified peace to all men, three stars stood for Pernambuco, Paraíba do Norte and Rio Grande do Norte, and the sun for the equator. Space was left for other stars as more provinces declared for the republic. Padre Ribeiro, longing for the day on which he could cast aside his cassock, drafted posters proclaiming support for the Fatherland, Our Lady, the Holy Catholic Religion and Death to Aristocrats. In the meanwhile the defenders of the republic promoted themselves to high rank and voted an increase in the troopers' pay. But they could not actually pay them, any more than could the governor. The provisional government had found only 6000 *contos* in the treasury, and instead of setting about raising more revenue, it repealed unpopular taxes, declared a free trade in Brazilwood and discussed where to site a new federal capital. While they wasted time, so the forces of reaction began to gather strength.

Governor Caetano Pinto was arrested on arrival in Rio de Janeiro for having made an accommodation with rebels, and was to spend four years in detention on the Ilha das Cobras, in the middle of Guanabara bay. Dom John sent in haste to Lisbon for more veteran Peninsular volunteers, the Bank of Brazil was ordered to lend the government a million cruzados (about £60,000) and regular troops were recalled from watching Indians in Minas Gerais and São Paulo. Soon the capital was swarming with soldiers from the outback, swelling the ranks of the 7000 militia volunteers in Rio de Janeiro itself. Dom John varied his daily journey from São Cristovão to the Chapel Royal (where he liked to arrive early from time to time to see that the clergy were punctual for mass) by walking 'to universal astonishment' to the Arsenal, where the expedition was assembling that was to restore Pernambuco to loyalty.[7] In Salvador the militia had been mustered, and at the end of March the Governor of Bahia, the Conde dos Arcos, sent two corvettes and a schooner to blockade Recife. A rebel priest, on a mission to raise Bahia, was discovered hidden in a cargo of coconuts on one of the balsa-wood rafts (*jangadas*) that plied the coastal trade. On 2 April, Admiral Rodrigo Lobo, recalled from the

Plate, sailed with reinforcements for the blockade, and a month later four regiments set off for Pernambuco under the command of its new governor, a Peninsular veteran, Luiz do Rego, who had just arrived from Lisbon.

The rebel junta seemed mesmerized by its danger. One hundred and fifty years had elapsed since the glorious days when the Dutch were expelled from the province by the combined efforts of Portuguese regulars and Brazilian irregulars. Military action since then had been a matter of uniforms and parades from which most officers managed to absent themselves. At no time did the republic take any bold steps that might have enabled it, if not to survive, at least to expire with honour. One by one the confederate provinces fell away. Eight hundred loyalist militiamen, calling themselves 'Scipios' after the unbeaten Roman general, marched out of Bahia to rout a rebel force in Alagoas. Rio Grande do Norte declared for *El-Rei* as soon as the Paraíba patriots withdrew to strike down counter-revolution in their own province. On 16 April, Admiral Lobo called on the junta in Recife to surrender or be shot out of hand. Padre Ribeiro and two Franciscan friars formed *guerilhas* to raise the countryside as it had once been raised against the Dutch. Militia-Captain Silva Pedroso, discovering that the soul of the revolution had entered into himself, hauled deserters from the gaols, and, crying that revolutions only sustained themselves on blood, had them publicly shot. Apart from the slaves who volunteered for armed service in return for freedom, the public put its head down. Those who could fled the city. Those who could not, and they were mostly the poor, roamed the streets hungrily, breaking into the shuttered shops and looting.

In a bold move, Martins, who had never seen a battalion of troops in battle order, marched south at the head of such troopers as could be persuaded to follow him to rally the faint-hearted planters behind the flag. Meanwhile, on 11 May, the Portuguese merchants clubbed together to offer the junta half a million francs to pack their bags and go. On 17 May, Martins met the 'Scipios' at Serinhão, in a brush between the incapable and the incompetent. The latter won. Martins was captured and Lobo refused an offer of conditional surrender from the remaining junta. Its moment of destiny was now approaching. Dictatorial powers were conferred on Domingos Teotônio Jorge, who demanded free passes from Lobo in return for the lives of his Portuguese prisoners. When this ultimatum expired unanswered on 19 May, he marched out of Recife at the head of two infantry regiments. At once the streets filled with jubilant Portuguese, leading the fickle mob in cheers for Admiral Lobo, who came ashore and found the city wholly loyal. Three days later a detachment of Indians armed with bows and arrows arrived and showed themselves more effective at policing the city than either the armed Portuguese citizenry, most of whom had been drunk for two days, or the 'Scipios' who followed them.

The dictator and his rebel survivors met Ribeiro's *guerilhas* at Engenho Paulista, where they held a council of war. Padre Ribeiro left it to hang himself. The others went off into the *mato*. The troopers, anxious to guard the honour of the republic, returned to Recife with the treasure chests unopened. Admiral Lobo ordered a Te Deum and opened the theatre for a *laus perenne* lasting three days and nights. The Portuguese merchants spent their half million francs instead on masses and sermons on the evils of Jacobinism. The freed slaves were restored to their masters and brutally flogged. One by one the rebel leaders were tracked down. Padre Ribeiro's body was disinterred and his head hacked off for public display. Martins was hanged along with the *juiz de fora*, Mendonça, and three priests. Silva Pedroso and Carlos Antônio were shipped to Salvador in chains like slaves and kept in durance made particularly vile by the company of flogged slaves, murderers and pimps. On 29 June the new governor arrived. Luiz do Rego was not disposed to mercy. The head of Domingos Teotônio Jorge went to grin over Olinda; Barros Lima and two others were hanged. The governor also signed warrants for the execution of five Paraíba rebels, including another priest. There the deaths stopped, for Dom John was acclaimed King of Portugal and Brazil in February 1818, and he declared an end to blood-letting. The First Infantry Regiment was packed off to Montevideo for allowing rebellion to survive for 74 days. Women who had had their hair cut short in republican style hid it under bob-caps until it grew again in honour of the king. But the prosecutions continued for four years until the prisons of Salvador and Recife were full.

Stendhal, tired of waiting for a revolution somewhere, preferably in England, wrote in his diary: 'This admirable insurrection in Brazil is the greatest thing to have happened and suggests that liberty is like the plague ... There is only one remedy for liberty — and that is concession.'[8] Luiz do Rego, however, put his faith in oppression. The causes of the revolt were neither examined nor understood. One theory was that high cotton prices during the Anglo-American war of 1812–13 had tempted planters to put more land under cotton at the expense of cheap home-grown food, which then, after a prolonged drought, became scarce.[9] The government in Rio blamed the freemasons. Commodore William Bowles, commanding on the South America station, reckoned it was the prelude to a black uprising.[10] The local historian blamed *mazombo* resentment at the tithe on agricultural produce and urban housing, none of which was spent in Pernambuco. 'Lighter arbitrary taxation than this had impelled the English colonies to deny the protection the mother country insisted on giving them.'[11] As a *mazombo* himself, he came nearest the truth. At the heart of the revolt was not only a protest against non-representational government but a bid for independence of both Rio de Janeiro and Lisbon, a theme to recur more than once in the subsequent history of the province. Because the heart went so quickly out of the revolt, the court was inclined to treat it as the latest if the most serious of a long list of incidents between *reinóis* and *mazombos*. It was a view reinforced by a curious incident that occurred soon after the revolt was finally crushed. Dom John had summoned more hard-bitten Peninsular veterans to Brazil to keep the lid on the pot. When they arrived they behaved with such a high hand that a tattoo to celebrate Dom Pedro's 20th birthday in 1818 had to be cancelled when the organizers learned that the loyal Bahian 'Scipios' and the Voluntários d'El Rei were preparing to settle their scores during the battle manoeuvres.[12]

The Recife business could have been passed over as something peculiarly Brazilian had it not sparked off a second, abortive revolt in Lisbon. Discontent in the *Reino* had been simmering since the end of the war, which, despite the valour of the Portuguese army, had given Portugal nothing. How long, asked the junior officers, was Sir William Beresford to be allowed to treat her as an occupied country? Perhaps the time had come to change the dynasty again, as once upon a time they had transferred sovereignty from the House of Aviz to the House of Braganza. The Braganzas could stay in Brazil if that was what they preferred, and in their place they would enthrone the Duke of Luxembourg's nephew, the half-French Duque de Cadaval. In May 1818, while Beresford was in Caldas, where mutinous troops had refused to embark for Pernambuco, General Gomes Freire, Grand Master of the Knights of the Cross (despite its chivalric title a freemasonic lodge) and formerly commander of Napoleon's Portuguese legion, led the garrison into Lisbon's streets to declare for a Cortes and constitutional monarchy.

Beresford acted with terrible and unexpected speed. Gomes Freire and his associates were arrested and tried in camera. Eight of the ringleaders were hanged, their bodies incinerated and ashes cast into the sea. Four other victims were beheaded. The loyal officers and men, whom Beresford had no money to pay, were appalled by the savagery, so much greater than that which was meted out to the larger *Inconfidência* in Recife. Beresford made light of the conspiracy but Castlereagh saw the danger ahead and urged Dom John to return to the *Reino* or send his son as viceroy before he lost it for ever. He even sent Canning as an official ambassador to Lisbon to meet him. But Canning waited in vain. Instead, Dom John on 3 March 1818 banned all masonic societies in both kingdoms, acknowledging the existence of liberal conspiracy but doing nothing to disarm it. The Brazilians resented the ban as an attack on the only legitimate vehicle for national self-expression they had. The Portuguese dissidents, determined to succeed where Gomes Freire failed, and to rid Portugal of her British general staff, went deeper underground.[13] The cauldron continued to seethe and bubble while Dom John returned thankfully to the masses of Marcos Portugal and José Maurício, and the loyal tributes of his faithful people in Rio de Janeiro.

11· The Kingdom of Brazil: Church

*'The African has been the principal instrument in the occupation
and development of our land by the European . . . Where he has not
yet been the land is just as the first discoverers saw it'* —

Joaquim Nabuco, in 1883

*'Je n'ai vu de lieu où le Christianisme parut avec plus d'éclat qu'en
cette ville, soit par la richesse et la multitude des Eglises, des Couvens
et des Gentishommes, des Dames et des Courtisannes'* —

François Correal, *Voyages aux Indes Orientales*, Amsterdam, 1722,
describing Salvador da Bahia

The kingdom which Dom John had brought into existence was now
beginning to show life of its own. For though he had established in
the colony all the institutions and ceremonials of the ancient kingdom
he had left, it was a very different place, inhabited by very different
people. The taciturn Portuguese and the melancholic Indian were
minorities in a land where the larger part of humanity derived some
or all of its genes from Africa. And it was that African inheritance
which brought the note of joy to life which visitors found (and still
find) so striking, despite the brutal cruelties of slavery. Indeed, one of
Africa's great gifts to the world developed in the Brazilian *senzala*.[1]

For unless the slave could dance he died. Dancing kept him alive
across the middle passage when he was allowed on deck, it punctuated
with its only moments of pleasure a life of otherwise hopeless drudgery.
The main form was the *batuque*, danced with the men and women in
concentric circles, clapping their hands and stamping their feet to
the beat that is now famous throughout the world, accompanied by
drums and bells. It originated in Angola, and its principal movement,
the *semba*, was when the man changed his partner by pressing his
navel against the woman's. One old India hand found the orgies of
the nautch 'never equalled (the *batuque*) for flagrancy'.[2] It was also

a fine occasion for a punch-up. In 1814 some 600 slaves ran amok after a *batuque* in Salvador, and for a moment people thought it was the beginning of an insurrection. The city fathers asked the governor to ban something so dangerously exciting. The governor decided otherwise. In his view, far from extending the brotherhood of the oppressed, the *batuque* was a potent source of inter-tribal conflict and helped to keep the slave nations divided. In the white south, owners took no risks. The *batuque* was banned in Curitiba on pain of 50 lashes and 30 days in prison.[3]

Today's samba bears little relationship to the *semba* movement of the *batuque*. The parades and costumes of the Brazilian carnivals which are now mainly tourist attractions were imported from Madeira during the 19th century, and the dance has been adapted to fit a processional defile of opulent splendour, a far cry from the beaten earth outside the slave cabins where it was originally danced. Only the beat of the drum and the lascivious contortions of the dancers can take us back in imagination to its origins. Carnival in Brazil was originally celebrated by something far more Indo-European, the *entrudo*, a frolic which bore a marked resemblance to the rain festivals of south Europe and the Hindu Indian *holi*. Hollow spheres of wax filled with water or flour were hurled at all and sundry like snowballs. No one was secure, neither the woman in her finery nor the Commander of Christ in his opera box. Dom Pedro was an enthusiastic player of the *entrudo*, carrying on the burlesque even as a crowned head. Slaves were particularly addicted, often wholly masked in flour until the Ave Maria closed the day's excitement.[4]

Brazil belonged to the Catholic south, but the tenets of that church commanded a light and easy loyalty. The colony had been spared both the Inquisition and ecclesiastical triumphalism. Despite the traditional privileges and respect accorded to the church in a Catholic land, religious fervour was tempered by the ignorance and indolence that usually accompanies a shortage of clergy. In 1456, the pope had conceded to the Grand Master of the Order of Christ the 'spiritual' revenues of Ultramar, and as the king was always the grand master, it was he and not the church who received the customary tithe, now to all intents and purposes a form of income tax, after revenue from customs duty the principle source of government income. In return he had assumed responsibility for all clerical stipends, and these were mean enough to ensure that the clergy were generally hard up. The primate of Brazil was in Salvador, and there were five other bishops, two of them with sees *in partibus infidelium*. None of them appeared to enjoy what in Britain would have been considered necessary to men of their rank. If the higher clergy found it hard to make both ends meet, the lower clergy lived pretty near the breadline. The main evangelists of Brazil had been the Society of Jesus, and following its expulsion in 1759 the bishops had tried to shoulder the burden of the Christian apostolate, borne by that maligned society with a distinction parallelled in few other mission fields. With some 1000 priests to a population of 800,000 in the four southern and central dioceses alone, and that population spread over an area the size of all Europe west of the Elbe, it was difficult for the bishops to visit all the clergy and more difficult to discipline them. It was easier to keep an eye on them in the more thickly populated coastal towns, but in the interior few brought either distinction or credit to their cloth.

The first missionaries to the Highland Mines were *bandeirante* priests, usually vagrant friars who had joined the Indian manhunts or the gold rush. So poor were the rewards of clerical life, in this world at least, that the seminary in Mariana, near Ouro Preto, founded in 1750 to bring a decent Christianity to the interior, was closed in 1811 because it could recruit neither teachers nor seminarians. Those who had originally enrolled had mostly failed in other avocations, being unpaid foot-soldiers, disappointed gold-diggers, mulattos seeking to better themselves and bastards who were normally denied access to the priesthood.[5] Many of the priests who had persisted to ordination had to support themselves and their common-law wives and children by running businesses or farms, like Father Freitas, who had opened the Morro Velho goldmine, and Father Pedro, whom Koster met in Pernambuco running a profitable sugar-mill with army deserters and criminals 'of honour', and whose lands were patrolled by bloodhounds.[6] Debt or tax-collectors rash enough to trespass were put to work on his treadmill. Travellers to Minas Gerais were all indebted to Father Correa, at whose farm on the border of the province their mules were well shod and rice was sold at half the price charged on the other side of the border post.[7]

On the whole, the Brazilian clergy were temperate men, assiduous at looking after the sick and charitable as far as their means permitted. Some of them had pretensions to scholarship and were keen amateur naturalists, like the author of the *Flora Fluminensis* which had attracted Saint-Hilaire to Brazil. Some had extensive libraries, like Canon Luiz Victor Vieira in Minas Gerais, who had collected the works of

Condillac, Montesquieu and Voltaire and who subscribed to Diderot's *Encyclopédie*. The parish priest of Santa Lucia, a tiny township in Goiás, had collected all the best works of the age of Louis XIV.[8] But if they observed most of the rules of the church, celibacy was not among them. It was not expected of the country clergy, and Martius stayed with one young priest in Minas Gerais who, surrounded by his mulatta women and children, 'seemed worthily to emulate the hermit in *The Decameron*'. His library consisted of Ovid's *Ars Amatoria*.[9] One cleric, who had himself carried in a sedan chair by the two sons his cook had borne him, aroused general disgust — not at his parenthood but at putting his by-blows to work like slaves.[10] Saint-Hilaire, good Catholic that he was, was troubled to find that the Brazilian clergy lived 'in a habitual state of concubinage'.[11] The harshest opinion was uttered by José Bonifácio de Andrada, who was outraged to find the clergy 'for the most part ignorant and corrupt, the first to use slaves to enrich themselves through commerce or agriculture and often the first to set up with wretched women in a sort of Turkish harem'.[12] The priesthood did not attract the sons of rich or educated families and there was a prejudice against celibacy among a people who were constantly urged to be fruitful and multiply. In 1823, a clerical deputy proposed that the Legislative Assembly should invite the pope to abolish clerical celibacy as 'not being enjoined on the clergy by divine law, but a source of immorality'.[13]

Many of the clergy in the cities belonged to the religious orders. The Benedictines were the richest; the Carmelites ran efficient farms with a big, native-born slave force; and the Franciscans were generally thought to be the worst behaved but the most charitable. St Anthony of Padua (being originally Portuguese) enjoyed the rank of lieutenant-colonel from 1814 to 1911, and his monthly pay was distributed to the swarms of beggars who waited at his convent gates. No order had been able to capture the loyalty of the people like the Jesuits, but individual priests were to find their niches in the Brazilian pantheon for their contribution to science or for their part in the national epic. Many of them were keen 'Academicians' and suffered for their opinions on the gallows, especially after the Recife rebellion. Lieutenant Prior was told in 1813 that the Archbishop of Salvador was a freemason and that a portrait of George IV as prince regent in full masonic regalia had been exposed in a church in the city.[14] And four years after the rebellion, the Governor of Recife confined all the mendicant friars to their convents as dangerous Jacobins. Seven of the first 49 deputies to the Constituent Assembly in 1822 were in holy orders (one was the Bishop of Rio), and in 1825, the Carmelite friar, Frei Caneca, who had drawn up the constitution for the Pernambuco Equatorial Republic, was to be shot after another attempt at a revolutionary republic in 1825. A secular priest, Father Feijó, served as Regent of Brazil from 1835 to 1837.

The Nuremburg artist, Rugendas, thought that the respect accorded to the clergy who were neither polymaths nor heroes was one of the finest and most characteristic features of the moral state of Brazil. 'They are counsellors and friends of the family, consolers and protectors of the oppressed and mediators in dissension and strife.'[15] If true, they could hardly have hoped for a better commendation, but their helplessness in alleviating the lot of the slave, especially on the new coffee plantations in the south, has already been described. But they were stitched into the fabric of the colony as an essential part of its social cohesion and if the clergy did little to challenge its basic institutions, they were sufficiently public-spirited to take a lead in local affairs and, when the opportunity came, to enter politics. By and large, they had little more education than their parishioners required. For the Brazilian was the devotee of a religion without subtlety or theology. He was ready to recognize the basically pessimistic and suffering side of humanity by an adherence to cults redolent of pain and desolation: Our Lord of Suffering, the Dead Lord, the Lord of the Sepulchre, Good Jesus of the Flagellation, Our Lord of the Agony. But these devotions were 'without obligation or rigour, intimate and familiar, and dispensed the faithful from all exertion, diligence or tyranny over himself'.[16] If fireworks were a passport to heaven, the people of Salvador were sure of salvation, and the Reverend Robert Walsh reckoned that the people of Rio de Janeiro spent £15,000 a year on wax and gunpowder for their *festas*.[17]

The faithful, moreover, were not much given to confession, so that 'the pastor's office was not onerous unless he chose to make it so'.[18] Those that did were the priests who served in the outback. There the priest was a stranger, often little more than a consecrated pedlar who passed by once or twice a year with an altar slung over his pack-saddle and faculties to hear confessions tucked in the band of his hat. His fees and offerings might amount to little more than £150 a year, 'hardly earned if the inconveniences and privations they must undergo to obtain it are taken into consideration'.[19] Perhaps that was why the parish priest of São João d'El Rei told Saint-Hilaire that the pastors in the interior treated most moral offences as a lark (*uma brincadeira*).[20]

Article XII of the Treaty of Commerce with Britain had allowed non-Catholic foreigners to build places of worship so long as they did not look like churches or advertise their services. When the papal nuncio protested, the Bishop of Rio told him that though the English had no religion, they were a proud and obstinate people. 'If you oppose them they persist and make it an affair of infinite importance, but if you concede to their wishes the chapel will be built and nobody will ever go near it'.[21] Protestant travellers to Brazil were not too greatly shocked by what they saw. Lord Macartney in 1792 had been agreeably surprised to find neither the friars nor the nuns 'at all disposed to run into the gloomy excesses of devotion, and nothing could be more sprightly than the conversation of the latter with strangers at the convent gates'.[22] Protestant visitors generally approved of the relative absence of nuns. In the great Ajuda convent in Rio de Janeiro, Robert Walsh met only 28, mostly old. For in underpopulated Brazil there was as great a prejudice against religious chastity for women as there was indulgence for concubinage among priests. There were no Maria Monks in Brazil. Indeed, outside the coastal cities there were no nunneries, and in the Highland Mines a royal decree had prevented the alienation of mining land to an immortal corporation, so that no religious houses could be established. In the coastal cities nuns looked after orphans and refractory wives; in the interior they were the charge of lay women in special asylums (*recolhimentos*). In 1808 the secular clergy in Rio de Janeiro were thought to number no more than 200, regulars 120 and nuns 60. 'These, then, are the many convents and excessive number of priests and friars for which Rio, according to foreigners, is famous.'[23] Most of the clergy were white. Despite the long years of evangelization, few Indians had been ordained and only a small number of the black and mulatto priests were Brazilian-born, except in Bahia. Most of them came from São Thomé or Portuguese Africa.[24]

For the black man, a religious feast was pretty well his only chance of a day off. He had a special devotion to Our Lady of the Rosary, depicted as a black Madonna. On her feast day, the slaves from the area of the lower Congo on the plantations and in the mining towns used to elect a King and Queen of the Congo. These monarchs 'reigned' until they abdicated or were replaced. They were not necessarily husband and wife, and they did not have to abdicate together. They were crowned by the parish priest after a solemn mass, after which there was a grand procession and feast. These straw monarchs were usually a pretty woebegone pair, but sometimes they were of chiefly caste in their country of origin and enjoyed a kind of ritual jurisdiction over their fellow-countrymen. On some estates, the 'Congo King' was used like the *kapo* in a Nazi concentration camp, to keep a watch on his 'subjects' and report any misdemeanour. The ceremony of coronation was known as the *Congada* and the dances that accompanied it enacted the ritual of an ancient African court. The king received ambassadors and declared war (as a Christian monarch) on pagans who were then overthrown in an energetic battle dance.[25]

Christianity sat lightly on most Brazilians, but lightest of all on the blacks. Among the Nagôs of Nigeria were often shamans or fetishist holy men who resisted the acculturation of Christianity. This was often easier for them as they were *pretos da ganha* and could move about with relative freedom, keeping their tribal contacts in the city. With them had come their tribal gods, the *orixás*, or possessing spirits, disguised as Christian saints and invoked in elaborate rituals and dances. Xangô, masquerading as St John the Baptist, and the Ibeji twin deities as SS Cosman and Damian were venerated as powerful thaumaturges. Yemanjá, the goddess of the waters, shared similar attributes to Our Lady of the Immaculate Conception, standing on her new moon. The Yoruba war-god, Ogun, appeared as St George, Iansa or Oxossil, goddess of storms, as St Barbara, the patron saint of gunners. These Nigerian *orixás* entered into a person's body during a state of ecstasy induced by a mixture of drink, tobacco and dancing, and reigned there temporarily, giving utterance occasionally by means of strange squeaks and spasms that only the holy man could interpret — or woman (they were known as *paes* or *maes de santos*, fathers or mothers of the holy spirits).

These *orixás* were also adopted by slaves from southern Bantu tribes as their ancestral deities and became master-spirits requiring worship. The *caboclos*, urbanized Indians and half-breeds, likewise assimilated the spirits of their pantheon to both Christian and Nagô hagiology, and throughout the 19th and 20th centuries their cults have survived until, today, spiritism is probably the dominant religion of Brazil. The *candomblés* of Bahia are expressions of comparatively pure spiritual expression, often with music and hymns, like pagan congregationalism. The *macumba* rites of Rio de Janeiro have something of everything, black magic, maledictory spells, glossolalia, ecstasy and spirit healing.

Umbanda, a word of African origin, though claiming links with Sanskrit, seeks to endow an Asiatic theology and a Christian ethos with an Afro-American pantheon in worship of the world spirit. This religious syncretism is described today as 'a proletarian manifestation of Brazil's racial democracy', but in origin it provided the uprooted and disorientated blacks with something that did not belong to their masters and gave them black gods as powerful as, if not more powerful than, the white saints whose powers they usurped.[26]

The corporal acts of mercy were the responsibility of lay brotherhoods (*irmandades*), subscription societies whose members were protected in health, nursed in sickness and buried in style. They built and maintained churches, provided for the sick, visited the imprisoned, solaced the condemned, buried the dead and prayed for the souls in purgatory. Black confraternities, made up of free blacks and mulattos, also redeemed other slaves and provided the same services as the white for their members. In death the fraternities often saw to it that the black was accorded equal respect to the white. Each church had its *irmandade*, whose members ensured that the patronal feat was celebrated with suitable magnificence and beautified it in their wills. The brotherhoods also supported hospitals, the most famous being the Santa Casas da Misericórdia in Salvador and Rio, open night and day to receive the sick and homeless without distinction of race, colour or sex, bond and free. The royal governess, Maria Graham, found the Rio *santa casa* very cold and damp and thought that many of its patients died soon after admittance, and another visitor reckoned that, of its 7000 admissions each year, 1000 died. But in poor societies the sick only go to hospital when it is too late to provide them with more than a decent death. Robert Walsh in 1827 found the place clean, even though he was told that there were 670 patients crammed into three lines of beds. The foundling hospital, also maintained by the brotherhood with revenue from lotteries, had no better record, since barely a third of the children thrust through the revolving doors survived into adult life. Many were mortally sick when they were delivered, and some already dead, left there for burial. Perhaps 1000 infants were received each year, but many were put straight out to nurse and adoption and never accounted for thereafter.[27]

Rio de Janeiro had a wicked reputation for sickness, and from the constant sound of handbells accompanying the viaticum to the dying and church bells tolling the dead to their graves, the royal librarian reckoned it must be more unhealthy even than Africa. In 1811 the

Misericórdia buried 300 Portuguese citizens.[28] There was not much good medicine in the cities; in the interior, treatment was often kill or cure, practised by the 18th-century equivalent of 'bare-foot doctors' licensed to practise after a perfunctory oral examination from an examiner whose knowledge of medicine was confined to a couple of textbooks. Apothecaries were all acquainted with William Cullen's *Materia Medica* in a French edition, but most prescriptions owed more to Dr Dulcamara, and the influence of the greatest pharmacologist of his time paled to insignificance before the pharmacopoeia of Brazil. A man bitten by a snake expected to die unless he could find a *curador*, either an Indian or a *cafuzo*, to suck the poison from the bite, whisper incantations and apply a poultice made from the black root (*Chiococco anguifuga*).[29] Armadillo's blood or rattlesnake broth were prescribed cures for syphilis in Minas Gerais.[30] Snake-skin pounded into a herb broth was a common unguent made up in the pharmacies of the *Santas Casas* as late as 1820, and when no other remedy was available, the blood of a black cock was considered more effective than nothing. Dulcified mercury was taken for fever and sufferers from rheumatism in the damp *senzalas* allowed themselves to be bled by having made in the skin an incision over which a cow's horn was fixed in such a way that the vacuum created drew out a limited amount of blood over an extended period of time. It was a not uncommon sight to see half-naked bodies lying out on Sundays, covered with small horns like exhausted cuckolds.[31] Quacks and shamans, known as *curiosos*, often acquired considerable homoeopathic skills, and naturalists were often assumed to be versed in medical lore and expected to be free with their medicine chests.[32] Martius was set on in Minas Novas by a mulatto with a sword who refused to believe he was not a doctor.[33]

The commonest ailments were dysentery, syphilis, hydrocele, prickly heat, festering bites and fevers of alarming virulence. Smallpox was only sporadic, for vaccination was widespread at the end of the 18th century, though it continued to ravage the Indians. Outside the Amazon basin there were no endemic fevers, but a man once stricken worsened rapidly and often died. Some people attributed much illness to the intemperate consumption of sugar-cane brandy, but *cachaça* has probably kept more people alive than it has killed. More often than not a man died of the treatment he received, and this was one reason why the English insisted on having their own seamen's hospital across the bay at Niteroi.

12· The Kingdom of Brazil: State

*'There reigns in Brazil a vast system of subornment: everyone is venal;
a few cruzados satisfy the consciences of the judges; justice is sold like a
piece of private property to him who pays the most'*—

Karl Siedler, *Zehn Jahren in Brasilien*, 1835

*'The police here is in a wretched state. The lure of the dagger is
so frequent, that the secret murders generally average 200 yearly
between the upper and lower town'*—

Maria Graham, Salvador da Bahia, Friday, 19 October 1821

One of the passengers with Dom John on his voyage across the
Atlantic was the Surgeon-Major of Portugal. José Correa Picanço was
actually a native of Pernambuco, and it was his advice that prompted
the regent to decree the foundation of a school of anatomy and surgery
in Salvador on 18 February 1808. A second school, in Rio, was set up
in the military hospital under the Surgeon-Major of Angola. A third
school was located in the Rio *santa casa* in 1813. Hitherto Brazilians
had gone to Coimbra or to Montpellier to study medicine (112 in the
course of the 18th century), but few of them returned to practise in
the colony. In 1789 there were only four university-qualified doctors
in Rio de Janeiro. Robert Walsh was more impressed by the military
hospital than the *santa casa* and thought it was the equal of any
institution in Europe; and the painter Debret in 1831 thought that
'the majority of the new hospitals in Brazil can rival in more than
one respect those of France and have the advantage of a locale that
combines the needs of the sick with the exigencies of public health'.[1]
The sea, that great dustbin and disinfectant, was never far away.

The expulsion of the Jesuits had not been followed, despite Pombal's
hopes, by a 'reformation, but by the destruction, pure and simple, of
the whole colonial system of Jesuit teaching'.[2] The 25 houses, 36
missions and 17 colleges of the society were replaced by dominies

licensed by the crown. They bore the grand titles of regius professor (*professor regio*), but in 1808 there were only 17 of them teaching the simple skills of reading and writing, 15 of them teaching Latin grammar, 6 of them rhetoric, 3 Greek, and 3 philosophy, divided between Rio de Janeiro, Salvador, São Luiz, Belém, Recife and the three gold cities of Vila Rica, Sabará and São João d'El Rei. They were paid from a tax on *cachaça*, but had they actually received the value of that tax, they would have been rich. As it was they had to rely on a tax on butcher's meat, which was also raised on their behalf.[3] From the ministrations of this royal schoolmaster, a child could go on to a seminary, and from there either into the church or on to Coimbra university. Only one seminary, that at Olinda, had a syllabus that covered more than the barest minimum required for ordination. Those who went to Coimbra usually made their careers outside the colony, but those that came back were either in orders or else scions of the local gentry, who expected them to carry on the tradition of their caste, which was to manage the estate or hold a number of sinecures. With the arrival of the court there was a rash of private schools in the capital, including special schools for girls, teaching French and music; and in 1827 Robert Walsh found schools for the three Rs in nearly every street in Rio de Janeiro, open to blacks and whites. He was told that 'mechanics' were encouraged to acquire an education to fit them for the army, the navy or the church, the traditional avocations of the privileged, but was almost certainly conned. Formal education remained for another century the almost exclusive privilege of those with money, but within a generation the education of both girls and boys outside the home had become a regular feature of life among the monied classes. This did not mean that it was confined to whites. Black and mulatto engineers, lawyers and journalists, were to achieve national distinction in 19th-century Brazil

In 1808 Dom Rodrigo de Souza Coutinho founded a naval academy in the hospice of the Benedictine monastery of São Bento in Rio, and two years later he transformed the artillery school (set up in 1795) into a military academy. This was to provide regular training to Brazilian-born officers as well as to provide a seven-year course in the exact sciences for the engineers, surveyors and cartographers who were to develop the immense colony. The academy moved into buildings intended earlier for the new cathedral, and Dom Rodrigo himself devised the syllabus that earned for him the soubriquet 'Dr Hodge-Podge' ('Doutor Trapalhada').[4] A chair in economics for Silva Lisboa was founded in Salvador, and in Rio de Janeiro the Chamber of Commerce, established in 1810, offered courses in agriculture (1812), chemistry (1817) and technical drawing (1818). The minister's utilitarian preoccupation with professional and technical education may have given him a Napoleonic prejudice against the traditional university, but, having transported the whole apparatus of government across the ocean, his first preoccupation was to have it properly serviced. In 1816 the merchants of Brazil offered to buy shares in the Bank of Brazil to establish an academic institute modelled on the contemporary German *Hochschule*, but the money was diverted by royal decree of 12 August to found the Royal School of Sciences, Arts and Crafts for the team of artists that had accompanied the Duc de Luxembourg to Rio de Janeiro. Only in 1827, with the schools of law in São Paulo and Recife, were juridical and social studies added to the other disciplines available to Brazilians, but the awesome influence of the Coimbra establishment prevented the foundation of a university in Brazil until long after independence.

The sudden stimulus to self-improvement that followed the arrival of the court was greatly fortified by the establishment of the Royal Press on 13 May 1808. Though what it printed was tame — government decrees, royal panegyrics, Brazil's first newspaper, the twice-weekly *Gazeta do Rio de Janeiro* — the fact that it existed was revolution enough. Between 1808 and 1833 it produced 1,154 titles: books on commerce and political economy, moral philosophy, poetics, dramatics, nautical almanacs, dictionaries, textbooks, treatises on diseases among blacks, Aguiar's translation of Pope's *Essay on Man*, *A History of Extraordinary Illusions and Supernatural Influences*, and the first Portuguese translation of Southey's *History of Brazil*. In 1821, Rio had a daily newspaper, *O Diário*, but by then the government no longer had a monopoly of newsprint. From 1808, too, books and newspapers entered Brazil freely on British ships, despite a feeble attempt at control by the police intendant. Not that Brazilians have ever been great readers. The Braganza library, with its 60,000 to 70,000 volumes, was freely open to the public but little used. In 1823 Maria Graham thought that few books had been added to the collection for 60 years, and a further 150 years of education have not refuted the monk among São Bento's worm-eaten volumes who told his British visitor that Brazil 'was not a country to read in'.[5]

Dom John apart, the royal family hardly read at all, and not a single member of the nobility subscribed in 1833 to the new edition of Father

Casal's *Corográfia Brazilica*, then the most compendious work on the Brazil they inhabited. This lack of interest was almost wilful; 'one of the major inconveniences the Brazilians experienced after the arrival of the king', observed Saint-Hilaire, 'was to be governed by men who knew nothing about America. They judged the country rich when it is poor and the inhabitants stupid when they are intelligent and can learn everything.'[6] If the French botanist was unfair to Dom Rodrigo, whom he never knew and who had tried to promote a knowledge of the country among his fellow Portuguese, he was otherwise right.

Given the indifference of the Portuguese who arrived unwillingly in 1808 and were forced to stay for 13 years instead of 13 months, the unpopularity of those who were in the colony when they arrived, the importation of a whole set of social institutions not entirely welcome to the indigenous inhabitants, especially recruitment for an unwanted war in the south, the ingrained attitude of violence towards slaves and Indians, it was surprising that the social cauldron did not constantly boil over into strife. But 'no greater quantity of vice exists here than in London', was one visitor's view, and he wished that murder was as seldom committed in the civilized countries of Europe.[7] Perhaps it was not as rare as he thought. The royal librarian reported 22 homicides in five days during 1813, even though the forces of law and order were very visible, parading through the streets 'with huge swords that rattle on the pavements *in terrorem* to offenders', suspected of half the robberies committed in the cities.[8] For the 'police powers were too great for the habits and mental culture of men who had been selected to it rather from their personal knowledge of bad characters than their claims to a good one!'[9] Despite the fondness of the poor blacks and English sailors for cheap rum, the only drunkards the Reverend Robert Walsh encountered in Rio de Janeiro were policemen.[10]

The intendant of police was not only responsible for law and order but also for public works, the second usually being constructed by the labour of those who had fallen out with the first. Not all these were necessarily criminals, for justice in Brazil was slow, corrupt and unequal. This was not because the laws were bad, for Portuguese legislation was among the fairest and most humane in the world and the doctors of Coimbra were well trained in drafting *alvarás, decretos* and all the other instruments of justice. The trouble lay with the human agents of this formidable corpus of law. For judicial and administrative purposes, Brazil was divided into *comarcas*, the nearest equivalent to a county, of which the principal officer was the *ouvidor corregedor*, like

Carlos Antônio de Andrada in Olinda. He was appointed by the crown for a period of three years and responsible for civil, criminal and even ecclesiastical jurisdiction, and expected to tour like a district judge on circuit. More often than not he was unwilling to brave the discomforts of the journey and the hostility of the planters who had their own ideas about dispensing justice. It was usually less tiresome, and more profitable, to delay or even suppress cases than to deal with them. Under the *ouvidor* was the *juiz de fora*, a district magistrate like the Recife rebel, Luiz de Mendonça. He was also nominated by the crown, but very willing to take his cue from his superior. Under him was the *juiz ordinário*, a justice of the peace, elected by the notables of the district, who was sometimes barely literate, with a legal education frequently gained in prison. Their emoluments were fixed, and had been fixed for a long time, so that their income came from 'closing their eyes'.[11] An *ouvidor* was generally held to earn in this way more than four times his salary and the most contented Brazilians were probably those who lived furthest away from the seats of justice.[12]

There were assize courts in Salvador and Recife (courts *de relação*) with their own judges, and from these appeal could be made to the appeal court (Casa de Suplicação) in Rio. The supreme tribunal, brought to Rio de Janeiro with Dom John, was the Mesa de Desembargo do Paço. Its function was to judge precedents and privileges, set aside or modify the judgments of the lesser courts and restore property to those unjustly deprived of it. It worked, like all supreme courts, with stately concern for decorum and ceremonial. But parallel to and confusing the work of civil justice was the work of local government, which had retained about as much of its early colonial democracy as the Venetian republic. The local oligarchy constituted a local senate, the *senado da câmara*; they were the *homens bons* acceptable to the captain-general or governor. Senators, or rather *vereadores*, presided over by the *juiz de fora* or the *juiz ordinário*, were responsible for public works like water and sewage, roads and bridges, the education of abandoned children and the collection of local taxes. They were elected by parish councils, and though they were usually local pillars of conservatism, they were none the less sometimes the authentic voice of the local population, even, as with the *senado da câmara* in Rio, a national voice. In most places, however, most of the time, they met twice a week to act as the torpid agents of the privileged society that elected them.

The church, too, had its juridical organization. It was entitled to have all cases in which it was a party heard before its own court, the Board of Conscience and Holy Orders (Mesa da Conciência e Ordens); but most people would have been more aware of the marriage judge (*juiz de casamentos*), whose original function was to prevent the marriage of Christians to Jews or pagans, but who now effectively ensured that a great number of the poor never got married at all.

Overseeing and underpinning these agents of order were the armed forces, a grand designation for disaffected Portuguese regulars commanded by the governor or captain-general of the province, and the local *ordenanças* and militia. The first were rural musters of all males between 16 and 60, called up irregularly as a protection against marauding Indians or runaway slaves. The militia were a sort of territorial army, made up of local men who paraded regularly and could be called out to meet any emergency. Its officers pre-empted rank according to social status, so that the cloud of colonels which ruled north-east Brazil for a century and a half was an elite corps of planters and ranchers without a military idea in their heads but a following of gunmen armed from public funds. The captain-major (*capitão-mor*) had powers of arrest and his staff officers liked to wear bright uniforms — the ones in Pernambuco, mindful of their glorious wars against the Dutch, with broad yellow facings, cuffs up to the elbows, feathered hats, ridiculously long swords and nankeen pantaloons stuffed into broad boots which bulged preposterously at the thigh, almost straight out of Rembrandt's *Captain Banning Cocq's Night Watch*.[13] The gentry, too, liked to wear their uniforms on formal occasions, to give the impression of a martial vigour largely alien to their natures.[14]

For fighting was not comfortable to the stomach of either Portuguese or Brazilians. Militia service was compulsory, but substitutes could always be arranged. Militiamen had their slaves to carry their muskets, drums and colours, and walked to parade carrying parasols instead.[15] They frequently looked and behaved like liveried retainers, and one *mazombo* millionaire, commanding the First Cavalry Regiment of the Capitania of Rio, paid for the chargers, uniforms and ironmongery from his own pocket, so that it looked smart on parade, whatever its fighting quality. The regular regiments were less smart and more dangerous. Largely recruited from the riff-raff of town and countryside, the troopers signed on for 16 years and it was generally believed that the impressment of so many vagabonds and thieves into a regular force contributed more to the safety of travellers on the roads than all their military duties. Every family with two or more unmarried sons could be called on to send one into the army unless it could buy him off. Sons frequently took to the *mato* on the approach of the recruiting sergeant, and even married men were unwilling to venture out without an exemption certificate from the *capitão-mor*.[16]

For the Indians and free blacks, not eligible for service in the line, there were militia regiments like the Old and New Henriques, called after the black, Henrique Dias, who fought with great distinction against the Dutch. It was a member of the Black Henriques Regiment who took umbrage in Recife at a slighting remark about Brazilians that sparked off the revolt there, but, that incident apart, the Henriques were better disciplined and turned out than white regulars, a third of whose pay, usually years in arrears, was docked to pay for new uniforms which should have been provided, but usually were not, every other year. The regulars, moreover, were on incessant duty in the interior, where, with empty pockets and down at heel, they made a living on the side, selling permits and protection.[17] In the towns they took other jobs, parading twelve times a year to collect their pay and passing on to their officers a percentage of their earnings.[18] An army of vagrants and unmarried men could hardly be expected to fight to the death for hearth and home, and the regular regiments throughout early Brazilian history earned few laurels for Brazilian arms.

Brazil achieved independence without a military hero. Spanish America had her Bolívar, San Martín, Iturbide, Sucre, but Brazilians are hard put to it to remember the names of any officers, Portuguese or Brazilian, during the same period of their history. If anyone, they own a heroine, a runaway farmer's girl, Maria Quitéria, who donned a uniform and served as an infantryman against the Portuguese in Bahia in 1823.[19] The Spanish Americans lost something like 100,000 dead and wounded in their struggle to expel the Spaniards and the persistent rancour of Old Spain drove the successor governments into heavy military spending, upon which they often succumbed to military juntas.

Brazil escaped all this, partly because neither Portuguese nor Brazilian liked the actual business of fighting. At no time were there many Portuguese-born troops in the colony, and the regulars, mostly Brazilian-born, numbered only about 2000 in all. Part-time soldiers had been sufficient for most purposes, except frontier duty, whether against Indians or Spaniards. Most full-time officers were, however, Portuguese-born. Poor prospects had always deterred Brazilians from a career in the Portuguese army so that Portuguese regulars had been required to stiffen colonial rule. In the transition from colony to empire, military action was almost exclusively led by Portuguese officers. Portuguese officers suppressed the creole rising in Recife in 1817; they led the demand for a constitution in 1820 and 1821, and swore an oath of loyalty to the (Portuguese-born) emperor of an independent nation in 1822. At the command of that same emperor they dispersed the Constituent Assembly, and in the uneasy years that followed they equated the criticism that their Portuguese birth precluded them from being good Brazilians with attacks on their honour and integrity. In the end they dragged the emperor down with them. Their performance on the field of battle did little to redeem their birth, and it was an army led by Portuguese officers which blundered its way through the long and bloody wars in Uruguay. There were no mute inglorious Bolívars eating out their hearts on the sugar estates of the north-east or the farms of Minas Gerais and São Paulo. The white Brazilian liked the grandeur of military life, but not the servitude, and it was fortunate that, when the crunch came, the Portuguese officers in their midst chose loyalty to the house of Braganza rather than to Portugal.[20]

13· Constitution, 1820–21

'Delay is the radical fault of this government — I ought, perhaps, to say: absolute inaction' —

Edward Thornton, British Ambassador in Rio de Janeiro

'Se queres inda reinar Olha beato João Deves ir para Portugal E assinar a Constituição' ('If you want to go on being king, good King John, you had better get back to Portugal and sign the Constitution') —

Pasquinade in Rio, 1821

The revolts in both Recife and Lisbon were protests against a remote and apathetic court. Age and decrepitude marked the conduct of government, for the councillors of state who had crossed the Atlantic with Dom John were dying off, and Dom John's most trusted adviser, the 65-year-old Conde da Barca, who conducted the business of a different ministry each day of the week, died on 2 June 1817. New blood was desperately needed and, casting round for someone experienced in the ways of post-Napoleonic Europe, Dom John recalled his envoy in London, the 46-year-old Dom Pedro de Souza Holstein, Conde de Palmela, to be his minister of foreign affairs. He was a kinsman of the still lamented Dom Rodrigo de Souza Coutinho, and they both boasted descent from King Alfonso III. Palmela's golden youth had been spent in the diplomatic service, in the embassies in Rome, Madrid and, latterly, London. He had led the Portuguese delegation to the Congress of Vienna. A full member of the period's equivalent to the 'jet-set' he had had a passionate affair with Madame de Staël in 1804, which cast him beautifully for the role of Oswald in that formidable lady's *Corinne*. He had been Wellington's Portuguese interpreter during the Peninsular Campaign and was, partly as a result, to be the only Portuguese minister for whom the British government had any respect. Since 1815 he had regularly attended the salons

Rio de Janeiro, a watercolour by Thomas Ender, painted from the Convent of Santo Antonio 1817–18, showing the familiar Sugar Loaf mountain in the far distance.

Dom John VI, from a painting by Luis Sequeira in the Imperial Museum of Petropolis.

O Grito de Ipiranga (The Cry of Ipiranga): Dom Pedro proclaims the Independence of Brazil on the banks of the Ipiranga river near São Paulo on 7 September 1822. (From a painting by François Renée Moreaux in the Imperial Museum of Petropolis.)

Above. A street scene in Recife, centre of two revolutionary movements in 1817 and 1823.
Below. Afternoon refreshments in the Palace Square, Rio de Janeiro, from a watercolour by Jean-Baptiste Debret

The *Capitão do Mato* or Bush Captain, engraved from an
original by Johann Moritz Rugendas. The Bush Captain's task
was to recapture runaway slaves.

Above. The *Batuque* was the slaves' most popular diversion and the origin of the Samba. *Below*. A Bahian family at table, showing the slovenly finery of rich Brazilians among the squalor of domestic slavery. (Both engravings from *Travels in Brazil* by J.-B. Spix and Philip von Martius.)

A Botocudo family on the march. A watercolour dated 1816 by Prince Maximilian zu Wied-Neuwied, from his *Journey to Brazil*, showing the distended lower lip characteristic of this tribe.

Dom Pedro I in 1822, from a painting by Henrique da Silva in the Imperial Museum of Petropolis. Dom Pedro is shown in imperial robes, with the newly made crown by his side.

of Madame de Lieven and Lady Holland, and for the moment he was too fascinated by the influence of society, especially of society ladies, upon politics to remove himself with any haste to a continent where there were neither. He was not to reach Rio de Janeiro before December 1820.

Dom John in the meantime entrusted that ministry and responsibility for home affairs to the son of a poor advocate from Portuguese Estremadura, Tomás Antônio de Vilanova Portugal. He had first come to the king's notice by the way he handled a border dispute with Spain, and had been elevated first to high court judge (*desembargador do paço*) and then lord chancellor (*chanceler-mor*), becoming not only a lion under the throne but one of Dom John's few personal friends, the only man to whom he could turn for disinterested advice. Unfortunately Tomás Antônio's advice generally supported Dom John's favourite course of action — to do nothing.

That preference of Dom John's had worn down the formidable Lord Strangford. Henry Chamberlain was no match for it. He lacked his former chief's effortless superiority and was inclined to preach. The rest of the diplomatic corps were nonentities. Balk Polev, the Russian envoy, had come down from Washington and often forgot that Brazil was not another Haiti. His biggest gaffe was to refer to the Conde da Barca as the 'Conde de Limonada'. (Le Comte, later le Duc, de Limonade was actually the mulatto secretary to King Henri-Christophe of Haiti, and later his foreign secretary.) The king had Polev recalled when he asked for his creditors to be imprisoned for dunning him.[1] The papal nuncio was in Dom John's pocket, because only the genial king's loans enabled him to keep his rapacious household at bay. The Austrian minister, von Elz, who had arrived with Dona Leopoldina, kept his embassy like a redoubt and was too mean to unpack his Meissen banqueting set in case it was broken or stolen. Thomas Sumter of the United States of America was remote and prickly, and Casa Irujo, representing Spain, was virtually the envoy of a hostile power. The French chargé, Colonel Maler, saw Bonapartist spies everywhere.

Bonapartist flotsam there certainly was, and Maler sent long reports on all of them to the police intendant. Among them were Madame de Ranchoup, wife of the former French consul-general in Stockholm and one of Napoleon's mistresses in Egypt, Colonel Cailhé, a professional gambler, Maître Lacombe and the dancers of the Opera, dressmakers in the Rua Ouvidor, Professor Lebreton, the director of the Fine Arts

Academy, a reputed general from La Grande Armée and a supposed daughter of General Pichegru. Plots to rescue Napoleon from St Helena and bring him to South America thickened and thinned, thickest when, by what was almost pure coincidence, the Comte de Paulaincourt was put ashore in Rio Grande do Norte from an American ship just after the Recife revolt. Ostensibly he had come to botanize, but Maler was confident that he was contacting a Bonapartist cell in Paraíba, whose intentions were to spirit the former emperor across to the Equatorial Republic of Pernambuco, what destiny there to fulfil was never made clear. He and his associates were all arrested, but nothing could be discovered to incriminate them. Even though his quarry had escaped him, Maler continued to think that the king was absurdly complaisant, and so were the British.[2]

Von Elz had brought with him not only Dom John's new daughter-in-law, but also an invitation from Metternich for the king to return to Portugal as soon as possible. Dom John put it on one side with all the others. Home was here in Rio, where he had a new daughter-in-law to entertain, and where he was shortly to be acclaimed as king. Dona Leopoldina, her plain and wholesome face glowing from its two cosmetics, wind and rain, was delighted with her 19-year-old groom, with whom she was united in November 1817. Dom Pedro was a thoroughbred stallion, mettlesome without being dangerous, a handsome fellow in his way, well-shaped and, like his bride, fond of hard exercise, careless in dress and a good trencherman. 'Educated by and with negro boys,' was Lord Ponsonby's sour comment in 1826, 'he has ever since lived since he came to man's estate with prostitutes, pimps and horse-dealers, and his learning, morals and manners correspond exactly with the sources whence they were drawn.'[3] The description was unfair. If he could be ill-mannered he was never ill-natured. He was generous with inferiors, brisk with equals, impatient of etiquette, over-fond of practical jokes and taverneering. He liked to wake his household every morning by firing a fowling piece in the palace corridors. There was a Falstaff to this Prince Hal, his secretary, a louche Portuguese, son of one of the court jewellers, whose nickname, 'A Chalaça' ('The Dirty Joke'), was a clue to his hold over the prince.[4] Yet like Prince Hal, Dom Pedro was no hobbledehoy. He had a keen musical sense, though as emperor he preferred conducting a Negro band on the *fazenda* of Santa Cruz to a *soirée musicale* at São Cristovão. He knew some Latin, more French and a lot of English bad language that he and his wife learned from an English groom. A good judge of horseflesh, he enjoyed a variety of women, but only lost his head over one — the Paulista beauty, Domitila de Castro Canto e Melo. His storms of wilfulness and bad temper were followed by periods of sunshine that no one could resist, and those who served him were by turns exasperated and captivated by his weathercock nature.

Dom Pedro rushed into hymeneal action while his father planned a reception worthy of an emperor's daughter. What with that, his acclamation and Dom Pedro's 20th birthday, Rio de Janeiro seemed to have taken the place vacated by Venice in the world of public pleasure, and the raven voices of the Old World were rendered inaudible. Dom John indeed became quite vexed at all these suggestions that he should go back to Lisbon. Why *should* he return to Lisbon to be once more a puppet, played alternately by Britain's fleet and France's army, when, if he took himself off to São Paulo, 70,000 armed men could not dislodge him?[5] Why, too, should he sacrifice a natural frontier on the Plate just to allow British trade to flow freely to Buenos Aires? And it did look as if the Portuguese gamble had come off. General Lecor, now Baron Laguna, was proving remarkably successful in wooing the Orientals from both Old and New Spain. The creoles in Buenos Aires were content to allow Laguna to cut Artigas down to size and, despite the bellicose noises emanating from Madrid, the Spaniards were not averse to letting the Portuguese suppress rebellion in one of their colonies.

To the British foreign secretary the picture looked quite different. Unless Portugal abandoned the Banda Oriental, war on the Plate was inevitable, to the certain misery of all involved, not least British business houses with interests in the area. The Plate dream, however, was the principal spell that bound Dom John to Brazil like Rinaldo to the arms of Armida. Between 1817 and 1820, the Oriental resistance flagged, and with Buenos Aires implacably hostile, the Chief of the Orientals knew that the game was up. On 5 September 1820, Artigas led his last band of faithful *gaúchos* into the prison state that was Dr Francia's Paraguay, never to return. The long war of attrition seemed to have ended and Laguna now proceeded to woo the Orientals into the kingdom of Brazil. He came as near as any Portuguese could to success. He and his officers married local girls; Brazilian cattle rustlers were flushed out and their victims compensated; schools were opened, roads and warehouses built. Soon there was more traffic into Montevideo than at any time since the English invasions. The southern nightmare nearly turned into a pleasant dream.

It was not to be. If Old Spain could not accept the loss of a colony, New Spain could not accept its return to Madrid. Neither New nor Old Spain could agree to its becoming part of the Portuguese empire and were not deceived by another seemingly innocent suggestion that the Banda should become an independent duchy under the half-Spanish, half-Portuguese Infante Dom Sebastian, the son of Don Pedro Carlos y Borbon and Dona Maria Teresa, and so Dom John's grandson and King Ferdinand's great-nephew and second cousin. Moreover, the British government, having resolved to keep the continental powers from meddling in South America, had offered to mediate between Spain and her colonies, and mediation there would be.

At that moment, as Castlereagh and Metternich had feared, people rather than politicians upset the nicer systems of diplomacy. Like a phoenix from the ashes of Gomes Freire rose the cry for representational government in Portugal and the calling of the Ancient Cortes of the Realm. In a few days the prestige of a government made in England vanished like a cloud and the Portuguese people managed at last to force themselves upon the attention of their absentee monarch in a way that could no longer be ignored.

At the close of the Napoleonic war, the morale of the Portuguese army stood higher than at any time since the liberation of the kingdom from Spain in the 1660s, but for six years afterwards an absent monarch had allowed the British commander-in-chief to treat his soldiers like sepoys. The *afrancesados* like Gomes Freire, who had fought with rather than against the French and who had as a result imbibed some of the stern republicanism of the Napoleonic army, had challenged that command unsuccessfully. But the savagery with which Beresford had treated the rebels strained, while his subsequent failure to find their arrears of pay in Brazil frayed, the loyalty of the troops that remained faithful to Dom John. In January 1820, the Spanish troops in Cádiz mutinied rather than embark for South America and a colonial war. King Ferdinand bowed to the sudden storm that swept his kingdom as a result and promised to reintroduce the Constitution of 1812. Beresford, knowing that the contagion must spread, sailed for Brazil in April in a second attempt to persuade Dom John to return to Lisbon with money to pay the troops. The king could not be persuaded to go and distrusted the wild youth of Dom Pedro too much to send him in his place. On 13 August, Beresford set sail again for Lisbon with money but no king. He had been 11 days at sea when the unpaid troops in Oporto paraded in the main square and called for his dismissal as regent, the recall of the king and the formation of a revolutionary junta. By 15 September, Gomes Freire was vindicated. A second revolutionary junta in Lisbon ordered the Regency Council to summon a National Congress before decreeing its own dissolution.

The news from Oporto reached Rio on 17 October. Beresford's worst fears had been justified and Castlereagh proved right. Dom John must act at once to save what he could from the wreck of his power 'which by bad management and unfounded jealousy of and indifference to our counsels', Castlereagh could not resist observing primly, 'His Majesty has exposed to utter dissolution'.[6] To the timid monarch, a return to Portugal now seemed an even more hazardous venture than his flight to Brazil in 1807. Yet if he sent Dom Pedro, the young prince might allow himself to be proclaimed king on arrival. So with the help of Dom Tomás Antônio he drafted a temporizing injunction. Only His Most Faithful Majesty could summon the Cortes, but he was prepared to ratify the present irregularity provided that the deliberations of that assembly followed the uses, customs and fundamental laws of the *Reino*. Once reassured on this point, Dom John would send a viceroy, or even return himself. When Palmela at last arrived in December, he warned the king that revolution was a great deal nearer than Lisbon. The new Austrian envoy, von Stürmer, while in Salvador waiting for his ship to water, had been alarmed to hear talk of a constitutional movement in Brazil. The only way to prevent the turmoil from crossing the Atlantic was to grant a charter like the one that Louis XVIII had granted the French and to send Dom Pedro to Lisbon to preside over the Cortes. The Portuguese would no longer tolerate a political system inferior to that of every other state in Western Europe, Spain included. 'Delay in a crisis like this,' he concluded solemnly, 'is a century lost!'[7]

Tomás Antônio flatly disagreed. Only when the Cortes had submitted its proposals should Dom John decide whom to send to Lisbon. Until then he should not leave the safety of Brazil. Portugal, moreover, would soon show that she was as incapable of action independent of Brazil as Hanover of England.[8] 'Should the Royal Family return to Lisbon?' he asked the reading public in an anonymous pamphlet. Decidedly not! For Dom John to try to rule Brazil from Lisbon would be like Louis XVIII trying to rule France from Martinique. The new kingdom would soon shake off the dominion of the old and, without Brazil, Portugal must sink into impotence.[9]

The lion under the throne had spoken with an almost complete lack of equivocation. Edward Thornton, who had arrived as British minister at much the same time as Dona Leopoldina, tried to have the pamphlet suppressed as an insult to his government, which had consistently urged the return of the monarch to Lisbon as the sole effective means of preserving the United Kingdom. The pamphlet also angered Palmela, who thought its reasoning benighted. It maddened Dona Carlota, who emerged from her semi-retirement on Flagstaff Hill to support Palmela, not because she believed in a charter but because she wanted to get back to Portugal to rally the forces of reaction. It aroused an intense suspicion among Brazilians that ministers were ready to accept a constitution in faraway Portugal but not in Brazil. It so cast down Dom Pedro, who was burning to occupy a stage of his own, that he talked openly of slipping away on his own on board a British ship.[10] It seemed to please Dom John alone, who knew that its conclusions were just. Reluctantly he agreed to the council's recommendation that Dom Pedro's energy be used; he should return to Lisbon not as his father's viceroy but as his constable to hear what the Cortes had to say. Dona Leopoldina, expecting her second child, took alarm and begged him to stay at least until it was born. Von Stürmer cajoled her to put duty before comfort. Palmela threatened to resign and Thornton fretted helplessly when, on 17 February 1821, the news broke in the capital like a thunderclap that constitutional fever had jumped the Atlantic and infected Belém do Pará and Salvador da Bahia.

A fourth-year law student from Coimbra started the upheaval in Belém. Arriving home for the holidays on 10 December 1820, he lost no time in preaching constitutional insurrection to the members of the local lodge, and on 1 January 1821 the First Regiment of the Line marched into the town square, demanding a constitution like their *confrères* in Oporto. On 5 February the revolutionary junta sent its emissaries into the interior and the student back to Lisbon to announce that Pará recognized the sovereignty of the National Congress.[11] On 10 February, the garrison in Salvador followed suit. After a token resistance, the governor was dispatched to Rio on board HMS *Icarus* with a letter from the inevitable junta. The Bahians, it was careful to point out, were not rebels like the Pernambucans of 1817. Their loyalty to *El-Rei* was second to none, certainly not to that of their compatriots across the water who had been forgiven for calling into being the Sovereign Cortes. The colonial system, however, had become merely a patchwork of local tyrannies. A glance at the unpopular English showed that their monarchy was based as firmly on Magna Carta as on a rock. Even the two Ferdinands, of Spain and of the Two Sicilies, were now constitutional monarchs. Could Dom John be less than they?[12] A few days later, the junta recognized the supreme authority of the Cortes in Lisbon and extended the hand of constitutional fraternity to Luiz do Rego in Recife. Do Rego, who commanded Portuguese regulars, recognized the need for a little judicious democracy, convened the *câmara* and asked the king for a constitution. At the same time he advised the people of Pernambuco, and of Maranhão, to keep the law.[13]

HMS *Icarus* reached Rio on 17 February 1821. To Palmela revolution was now inevitable unless Dom John went at once to Portugal with a charter in his pocket. He had one already drafted and had made no secret of its contents to a not very discreet circle of Portuguese officers in Rio. Dom John sounded out his lion. Tomás Antônio advised him on the 23rd to grant a charter for Portugal and leave the matter of Brazil till later. To ensure that a constitution made in Portugal might be applicable to Brazil, he should appoint a special committee of 20 wise men to prepare the way. Dom John thought this advice prudent and was surprised to find that his decree setting up the committee elicited no local enthusiasm. The Portuguese in Rio, for the most part rich merchants and senior army officers, did not want two constitutions and, by implication, two separate kingdoms. They wanted the Portuguese constitution as soon as it was ready. Palmela, discreetly informed of public feeling by the police intendant, led the chorus. Half-measures would be worse than none at all. Only the bold declaration of a constitution could prevent revolution in Rio de Janeiro itself.[14]

The options, however, were to be swept out of ministerial hands. Dona Carlota did not intend to lose her chance to escape from this detestable land. She had already once in her life posed as a good constitutionalist, and if her husband did not take her back to Portugal, then she would go on the shoulders of her son. Using two Portuguese priests as her go-betweens, she let it be known that if the garrison in Rio demanded the Portuguese constitution, then she would promise Dom Pedro's protection. Palmela received some of the more excitable officers and virtually promised them his charter.

The aces were now all firmly placed in their hands and when, on 25 February 1821, they heard that Tomás Antônio's Committee of 20 had spent its first meeting discussing but not endorsing Palmela's draft, they decided to bring matters to a head. In the early hours of the 26th, Dona Leopoldina being near her time, the conspirators went to São Cristovão to tell Dom Pedro that the garrison was on the march. The prince hurriedly dressed and rode to the Largo do Rocio, where the troops had assembled before the Opera House and elected their spokesmen. They would not disperse until Dom John had promised a constitution, dismissed his present ministers and convened a junta. Dom Pedro galloped back to the country palace, where his father handed him a decree, dated two days earlier, granting Brazil a charter.

In the *largo* the troops, mostly Portuguese veterans, had now been joined by a crowd of civilians who barracked the prince as he began to read the decree. 'Not that, not that,' they bawled. 'We want the constitution the Cortes will be writing.' Dom Pedro returned once more to São Cristovão, where his father was now in a state of acute panic. All the doors and windows had been locked, as if against a tropical rainstorm, while Palmela, grimly satisfied at the outcome of his unheeded warnings, declared that the soldiers now dictated all matters in the kingdom. Tomás Antônio advised the king to agree to the demands and accept nominations for a junta. The prince was back in the *largo* at seven o'clock the same morning. The 'constitutionalists' had already roused the *senadores da câmara* from their beds and conducted them to the theatre. There the bishop heard their oaths to the unwritten Portuguese constitution and swore in a junta of 12 men.[15]

There was a strong suspicion that Dom Pedro and the garrison were in collusion and that his reward, if Dom John proved difficult, would have been his acclamation as Dom Pedro IV of Portugal. The Austrian minister was sure, for one, that the prime movers of the sedition, the two dubious priests, an assassin, a thief, a jail-bird and the son of one of Beresford's victims of 1817, were all the kind of people with whom the prince chose to be friends. Whatever the truth, the two princes, Pedro and Miguel, swore to the constitution, and then Dom Pedro went off to invite his father to present himself before his faithful subjects in the *largo*. The hale and enthusiastic cheers which greeted his appearance sounded, to his nervous ear, very like those that had greeted Louis XVI on his way to Paris from Versailles in

1789. The people unhorsed his carriage and dragged it to the city palace, where the royal family, including Dona Carlota, gathered on the balcony to hear him whisper approval of everything his son had promised. To cheer him up, there was a performance that night of Rossini's *Cinderella*, during which the intervals were punctuated by vivas for *El-Rei*, the Holy Catholic Religion and the unknown constitution. Dom John, who was devoted to the work of the Swan of Pesaro, did not enjoy the performance. 'Long live the Sovereign People,' he muttered to himself on the way back to São Cristovão, 'but I am in my carriage and you are on foot.'[16]

Thornton, from the detachment of the British embassy, was sceptical about the future. The constitution, on which no one had set eyes, was acceptable not because it was good but because it was Portuguese. 'Such manifestations of a resolution to assert the supremacy of Portugal,' he wrote to Castlereagh on 14 March, 'cannot but have the effect of accelerating the separation of the two countries.'[17] For the moment, however, the Brazilians were being swept along by their Portuguese colleagues. Even the Bahia junta, now led by Carlos Antônio de Andrada, a constitutional hero for his part in the events in 1817, repudiated any suggestion of a special constitution for Brazil. But when the Pernambuco regiment had arrived in the Largo do Rocio on that eventful morning of 26 February, the Portuguese regiments had stood to arms in case the Brazilians came with a different objective. Thornton was right to see that the centre of gravity had shifted back across the Atlantic and that when the Brazilians realized this there would be a sharp reaction. As if to underline this shift, the Bahia junta suspended its provincial remittances to the government in Rio and corresponded only with the Supreme Cortes in Lisbon. The Voluntários d'El Rei, no longer willing to die in a South American cause, had mutinied in Montevideo. Above all, the Portuguese officers in Rio and Salvador wanted to get home to secure the commissions formerly held by the British, and the courtiers began to sigh once more for the cooler airs and gentler slopes of the mouth of the Tagus. For them the place of the monarch was in his ancient capital.[18]

The Supreme Cortes in Lisbon thought so too. On 10 January 1821, it sent a peremptory summons to Dom John to return, expressing its lively displeasure that delegates from Brazil had not yet joined the national congress. The junta in Rio, which had elevated itself into the Council of State, voted with one dissentient voice for the king's immediate return. Dom Pedro, father at last of a son born on 6 March, was to stay in Rio as his regent. At that the *câmara do senado*, representing the resident interests of the capital, the Brazilian office-holders who feared for their positions and the Brazilian merchants who feared a return to the bad old days of trading restrictions, begged the king not to leave them. The junta briskly replied that the greater good of the kingdom demanded it. Furthermore, Brazilian delegates should be elected to the Cortes as soon as possible. The Spanish 1812 constitution provided the model for election; each *comarca* would have an electoral college made up of elected representatives from each parish. Each college would send a delegate to Lisbon. On Holy Saturday, 21 April 1821, the 160 men elected by the parishes of Rio de Janeiro met in their fine new Exchange, joined quite irregularly by a swarm of petty officials and shopkeepers who were addressed by that assiduous demagogue, Father Macamboa, one of Dona Carlota's two familiars who had been used to bring out the garrison on 26 February. In the turmoil he created, there was a sudden and unexpected demand for the immediate adoption of the Spanish constitution. It seemed to come from two sources: the constitutional extremists, like Macamboa, who thought that the new junta was little different from the old Council of State, and agitated Brazilians, for whom the Portuguese constitution was only a phrase, unlike the Spanish, which was a fact, and who feared that once the court had returned to Lisbon it would forget all about Brazil.

From that moment events became confused. When the king and Council of State agreed to the Spanish constitution for as long as the Portuguese constitution lay in the mind of the Supreme Cortes in Lisbon, the largely Portuguese garrison in Rio suspected a *mazombo* ruse to keep the king in Brazil. Troops therefore were dispatched to watch the royal *quinta* of São Cristovão, at which the 'Spanish' constitutionalists in the Exchange became bolder. They demanded that the king should not leave the country without their consent, and when they heard that the ships prepared to escort him home were laden with all the nation's gold, they sent a *mazombo* general to seize the harbour forts to prevent their sailing. A second deputation was sent off to São Cristovão to thank the sovereign for the Spanish constitution, to the terror of Dom John, who imagined it was a Jacobin mob sent to drag him back to the city palace. The assembly in the Exchange in the meantime summoned the garrison commander to explain the movements of his troops. He professed not to know, though it was painfully clear that the Portuguese soldiery, both officers and men, were not going to surrender control of the revolution they had started. At four o'clock on Easter Sunday morning they surrounded the Exchange. Most of the electors had gone home, but someone fired a volley, at which the *Caçadores* battered in the doors and entered with fixed bayonets. In this miniature Brumaire, one elector and one soldier died, several electors jumped from the windows into the sea, others were manhandled and its elected secretary bayoneted in the arm. The ringleaders of the non-elected faction were arrested and the remainder, bruised and bewildered, were dispersed.

Again there were suspicions about the role Dom Pedro had played in all this. Had he connived at the dispersal of the electors to avoid a massacre? Had he gone further and actually inspired the coup because he feared the electors might prevent his father's leaving and thus his regency? When the delegation had asked Dom John for the Spanish constitution, its spokesman said that Dom Pedro had threatened to throw him out of the window.[19] Dom Pedro must have known that there was no force in Brazil capable of frustrating the intentions of the Peninsular veterans who made up the hard core of the garrison and that the future of his family depended on their continued loyalty to the ruling house. But whatever the prince's part in these events, Dom John was now convinced that Brazil was a more dangerous place than Portugal. Later that Sunday he annulled the Spanish constitution he had just granted and signed powers over to his son, 'so ample', thought Edward Thornton, 'as to erect the government almost to an independent monarchy'.[20] With another stroke of the pen, Dom John bid for national solidarity and gave all soldiers, Portuguese and Brazilian alike, the same pay. It was a postdated cheque on a bankrupt bank, for he was preparing to leave Rio with the same haste with which he had left Lisbon 14 years earlier. As he had emptied the treasury then, so now his courtiers, who held most of the shares in the Bank of Brazil, redeemed them and cleared the vaults of cash.[21]

Dom John had a few prophetic words for his son before he sailed. 'If Brazil wants to separate from Portugal, Pedro, let her do so under you, who have some respect for me, and not under any of these adventurers.' Did he have any particular adventurer in mind, or was he thinking of those Spanish American *caudillos* who had plunged the continent into civil war? As there were no Brazilian adventurers more alarming than the masons who had led the voting for the Spanish constitution, it is not surprising that Dom John later denied that he had ever said such a thing to his son.[22] On 25 April he and Dona Carlota boarded the *Dom João VI* with Dom Miguel and the mortal remains of Dona Maria I. In the escorting vessels went the councillors of state and 3000 other passengers. On board, too, were letters from various 'constitutionalists' in Rio to their friends in Lisbon, urging them to press for the early recall of the prince as no friend to liberal institutions.[23] Dona Carlota could not conceal her joy. She shook her skirts and flung her shoes into the water, so that she would not carry a speck of Brazilian dust with her. 'At last, at last,' she crowed, 'I am going back to a land inhabited by men.'[24]

This time the flight was more orderly. It had been organized by the same man who had organized the departure from Lisbon, Dom John's personal banker and domestic chamberlain, Joaquim de Azevedo, Visconde do Rio Seco.[25] But the uncertainties were as great as in 1807. The former ministers of state kept up, during nine weeks at sea, a circular correspondence on how the king should behave on arrival. They were in for a nasty shock. On 3 July the royal flotilla entered the mouth of the Tagus. By order of the Supreme Cortes, no one, not even His Most Faithful Majesty, was to be allowed on shore, because the reception arrangements were not complete. His ministers were told that they were effectively under shipboard arrest to protect them from the angry Lisbon crowd from whom they had kept their king too long. Every member of the committee that received Dom John on the 4th was a stranger to him. The military guard looked more like zouaves than soldiers who had defeated Masséna and Soult. The address he was given to read was so full of constitutional jargon that it was unintelligible, even to the deputies who listened to it. Dona Carlota refused either to go to the Cortes or to receive its members, and withdrew to the Queluz palace, there to plot its overthrow. Dom John was obliged to attend a requiem mass for Gomes Freire and the other victims of 1817. The timid monarch soon expressed the most lively regrets at leaving Brazil. 'There I was happy,' he sighed. 'There I was king.'[26]

14· Defiance, 1821–2

'Brasil é uma terra de macacos, de negrinhos apanhados na costa da Africa e de bananas' (Brazil is a land of monkeys, of niggers picked up on the coast of Africa and of bananas) —

> Manoel Fernandes Thomás, leader of the
> Portuguese liberal deputies in the Cortes

'They say in the streets; "If the constitution is no good for us, then to the Devil with it"' —

> Dom Pedro to Dom John, 14 December 1821

'It is impossible that an empire like Brazil can long remain the colony of a province like Portugal' —

> Anonymous pamphleteer, Rio, January 1822

Dom John had arrived in Lisbon to find the National Congress installed as a sovereign body, vigorously and wordily liberal. It had already decided what the constitution was going to look like and had received its first overseas deputies, from Pará. That these deputies were self-appointed, not elected, was for the moment a detail. More important was the growing conviction of the deputies from Portugal that they should never again play second fiddle to the giant across the ocean. For thirteen years money had flowed from Lisbon to Rio, decisions had come from the New World to the Old and men of Lisbon, Coimbra and Oporto had fought and died in obscure battles in Recife and Montevideo. Worst of all, the British had made the profits in Brazil, paying lower import duties on their goods than the Portuguese themselves, and the great Portuguese carrying trade had withered away. All that had been left them was the slave-trade and the British wanted to stop that. In 1820 only 57 Portuguese ships entered Rio de Janeiro harbour, a steep fall from the 810 of 1810. From 1806 to 1819 the value of Brazilian goods re-exported from Portugal had fallen from 14 million to 4 million cruzados. The government in Brazil may have been Portuguese in origin, but it had seemed resolved to reduce the metropolitan kingdom to 'a walking skeleton'.[1]

That must now change. The constitution would accord representation on the basis of one deputy to every 30,000 free citizens, and this arrangement would give Brazil only 70 deputies to Portugal's 130. The proud merchants of Oporto and Lisbon made little secret of their confidence that this would enable them to resume the privileges they had enjoyed in imperial trade before 1808, and from the very outset they were resolved to humiliate and subordinate Brazil to the sovereign will of Portugal. Their deputies in the Cortes never seemed to think that the Brazilians in their turn would never willingly return to their former colonial status.[2]

They started with Dom Pedro, refusing to recognize his appointment as regent, which the deputies formally annulled on 1 September. On 1 October 1821, they ordered the Brazilian provinces to replace their royal governors with elected juntas, each separately answerable to the Sovereign Cortes. Dom Pedro, moreover, should return at once to Lisbon to prepare himself for a trip round Europe, studying constitutional government. If he refused he would be stripped of all his titles and offices. Subsequent decrees dismantled the institutions of the kingdom of Brazil: first the parallel legal tribunals were suppressed, then the military and fine arts academies were closed. In March 1822, legislation was prepared to restrict Brazil's foreign trade to the limits prevailing before 1808. The manifest intention was total recolonization.

Up till now, the Brazilian deputies had been bemused by the proceedings in Lisbon and unwilling to challenge an elected assembly. Those from Pará, the first to arrive, were enthusiastically liberal, and their twelve colleagues from Pernambuco and Rio who arrived in August and September 1821 were ready to go along with the majority. Delegates from Maranhão and Bahia trickled in before the end of the year, but it was not until the arrival of the Paulista deputies in February 1822 that a new voice was heard in the chamber. It was that of Carlos Antônio de Andrada, who had left the prisons of Bahia for the heartland of the Andrada family and now appeared as the elected representative of the province of his birth. The deputies were astonished to hear from his lips that the São Paulo junta had given its deputies firm instructions to warn the assembly that the United Kingdom of Portugal, Brazil and Algarve could only survive if the citizens of both countries enjoyed equal civil and political rights. The king could reside alternately in Rio or Lisbon if he so wished, but Brazil and Portugal must have equal representation, and the two nations on a basis of equality must devise the laws that would govern their affairs in peace, war and trade. On 13 February, another Paulista deputy, Nicolau Vergueiro, actually Portuguese-born, gave the Cortes an unequivocal warning that Brazil wished to continue the union with Portugal but not on the terms proposed.

The Paulista certainties shook their fellow Brazilian deputies out of their trance. Soon they were a beleaguered minority united in their view that Brazil should never again be governed from Lisbon. Though there should have been 76 of them, only 46 ever reached Lisbon. The Minas deputies decided as early as January 1822 that the two countries were drifting apart and never left Brazil.[3] It took anything up to three months for news to cross the Atlantic, but many more for that news to sink into the collective mind that was the Sovereign Cortes. Brazil had changed in the last 14 years, and what was constitutional sauce for the Portuguese goose was good also for the Brazilian gander.

Dom John had on leaving endowed his son with a former viceroy, subsequently Governor of Bahia, as chief minister. So obvious a member of the old order as the Conde dos Arcos was scarcely likely to understand what was going on and the prince found from the start that the business of government was unexpectedly difficult. His first manifesto on law and order read like a threat to the liberals and masons, who kept themselves in almost permanent session in their clubs and academies. His next decrees, against arbitrary imprisonment, torture and an excessive tax on salt, were held to usurp the functions of the Cortes. When he tried to strengthen the garrison of Montevideo, the Portuguese officers in Rio suspected him of wanting to weaken the garrison there in preparation for a coup and refused to let him. His government, above all, was broke. Its estimated commitments were 1700 *contos* more than its revenue and the national debt was already running at 10,000 *contos*. Only one province, Pernambuco, under the indomitable Luiz do Rego, acknowledged that there was a government in Rio and continued to send its remittances. Dom Pedro, in setting a good example, had cleared all the grace-and-favour tenants from São Cristovão and reduced the horses in his stables from 1200 to 156. He even ordered the laundry to be done by the palace slaves. Though the expenses of royalty had been reduced by nearly half, the fabric of government was very thin and billowed perilously at every breath from across the Atlantic.

The Cortes had promulgated the bases on which the new constitution should be written in March 1821, and these reached Brazil in mid-May. As Article 2 stipulated that Portuguese America, Africa and Asia had the right to submit them to representative assemblies before acceptance, dos Arcos advised that this should now be done. General Caula, who held the war portfolio in the junta, distrusted delay and thought that as the junta was a representative body it had the right to approve the bases straight away. On 2 June the Arts and Commerce Lodge, largely composed of the Portuguese-born officers in Rio de Janeiro, met in inaugural session. Two days later Dom Pedro heard that the Third Caçadores were planning to march on the Largo do Rocio for a repeat performance of 26 February. The prince booted and spurred at once, rode to their barracks at dawn the following day and ordered them on their loyalty not to disturb the peace; but as soon as his back was turned, they were on the move. By mid-morning on 5 June, nearly all the Portuguese military units had joined them in the *largo* with their commander, Lieutenant-General Jorge Avilez, at their head.

The prince, who never lacked courage, decided to confront them as he had done before. They demanded the dismissal and expulsion of dos Arcos from Brazil, the unconditional acceptance of the constitutional bases and the election of a new junta answerable to the Cortes in Lisbon, not to the prince as regent in Rio. For dos Arcos he could do nothing, but the other demands Dom Pedro would only accept if other voices, more representative of informed opinion, wished him to do so. He ordered the *senado da câmara* and the parochial electors to reassemble in the Opera House, where the hapless secretary, José Clemente Pereira, a long-time Portuguese-born resident in Rio, his bayoneted arm still sore from the last meeting, was nominated president and instructed to see to the election of a junta in full view of Avilez and his Praetorian guard sitting in the stalls. In fact the presence of many Brazilian officers nerved the assembly to choose a nine-man body which was not packed by creatures of the military. Dom Pedro warned them as he stalked out: 'You can manage as best you can for I shall not come here a third time. Though,' he was heard to mutter, 'God knows where I shall go.'[4]

Humbler spirits than his would have felt the humiliation. His minister dismissed, himself treated as a refractory schoolboy, Dom

Pedro's authority had been reduced to a hollow shell. The new junta may have looked as if it was in the hands of safe men — the new chief of government was a high-court judge, the Bishop of Rio was its chairman — but no one knew where real power lay. Relations between the Portuguese and Brazilian soldiery, both officers and men, were so tense that shopkeepers kept their shutters down for fear of a riot, and even the masonic lodges thought it more prudent not to meet. To add to the sense of doom, Chilean and Peruvian privateers appeared off the coast and in July the unpaid garrison at Santos went on the rampage. Dom Pedro and Dona Leopoldina behaved with faultless circumspection. They appeared at all the social occasions of the military, especially the ball given by Avilez to celebrate the first anniversary of the Oporto declaration, and sat through sermons which were more concerned with the sovereignty of the people than the moral teaching of Jesus Christ.[5]

Dom Pedro felt the strain of a position for which nothing in his education had prepared him. Life in Portugal could not be worse than this perpetual stiltdance above the heads of a fearful and undecided people in an atmosphere sharp with knives. 'I beg Your Majesty,' he wrote to his father on 21 September, 'by all that is holy to dispense me from this distressing situation which must surely kill me. Horrible visions constantly surround me. Some are already under my eyes. Others more dreadful are in prospect.'[6] He knew that others beside his father read his letters and he was not above overstating his case; none the less we should not underestimate the dilemma of a man, only 23, with no one to whom he could turn for advice. One party of freemasons, both Portuguese and Brazilian, was plotting a republic on the Buenos Aires model, while another was bent on separation from Portugal. No one knew who could be trusted. Those who could afford to, left for their country *quintas*. Dom Pedro, suspected by some of his Portuguese officers of being a Bonaparte in Braganza clothing, dined in every mess, listened to the gratuitous advice of General Avilez and repudiated any suggestion that he had a mind of his own. To his father he swore that honour meant more to him than Brazil, that he was faithful to the king, the nation and the constitution.

The summons from the Cortes to return to Portugal arrived on 1 December 1821, like a blow across the face. Dom Pedro kept his temper and assured his father that obedience was second only to his eagerness to see Dom John again. But to allow Brazilians to read of the contempt with which they were held in Lisbon, he published the dispatch from the Cortes in a special number of the *Gazeta* on 11 December. There the astonished public read that their tribunals had been suppressed and that the writ of the government in Rio had ceased to run. But words can only wound not kill and, as the Cortes had not reinforced the garrison before promulgating such inflammatory decrees, the *Cariocas* of Rio de Janeiro were emboldened to identify themselves with their prince who had become, unexpectedly, one of them, to be saved from despiteful handling by Portuguese politicians who had learned nothing and forgotten nothing since 1807. Indignation was on so many lips that even the Portuguese merchants, fearing an epidemic of window-smashing, were as hot as any in their disapproval of the decrees. Though a frigate was prepared to take the prince home, no one expected him to board it as Dona Leopoldina was once more pregnant. On 14 December, Dom Pedro wrote again to his father. If he obeyed the Cortes, revolution in Brazil must surely follow. The people would rise to stop him.

The people were certainly being organized. As soon as the decrees had been published, men rode forth to Vila Rica and São Paulo to rally support and, on 29 December, 8000 signatures had been collected in the capital alone for a petition calling on the prince to stay. On 1 January 1822, a manifesto from the São Paulo junta, dated 24 December, called on him to defy the Cortes. A copy was sent to the *Mineiros*, urging them to raise a petition of their own. The Austrian minister, who was close to the princess royal, was sure that Dom Pedro had seen a letter from his father's old friend, Tomás Antônio, to a friend in Rio, urging him to advise the prince to stay. Could this be his father's voice?[7] By now Dona Leopoldina's Habsburg dander was up and she urged the publication of the São Paulo manifesto in the *Gazeta* on 8 January. It was full of ringing, sometimes offensive, phrases. 'The egregious, indecorous decree of the Cortes' was a deliberate move to divide and weaken the Brazilian people. If he accepted it, the prince would show himself to be craven, for he would become the slave of a tiny group of wreckers bent on destroying the edifice of government constructed since 1808. Even Ireland had a viceroy, so how could Brazil not have a representative of the executive power? Dom Pedro would have to answer to God for the rivers of blood that would flow if he left. If he stayed, the Paulistas would shed theirs to the last drop in his defence.[8]

The text had been agreed between the president of the São Paulo junta, the *reinol* aristocrat and captain-general, Carlos de Oeynhausen, and its *mazombo* secretary, the Intendant-General of Mines in the Kingdom of Portugal, José Bonifácio de Andrada e Silva. He was Carlos Antônio's elder brother, a true child of the century that had produced Benjamin Franklin, whom in later years, with his broad forehead and wispy white hair, he came to resemble. As with Franklin, nothing in his life had given any premonition of a political career. The active politician was Carlos Antônio. José Bonifácio was born in Santos in 1763 but had spent most of his adult life in Europe. He graduated from Coimbra and spent ten years travelling Europe, perfecting his knowledge of mineralogy. He is credited with the discovery of a silicate of aluminium, calcium and sodium found in Norwegian gneiss and called after the German mineralogist, Alfred Werner.[9] He was a fellow-student and colleague of Alexander Humboldt, and in 1803 returned to the *Reino* to be Intendant-General of Mines and Metals. He was also a lecturer at Coimbra and life secretary of the Royal Academy of Sciences in Lisbon. His sole political act up to the present had been when he took command of the battalion of Coimbra students against Marshal Soult.

In 1812, after nearly 30 years in Portugal, he applied for service in Brazil. His younger brother, Martim, was Director of Mines and Forests of São Paulo, and two of his Rhenish assistants, Eschwege and Varnhagen, were already in the colony. But in the event José Bonifácio did not return to the land of his birth until 1819. 'Like a second Pythagoras, introducing the science of Old Egypt into New Hellas,' he was on an official inspection of Brazilian mines when Carlos Antônio and Martim secured his election to the São Paulo junta. He immediately became its secretary. At nearly 60 he had the authority of his years and learning and, above all, what was to make him the Patriarch of Independence: a quality of vision, which was in short supply among his colleagues. He had learned to look on nature and to hear 'the still sad music of humanity'. He rallied to that humanity's defence with a muscular power of expression that made all the Andradas disliked in power and feared in opposition. In the São Paulo manifesto, the ruder colonial spirit broke through the vapid official style of Portuguese public documents and struck a resounding chord for those Brazilians who could read it and the many more who heard it read.

The Rio *câmara* met Dom Pedro on 9 January and endorsed the feelings of the São Paulo junta. 'The departure of Your Royal

Highness will be the fateful decree announcing the independence of his kingdom,' they told him. He should stay until the Cortes had had time to digest this truth. The prince, without prevarication, agreed. 'As it is for the good of all and for the general happiness of the nation, I have made up my mind. Tell the people I stay!'[10]

On 16 February 1822, the *câmara* officially informed the Sovereign Cortes of this decision, which is known in Brazilian history as *O Fico*, meaning 'the I stay'. Brazil, it was admonished, should be treated like a brother not a son, like a sovereign not a subject, as independent as Portugal herself, in union with that country on equal terms. These bold words did not, in fact, reflect the certainties of those in Rio who lived through the events that followed this momentous resolution. The prouder spirits among the Portuguese officers were finding Brazilian euphoria hard to stomach and a dispute in the foyer of the Opera on 11 January, sparked off a riot by a squad of drunken soldiers who ran through the streets smashing windows. It was explained away as a protest against the omnipresent merchandise of the British who had made the glass. More seriously, the *Voluntários d'El Rei*, back from Montevideo, declared that they would embark that night (12 January) for Portugal with the prince.[11]

If Dom Pedro lost his head he lost his throne. Brazilian and militia regiments, stiffened by the Black Henriques and a unit of Indians, streamed into the Campo Sant'Ana. There was a scramble to secure the artillery. General Avilez demanded that they should be disbanded. Dom Pedro curtly ordered him to withdraw the *Voluntários* to their barracks, whereupon Avilez resigned his command. Dom Pedro immediately replaced him by a Brazilian veteran of 79, General Curado. The Peninsula hero, furious at being thought no better than a *mazombo* whose only battle command had been in the Banda, put himself at the head of the mutineers. Civil war was imminent. Dona Leopoldina and the two royal children were sent to Santa Cruz while Dom Pedro prudently arranged for Maria Graham's husband, captain of HMS *Doris*, to give him the protection of the British flag if things went wrong. That night he sent to Minas and São Paulo for loyal reinforcements. Avilez and the *Voluntários* occupied Flagstaff Hill, hoping to overawe the Brazilians, but he commanded barely 2000 men and rumour put the men-at-arms in the *campo* at five times that number, with more coming in from the interior every hour. Avilez, moreover, had learned something other than warfare from his Peninsular experience. He had some understanding of the power of national feeling, for if the Portuguese in defence of their own soil had thwarted Napoleon's legions, their own fate far from home might be little different. And Dom Pedro had one asset worth more than a regiment of troops. He was a Braganza, son and heir of *El-Rei*. Veterans who had fought for nation, church and throne could not turn their guns on the king's son. When he offered them a chance to withdraw with honour across the bay to Praia Grande, Avilez accepted and crossed over on 14 January.

Avilez had not given up, for he expected reinforcements from Portugal at any moment. Dom Pedro knew this and as volunteers poured into Rio he put a ring of steel round Praia Grande. He then gave Avilez an ultimatum. He must embark his troops for Portugal by 4 February, when they would leave with three months' pay in their pockets. Avilez agreed, but when on 9 February they had not boarded the transports put at their disposal, Dom Pedro boarded the *União* frigate and addressed the general through a speaking-trumpet. He had until the following day to embark or else the *Voluntários* would receive 'such a breakfast of Brazilian shot as would make them glad to leave the country'.[12] Avilez knew when he was beaten. On 15 February the *Voluntários* began to leave Guanabara bay for ever. Dom Pedro had surprised himself, delighted his friends and confounded his enemies. He had shown none of the irresolution of his father, and his authority was now very different from the pale shadow of 5 June. Part of his success was due to popular Brazilian support, but most to his behaving like a king, hedged about by the divinity that Portuguese soldiers, both officers and men, respected. It was an asset possessed by no viceroy in Spanish America

There was one pathetic casualty of the fracas. None of the craven palace servants had dared to accompany Dona Leopoldina to Santa Cruz, and her year-old son died there of a fever contracted during the haste of the removal from São Cristovão. The sacrifice was symbolic. The prince could not leave now, for he was the pledge that Brazil and Portugal would not drift into the liberation wars that had convulsed the rest of the continent. Chile had by this time been liberated and the Spaniards were on the defensive in Alto Peru, now Bolivia. New Granada (Colombia) was free; in Venezuela the Spaniards were confined to two strongholds only. The Viceroy of Mexico had abdicated and in September 1821 General Iturbide entered Mexico City to reign as the first and last creole monarch in Spanish America. The cost in lives and treasure had been incalculable.

When, on 20 March, Castlereagh decided to ban the export of warlike stores to Brazil, he hoped that the prince could hold his own without them. Henry Chamberlain, the consul-general, was convinced that the former colony had become independent without knowing it.[13] It was reassuring for the secretary of state to learn that the new chief minister of this unwittingly independent state was not a creole adventurer but a Coimbra professor of mineralogy, nearly 60 years old.

José Bonifácio had arrived at São Cristovão on 16 January to pay his respects to the prince. Before he had time to wash, Dom Pedro offered him the Ministry of Home and Foreign Affairs.[14] At the time people were struck more by the fact that José Bonifácio was neither a *fidalgo* nor a *fazendeiro* than that he was Brazilian-born. But it was his Brazilian birth by which Dom Pedro set most store. The prince was sensitive to the gibe that Brazil had been a co-equal kingdom for six years, yet none of her sons was a councillor of state. José Bonifácio, moreover, had not been long out of Portugal and few *mazombos* had a better insight into the strength of Portuguese revanchism. He was a monarchist by conviction and an oligarch by nature. His constitutional ideas were inspired in part by Bonaparte, in part by Montesquieu, and he believed in mixed government with an impressive array of checks and balances: a chamber of deputies, a senate, a syndicate, consuls and what he chose to call after the Athenian republic an *archon*, which lesser mortals could call a king. He had theoretical objections to hereditary nobility, regular armies and slavery, great confidence in education, and a deep distrust of his fellow-masons who burst into print at the slightest encouragement.[15] His first concern was to bring the provincial juntas to heel behind Dom Pedro. That, to his logical mind, meant a Cortes not in Lisbon but in Rio. On 16 February he ordered the convening of a Council of Procurators of the provinces to monitor and adapt the decrees emanating from Portugal.

Public reaction was not enthusiastic. Conservatives feared that the procurators would become tools of the Paulista mavericks, while liberals scorned them as phantoms of popular government. But José Bonifácio was determined to vindicate the authority of the prince without the distraction of an assembly, and Dom Pedro trusted him so implicitly that republicans called him José Bonifácio's adjutant. Whenever he could find them, the new minister had the authors of disrespectful pasquinades locked away. 'I do what I can,' he told the Austrian envoy, who in turn reassured Metternich that the Brazilian minister was a legitimist like himself, 'but I am not a giant with a hundred arms and a hundred eyes.'[16] He was unscrupulous in his use of police informers to investigate plots and rumours of plots, and firm in their suppression, so that by the end of April the diplomatic community was in no more doubt that, for the first time since the little Brumaire of 5 June 1821, effective power had been restored to the throne.

Two events were to prove it. The reinforcements Avilez had been expecting passed him in mid-Atlantic. They were refused permission to land either at Recife or at Rio de Janeiro unless the troops signed on to serve with Brazilian regiments. Those who refused were sent back to Lisbon on 23 March. Immediately that threat was disposed of, Dom Pedro set off for Minas Gerais, where the junta was not in a co-operative mood.[17] The *Mineiros*, reckoning that since 1700 over 553 million cruzados had been raised from the quint on gold without an ounce of profit to the province, were as suspicious of a Cortes in Rio as of one in Lisbon, and unwilling to send their remittances to the capital. The prince's journey was a royal procession all the way. His manifesto to the *Mineiros*, full of grammatical errors from his own fist, called on them to be constitutional and have faith in him. 'You live for liberty, but I adore her. Unite with me and from this unity see the benefit to Brazil. You will hear Europe say: "Brazil is great and rich and those Brazilians know how to recognize their true rights and interests."' The historic *Mineiro* spirit now harnessed to the crown, the *Cariocas* were not slow to follow. One of the liberal journals, the *Revérbero*, of 30 April, urged him to cross the Rubicon and found a new empire. On 4 May the government announced that no decree of the Cortes had any validity in Brazil until it had been approved by Dom Pedro. On 13 May, the birthday of *El-Rei*, a delegation from the *câmara* invited Dom Pedro to accept the title of Protector and Perpetual Defender of Brazil, a title conjured up at a meeting of the Arts and Commerce Lodge, now largely purged of its Portuguese military members and enthusiastically Brazilian. The chief minister, disturbed by its Cromwellian echoes, agreed that the prince could be Perpetual Defender but not Protector.[18] On 23 May a second delegation begged Dom Pedro to call a general assembly of the Brazilian provinces.

Events were now moving too fast for José Bonifácio. Knowing the volatile spirit of the masons, whose views were strongly tinged by Spanish American republicanism, he intended to mobilize the forces of conservatism in the Council of Procurators, whose election he hurried forward. The parochial electors of Rio de Janeiro elected theirs on 1 June. One of them was the Portuguese-born Joaquim Gonçalves Ledo, a former clerk in the Arsenal, arch-priest of liberalism and editor of the *Revérbero*. Ledo and his colleagues immediately co-opted a third procurator, a Spanish-speaking deputy from Montevideo on his way to Lisbon to represent the Cisplatine State (a euphemism for the occupied Banda Oriental) in the Cortes there. Posing as elected deputies of the people of the capital, they petitioned Dom Pedro for a general assembly. José Bonifácio knew that his hand was being forced, but he could not afford to neglect any measure that might unite the prince to his subjects, both *mazombo* and *reinol*. Though he hoped to avoid a conflict with Portugal, it was 'written in the Book of Eternal Law that Brazil . . . must join the list of free nations', yet there were not a hundred men in the country who could be relied upon to defend her. On 3 June Dom Pedro signed a decree summoning a General Constituent and Legislative Assembly. Henry Chamberlain was convinced that José Bonifácio had decided on a final breach with Portugal.[19]

It was a victory for the Arts and Commerce Lodge, where liberals rehearsed the speeches they were going to make in the assembly. José Bonifácio allowed himself to be elected its grand master, but he distrusted the rhetoric which, in the heady atmosphere of free debate, tempted its inexperienced members into fatuities.[20] Not from among them would he find the committee of public safety Brazil might need if Portugal were determined to reassert her colonial authority. Above all he was repelled by the populist ideas of Gonçalves Ledo, now styled 'First Vigilante', an *exaltado*, almost a republican, who was making a dead-set at Dom Pedro. He did not want the prince's head filled with ideas of popular will, but Dom Pedro, as his wife ruefully remarked, 'loved all things new', and could not be kept out of the fray for long. On 2 June José Bonifácio founded his own Apostolate of the Noble Order of the Knights of the Holy Cross. It was not a masonic lodge as it did not seek to interpret the plans of the Great Architect, but it was resolved to 'defend by every measure the integrity, identity and independence of Brazil as a kingdom and the legitimate constitution of the state, ranging itself equally against despotism that could deform and anarchy that could destroy it'. Dom Pedro was invited to take the title of 'Archon King' with the name of Romulus; Gonçalves Ledo was tactfully enrolled as a founder member and the apostolate divided into three confraternities, taking as their names 'Independence or Death',

'Union and Tranquillity' and 'Firmness and Loyalty'.[21] The name of that first confraternity was to be heard again.

The *exaltados* were not to be outdone by these charades and redoubled their efforts to win the prince over. The Arts and Commerce Lodge transformed itself into the Grand Orient Lodge of Brazil and on 13 July admitted Dom Pedro with the name of Brother Guatimozim, called after the nephew of the last emperor of the Aztecs, who had defied another Cortes. They had plans to make him grand master in the place of the heavy-handed minister. He knew what they were up to, but he had other problems to face. Of the two provincial juntas, only two were safe: São Paulo's, under the baton of his younger brother, Martim, and Minas Gerais, still basking in the royal sun. Pernambuco had only just recognized Dom Pedro's regency. Luiz do Rego's cautious flirtation with constitutionalism had been unconvincing from the start and in August 1821 there was an attempt on his life. Forty-three suspects were rounded up and sent, not as expected to Rio, but to Lisbon. There they were released immediately. The victims of the man who had hammered the patriots of 1817 could not be anything but innocent in the eyes of a liberal and democratic Cortes. Knowing that he did not command the support of either *reinol* or *mazombo*, Luiz do Rego held the ring until the election of a new junta in January 1822, when he returned to Portugal.

On 1 June the Recife *vereadores* in the *câmara*, the church leaders and the military recognized Dom Pedro as regent. Five days later Belém do Pará acclaimed the prince. But Bahia had been in the grip of Portuguese soldiery since February. There the mainly *mazombo* junta had had to elect a successor to the old captain-general and there were two candidates. One was a Brazilian like themselves, the other was a hard-line Peninsular veteran, Inacio Luiz Madeira de Melo. The latter lost no time in establishing what he understood to be the will of the Cortes in Lisbon. On 19 February he seized control of Salvador, arrested his rival and shipped him off to Portugal. The coup cost over 100 lives, including the first martyr of Brazilian independence, the Franciscan Abbess of Lapa, Joana Angelica de Jesus, who, in covering the retreat of her nuns from a soldiery rendered more than ordinarily brutal and licentious by drink and *francs-tireurs*, was butchered at the door of her convent. Dom Pedro and Dona Leopoldina assisted at her requiem in Rio. Madeira put a brave face on his shame and established an iron grip on the city.

Madeira had clearly been influenced by the fate of his old comrade in arms in Recife. When the *vereadores* of Salvador decided to follow the example of their other north-eastern colleagues, they were prevented from meeting by Madeira's troops. A mulatto lawyer, Francisco Gomes de Brandão, using the pen name of Montezuma, protested in the Salvador newspaper. When Madeira tried to silence him, he escaped into the interior and on 25 June proclaimed Dom Pedro regent on behalf of the people of Bahia. A patriot cause was born and appealed to Rio de Janeiro for help. Madeira, like a second Avilez, would have to be dislodged by force.[22]

15· Independence, 1822

*'Brazil is ready to be united with Portugal but she will not march
in the direction the Cortes wants her to'*—
> Deputy Nicolau Pereira de Campos Vergueiro
> to the Cortes, 15 September 1822

*'Inda que não fosse herdeiro Seja já Pedro Primeiro.' (Since heir I
cannot be, at worst, I may as well be crowned Pedro the First.)*—
> A popular refrain in Rio, 1822

Both Dom Pedro and his chief minister knew that if the Cortes turned
ugly, then Salvador under Madeira would be the obvious beachhead
for a Portuguese expeditionary force. The former colonial capital
must, therefore, be recovered without delay. In July 1822, Brazil had
commissioned her first soldier of fortune, formerly one of Napoleon's
brigade commanders in Egypt, who had between 1810 and 1813
fought for the independence of New Granada (now Colombia). Pierre
Labatut was to invest Salvador by land while Commodore Rodrigo
Lamare blockaded it by sea. On 18 July the patriots, peddling the
sophism that no liberal, constitutional assembly could wilfully support
tyrants, called on the people of Bahia to conquer or die for the
prince, for *El-Rei* and, since Madeira could not be its legitimate
agent, the Cortes. The Portuguese general was offered and refused
100 *contos* to join the Brazilian cause and asked Lisbon for help.[1] On
1 August, Dom Pedro called on his people to resist the landing of
any Portuguese troops on Brazilian soil.

Dom Pedro had accepted the title of Perpetual Defender, and
against whom, if not the proud and contemptuous Cortes, should
he be defending his adopted land? Rumours from London spoke of
a secret pact between Lisbon and Madrid to unite forces against their
rebellious colonies and José Bonifácio's agent in London reported
that Lisbon had offered France the left bank of the Amazon in

return for positive assistance against the Brazilian 'rebels', a proposal she had refused to entertain. The Cortes was talking for its part of abandoning Montevideo and moving the garrison to Santa Catarina, whence it could revolutionize the slaves of the northern provinces and thus create space for Madeira to march south to meet them.[2] If half the rumours were true, the Brazilians had cause to worry. On 1 August, Dom Pedro urged his subjects: 'Let there be heard from you no other cry but "Union". From the Amazon to the Plate let there be no echo but "Independence"!'[3] It caught the *exaltado* mood perfectly. Disgusted by the way the elected deputies of Brazil had been treated in the Cortes, where, with a lack of finesse that could only be the result of constitutional madness, their Portuguese colleagues had united both Brazilian and Portuguese-born in opposition to any return to colonial status, the constitutionalists in Rio de Janeiro began to talk of separation. The traditional loyalty of the people to *El-Rei* would simply be transferred to his own flesh and blood, the patriot regent, Dom Pedro.

On 14 August, José Bonifácio made a public pronouncement to the world. Since Dom John was clearly only the slave of the Cortes, Brazil must shift for herself. She had no desire to change her head of state but she could acknowledge no authority that she had not chosen herself. In asking that the agents he had appointed in London, Washington and Paris should be recognized as the accredited agents of the Brazilian government, the minister was stating Brazil's *de facto* independence. Already in London, Felisberto Brant, scion of a rich Bahian planter family and graduate of the Lisbon College of Nobles, was negotiating the first of many loans that were to keep his country afloat. Antônio Gonçalves da Cruz, the former envoy of the 1817 Recife rebels, who had prudently stayed in the United States to pursue his business interests, moved to Washington to represent the country from which his native province had earlier wished to secede. Gameiro Pessoa was in Paris. Each was to make it very clearly understood that Brazil would close her ports to any nation that denied her rights to independence — a clear hint to the British, already worried about the security of their privileges under the 1810 treaty, and to the French, who hoped to negotiate similar privileges for themselves.[4] If Europe did not accept Brazil's open commercial system, José Bonifácio told the Austrian minister, she would close up like China and fight from behind her natural bastions of sea, forest, mountain, space and time.

José Bonifácio had never expected and now did not want any accommodation with the Cortes. His brusque contempt for its deliberations, however, had its critics, who feared he would push separation from Portugal to the point of no return. Many of them lived in his own heartland, and on 23 May 1822 the São Paulo junta had sacked its secretary, the minister's younger brother, Martim Francisco. The State Intendant of Mines and Forests had fallen out with the Paulista oligarchs, who resented his proud, despotic and arbitrary temper. His severe attacks on food speculators had been noble if clumsy, but his ultimate offence was to insist in rehanging a mutinous soldier, round whose neck the rope had broken but over whose body the *Misericórdia* had thrown its banner, claiming God's acquittal.[5] Interpreting his brother's dismissal as a gesture of resentment at his defiance of the Cortes, José Bonifácio persuaded Dom Pedro to bring him into the Council of Ministers, where he could be his brother's right hand. The mantle of royal protection now cast upon its former secretary, the Paulista junta fell into a state of mutual bickering. José Bonifácio thought it was time for Dom Pedro to repeat his triumph of the year before in Minas Gerais.

On the same day, 14 August, on which José Bonifácio had delivered his message to the world, the prince left Rio with an entourage of five. An instinctive populist, he would raise his escort from among the people and enter the city on their shoulders. He had not been gone a fortnight when the news reached Rio that the Cortes had cancelled his decree convoking the Council of Procurators, appointed him a new ministry and ordered the arrest of the authors of the São Paulo manifesto of January. Coming close behind rumours of a vast expedition assembling for the reconquest of Brazil, this was the last straw. A malign destiny seemed determined to see that the interests of Portugal and Brazil were never to meet on the floor of the Cortes. The three-month gap between the two countries meant that politicians on one side of the Atlantic took decisions in ignorance of what was happening on the other. There had been a time when the Cortes, understanding how badly its early decrees had been received in Rio de Janeiro, was prepared to be accommodating. Dom Pedro had not been recalled and it had been left to him to decide what instruments of state he needed. It had even proposed that the Brazilians should produce local amendments to the constitution when it was produced. But these early voices of reason were soon to be drowned in anger.

On 15 March, the day the Cortes published a project to return the carrying trade between the two countries to a Portuguese monopoly, two of Dom Pedro's letters were read in full house. The Portuguese deputies were outraged to hear that the Paulistas in their December manifesto had called on him to disobey the orders of the Sovereign Cortes and stay in Brazil. When they later learned of the ignominious expulsion of Avilez and his *Voluntários*, the news provoked a fierce clash between the most nationalist of the Portuguese deputies, Borges Carneiro, and the leader of the Brazilians, Carlos Antônio de Andrada. What dashed any hopes of reconciliation was Madeira's dispatch, arriving at the end of April, on the patriot siege of Salvador. Borges Carneiro demanded an expeditionary force to show that Portugal still had bulldogs to bring the fractious Brazilians to heel. Carlos Antônio poured scorn on such 'fatuous menaces'. Brazil had clubs, swords and bullets enough to deal with bulldogs!

Then in May came the news that Avilez's reinforcements had been turned back, that the Minas Gerais deputies had chosen to stay in Brazil, that Dom Pedro had decided to call a Council of Procurators and that the deputy from Montevideo to the Cortes had been waylaid in Rio and drafted to serve on it. *O Rapazinho*, that whipper-snapper, was growing insolent. On 10 June, Borges Carneiro moved that the São Paulo junta be arraigned for *lèse-majesté* and the Minas junta be called to account for not ordering its deputies to proceed to Lisbon. One of the Paulista deputies, Nicolau Vergueiro, warned the assembly not to rend the monarchy in two. Carlos Antônio promised civil war. So quickly had views hardened that when, a week later, the constitutional commission set up to advise on the position of Brazil put forward its proposals for a dual monarchy, based on separate national congresses and an imperial parliament to which each country should send 50 deputies, they were dismissed out of hand. Instead, the Portuguese majority deposed Dom Pedro's ministry and ordered the arrest of José Bonifácio. Borges Carneiro would not listen to talk of conciliation while Madeira was under siege. Like an angel of division, he accused Dom Pedro of turning a greedy eye on Portuguese Africa and Asia and urged the dispatch of a force to relieve Salvador. Carlos Antônio, now in his full fiery element, promised that every Brazilian deputy would hurl himself into the front line against aggression. 'If Brazil seeks separation and independence,' he cried, 'it will be my sacred duty to follow her.'[6] While the other Brazilian deputies were still trying to decide whether to put their names to the constitution which had been presented at last to the Cortes on 12 July, Dom Pedro declared Brazil independent.

As predicted, Dom Pedro's royal procession to São Paulo was a triumph. At each town he was acclaimed and the *ordenanças* paraded as his bodyguard, and when he reached São Paulo on 25 August he held the city in the palm of his hand. Only the refractory junta felt the draught of his displeasure. He spent the next few days riding in the open terrain near the *fazenda* of Piratinanga, where he set eyes for the first time on the strawberry and cream charms of his equerry's married sister, the future Brazilian Pompadour, Domitila de Castro Canto e Melo. He was to see her in more intimate detail over several nights before riding down to Santos on 5 September. Two days later he was returning without haste to São Paulo, when he was met by a courier galloping at full speed towards him with dispatches from Rio.

To this day no one knows all that the dispatch case contained, but it certainly carried copies of the offensive decrees from Lisbon and two letters from his wife, written in rapid sequence on 28 and 29 August. Dom Pedro was infuriated by what he read. Madeira had been reinforced and rumours that the first sails of the expected Portuguese armada had been sighted off the south of Rio de Janeiro on the 27th had put the capital in a panic. He must return at once. Only his presence, firmness and energy could save Brazil, for when 600 Portuguese soldiers had disembarked at Salvador from only two or three ships of war, 'our treacherous squadron just stood there, open-mouthed, watching them'.[7] There was also a letter from José Bonifácio, but Dona Leopoldina had said everything.

Dom Pedro cast the decrees to the ground and mounted his horse. The tiny party galloped up the neighbouring hill to the waiting escort by the banks of the Ipiranga. 'The time has come,' he shouted, his face pale with fury. 'It is "Independence or Death". We are no longer united with Portugal.' Plucking off his blue and white constitutional armband, he threw it away. His companions did the same, whereupon Dom Pedro drew his sword and raised it to the sky. 'I swear by my blood, my honour and by God that Brazil shall be free. "Independence or Death" will be our watchword. Green and gold our colours.' It was now 4.30 in the afternoon. An hour later they were in São Paulo, which was electrified by the vivas to independence from the São Paulo dragoons, led by Domitila's brother. Dom Pedro withdrew for a few minutes and composed the national anthem, which he sang that night in the theatre, after which a priest leaped on to a seat and called three cheers for the first King of Brazil. Garibaldi could not have done it better.[8]

A scene so like something out of an opera by Verdi suggests that some of the libretto had been written in advance. The prince was looking for a chance to make a dramatic gesture and José Bonifácio may have persuaded Dona Leopoldina to send the courier hotfoot to São Paulo to ensure that it was made there and not in the Grand Orient Lodge. He knew that the *exaltados* wanted to make the inevitable declaration of independence a masonic achievement, but before they could do so, Dom Pedro came racing back from São Paulo like 'a second Charles XII' in just five days to announce that Brazil, without the assistance of the Grand Orient, was already independent.[9] They lost no time in making the best of the situation. 'Independence or Death' was, after all, a masonic password (being the name of one of the *Apostolado* fraternities) and on 15 September the rank and file of the lodges voted to send agents into the provinces to rally them behind the throne. On the 16th, the tribune Gonçalves Ledo placarded Rio with handbills encouraging the people to 'acclaim the worthy hero, the magnanimous Pedro, our first Constitutional Emperor'. The new title caught like wildfire.[10] On 7 October the Grand Orient acclaimed Brother Guatimozim not only their grand master but also First Emperor and Perpetual Defender of Brazil. New Granada might have her *Libertador* but Brazil would have her *Imperador*.[11]

It was a better title than *archon*. It was better, even, than king. To legitimist and royalist ears, both in Brazil and in Europe, kings ruled more by grace of God than by will of the people and Brazil had a king already, the much loved *El-Rei*, Dom John VI. By Roman, Habsburg and Napoleonic precedent, emperors were created by election. They were not protected by divine sanction and were not necessarily of royal lineage. Emperors could be acclaimed, and indeed Dom Pedro was not America's first emperor, since Agustín I Iturbide of Mexico had been raised briefly to that dignity by the creole army on 18 May 1822, and the first emperor in the New World was the former slave, Jean-Jacques I Dessalines of Haiti, who reigned in 1805–6 until murdered by his successor, the Emperor Henri-Christophe. An emperor could, therefore, be presented to the world as reflecting popular choice every bit as convincingly as a republican president, so that Dom Pedro's 24th birthday, 12 October, was chosen to mark a happy marriage between liberty and legitimacy, solemnized on American soil. It was to be the high-water mark of masonic triumph. Dazzled by their own narcissism, the members of the Grand Orient Lodge believed that they had called the empire into being as the culmination of their liberal aspirations. Dom Pedro I was their creation, and throughout his short and tumultuous reign he was to have no sturdier partisans of imperial authority than the hitherto democratic and republican *exaltados*, like Gonçalves Ledo.

Maler and Marschall, those agents of conservative monarchy, were comforted by José Bonifácio's promise of stern measures against 'democracy'. Marschall may have been puzzled by Dom John's position should he ever return to Brazil, but was practical enough to warn Metternich that if he hoped to return as monarch, he would have himself to be acclaimed emperor. Brazil and Portugal were now irrevocably separate. José Bonifácio, for himself, was in no hurry to solve the puzzle of *El-Rei*. Continued warnings that 20,000 men were preparing for an expedition against Brazil made national unity the first prerequisite for security. The nicer issues of etiquette could be dealt with later.[12]

On 17 September, the breathless citizens of Rio de Janeiro had been warned to expect nothing more from Portugal than slavery and horrors. Anyone not prepared to declare his loyalty to the new sovereign and nation by wearing the green and gold armbands now obligatory for patriots must leave within the month. The national colours represented the new spring and the old gold upon which Brazil's nationhood was founded. Her ancient armillary sphere, long her heraldic device, was capped by the cross of the Order of Christ under whose auspices she had been colonized, and surrounded by 17 silver stars to represent the constituent provinces, on one side a sprig of the cotton tree and on the other a tobacco plant. The Campo Sant'Ana was prepared by the French team at the Fine Arts Academy with suitable tableaux for the acclamation. The royal party wore green and gold on 12 October, when, before a huge crowd and 6000 men in uniform, Dom Pedro accepted his new title from the president of the Rio *câmara*. There were vivas for everyone except the Cortes, and a salute of 101 guns. The British and French warships in the bay saluted the new flag — the British because they had already saluted the flags of the Spanish succession states, the French not to be outdone — after which the new emperor walked under a canopy borne by the senators of the *câmara* to the Chapel Royal for a Te Deum. This was followed by his first *beija-mão* as emperor and a drama at the theatre hurriedly prepared for the occasion and called, surprisingly, *The Independence of Scotland*.[13]

Both Dom Pedro and Dona Leopoldina wrote to their fathers to explain that they had not waited for the approval of the concert of Europe, since Dom Pedro could not have confronted both the Brazilian people and the Cortes single-handed. Forces beyond his power to control had put him at their head, but Maler, Marschall and Henry Chamberlain were all convinced that those forces were no more powerful than the masonic twins, Gonçalves Ledo and José Clemente Pereira.[14] The reaction of that concert was muted. As Brant had warned from London, the unilateral declaration of independence was too strong for legitimist stomachs.[15] Canning instructed his ambassador in Lisbon to express no opinion, for, he told the cabinet on 15 November, if Britain were to recognize the separation of the Braganza kingdoms, she could not logically refuse also to recognize the Spanish American states. In the long run, too, economic benefits should not be the sole determinants of recognition. The 1815 declaration that the slave-trade with Brazil could only be licensed if Brazil were a colony offered an opportunity to conclude the last major item of unfinished business that 'hangs about the neck of this country'.[16] The price of recognition could be its abolition by an independent Brazil. 'Let the Brazilian government relieve us . . . by frankly removing a traffic which, however it might be thought necessary to its cultivation as a colony, must be fatal to any wholesome increase of population and internal strength as an empire.'[17]

The French government still hoped to secure the same trade concessions from Brazil that her rival had secured from Portugal, and hinted strongly that they might be the price of recognition, but its envoy to Brazil had been embarrassed at a critical moment by having to explain away the French invasion of Spain in February 1823.[18] José Bonifácio had no love for the Spanish constitution, but Chateaubriand's earnest avowal of disinterested friendship struck his ear as false. As for Britain's resolve to hang the abolition of the slave-trade round the neck of the new nation as well as round her own, that was pure blackmail. And little support could be expected from the other English-speaking power. The new US consul-general, Condy Raguet, was a doughty enemy to British influence in the Americas, but he was also a staunch republican and a doctrinaire opponent of the imperial concept. That left Austria. The presence of a daughter of Francis II on the Brazilian throne was the best guarantee of Austrian support, even had Metternich not felt protective towards the idea of a hereditary, legitimate monarchy in the New World.

Of Dona Leopoldina, indeed, almost too much was expected. As a dutiful daughter she had also to be a dutiful wife. She had presided over the regency council which met when Dom Pedro was in São Paulo. It was she who called him back when the final breach came. Fortunately she saw nothing incongruous in being the daughter of the most conservative monarch in Western Europe and the wife of a constitutional monarch. 'The good Brazilian people' had put her husband on the throne to establish national unity and banish anarchy. The dread Constituent Assembly ('Our Cortes'), she told her father, would have no more ardent wish than to see commercial treaties signed with the Austrian dominions and another dynastic tie welding the two empires together.[19] José Bonifácio admired the hard-riding Habsburg princess as one of the hundred Brazilians whom he could trust to defend the new country. The support of so stalwart a champion of legitimacy as Prince Metternich was worth a few promises, and as the Austrian chancellor was likely, as his price of recognition, to ask only for a stable empire, that would be the chief minister's first concern.

Dom Pedro had come storming back from São Paulo because Commodore Lamare's blockade of Salvador had been so easily pierced by Madeira's reinforcements from Lisbon. The greater number of his sailors had been born in Portugal and Lamare feared that if he engaged the enemy closely, they would merely have delivered his ships into their hands. Both José Bonifácio and Dom Pedro knew that Lamare would have to be replaced. But by whom? The senior naval officer was Admiral Lobo, but he was also Portuguese-born and, worse still, stained for ever by the 1817 white terror in Pernambuco. There were no other officers with even Lamare's experience. Felisberto Brant, talent-spotting in London, had already suggested where they might look, and on 17 September 1822 the chief minister authorized the Brazilian consul in Buenos Aires to negotiate the hiring of an admiral, 'an audacious bandit, capable of anything, with only one object and desire — gold, equally ready to mount a magnificent enterprise or a petty meanness for the sake of an *escudo*'.[20]

Thomas Cochrane was, perhaps, the finest seaman of his time. After his stormy but brilliant war against Napoleon, egocentric, ill-tempered and hogtied to a grievance like a jealous husband to a nagging wife, he had in 1816 taken his still undiminished energy (and a special prize agent to protect his interest) to command Chile's naval forces against Spain. The campaign that followed was as brilliant as its leader was difficult, and by 1822 this stormy petrel was thinking of transferring his services to the 'struggle for the liberties of Greece ... [which] offered the fairest opportunity for enterprise and exertion'. Brazil, on the other hand, was nearer and might be fairer. What cashiered freebooter could resist the call of the new emperor himself? 'Venez, Milord, l'honneur vous invite, la gloire vous appelle. Venez, donnez nos armes navales cet ordre merveilleux et discipline incomparable de puissante Albion!'[21] Assured that he would be given a rank no lower than that he had held in Chile, he resigned that command on 29 November 1822 and set off for Rio de Janeiro, open, he asserted, either to decline or to accept Dom Pedro's offer, thus preserving 'a consistency of character', in case Brazil's should not be the sort of government 'I have been in the habit of supporting'. This 'fanatic for glory, a second Lafayette', was not sure that Brazil could afford him.[22]

He had good grounds for his anxiety. The new state was, within three months of declaring its independence, nearly £2 million in the red. A public subscription was launched to buy shares in the six fully manned ships of war that Brant was to hire or buy in London, and José Bonifácio was ready to hypothecate every asset in the treasury to pay for them.[23] Rich men, led by the emperor himself, dipped into their pockets to buy a brig or a schooner for the nation. In the event, the ships could not be bought; no one would accept payment in Rio de Janeiro. Instead shipwrights and artificers worked under Dom Pedro's supervision to overhaul and equip the few vessels that Dom John had left behind. But ships were only half what was wanted. There were 160 Portuguese-born naval officers in Brazil, 96 of them fit for service, but of these only 27 were prepared to serve. Ready as they might be to battle against Argentines or chase Chilean corsairs, they were not ready to fight in a fratricidal war. When a schooner and three transports carrying artillery to Lecor sailed instead into Montevideo to deliver their cargo to the Portuguese troops he was investing, the Brazilian government wondered whether Cochrane would be enough.

The arrival in Salvador on 6 November of Commodore Félix de Campos and a further 1200 men under escort of the *Dom João VI*, of 74 guns, and the *Perola* frigate, seemed proof that he was not. Five other foreign officers also signed on. The first was David Jewett, late of the US and Buenos Aires navies. John Taylor, first lieutenant in Captain Graham's HMS *Doris*, was in February 1823 appointed frigate captain before he was able to resign his commission in the Royal Navy and faced arrest for desertion if he could be taken without violating the Brazilian flag.[24] The others were Théodore Beaurepaire, late of the French and Portuguese navies, and Second-Lieutenants William Eyre and George Manson, RN. All except Manson were to end their careers as flag-officers in the Brazilian navy, as did Cochrane's flag-lieutenant, John Pascoe Grenfell, who followed his old chief from Chile. The enrolment of seamen was not so easy. Brazilians were landsmen; the only experienced sailors were Portuguese, slaves or *caboclos*. Six hundred British tars then should be enlisted in Britain. For a few months the enrolment of 'immigrant farmworkers and overseers' who happened to have served in the Royal Navy was brisk, despite the ban on service in foreign navies. Five years' service on pay no worse in most cases than they had earned on active service and the prospects of prize-money in the tropical sun were too alluring for men caught in the vice of a post-war depression. On January 1823 the first of them sailed for Rio, while illegal supplies of ordnance, munitions and naval stores were already on the high seas, paid for in diamonds. By May, 450 experienced officers and men had left for Brazil, a stupendous achievement by Brant, who had, in fact, promised more than his country could afford to pay. They were to earn every *mil-réis*.[25]

Almost simultaneously, a third expedition of 1600 men set out from Lisbon for Salvador.

16· War, 1822–3

'I must have sailors to end the war . . . I need scarcely say that I should prefer British seamen to all others' —

Lord Cochrane, *Narrative*, vol 2, p 55

'Thanks be to Providence that we see the nation represented by such worthy deputies. Would to God it could have been earlier' —

Dom Pedro I to the Constituent Assembly, 3 May 1823

The mercenaries could, if they were regularly paid, be relied on to fight the Portuguese. José Bonifácio could not be too sure of anyone else. He must seek out and crush the fifth column of the Portuguese-born whose loyalties, when put to the test, would be to the old country not to the new. At the same time he must contain the liberals and republicans, nurtured on the pernicious 'democracy' of Spanish America. The bastion of monarchy must not be undermined. When the incautious editor of a liberal broadsheet referred to 'Dom Pedro the First but Never a Second', he was instantly arrested and deported. The sessions of that *pepinière* of dangerous ideologies, the Grand Orient Lodge, were suspended and the police intendant was authorized to pay more for information about subversives. Dom Pedro was disturbed. Had he become grand master to preside over the demise of the lodge, or constitutional emperor to connive at tyranny?[1]

On 26 October he revoked the sentence of deportation on the editor and reprieved the Grand Orient. José Bonifácio and his ministry resigned at once. As no one could be found to succeed him, he was soon back in office, heading a large crowd chanting 'Pedro the First, Second, Third and Fourth'. A petition was signed by hundreds of citizens demanding the delation of the minister's opponents as factious demagogues. The police intendant was sacked and his successor arrested those Portuguese-born 'democrats' of the Grand Orient who had been José Bonifácio's rival rather than fellow-architects of independence. José Clemente Pereira, president of the *câmara*, who had first moved in the lodge that Dom Pedro should be acclaimed emperor, Canon Januario Barbosa, who had rallied the *Mineiros* behind the prince, and Gonçalves Ledo, the 'soul and mouthpiece' of all liberals in the capital, were sentenced to deportation to France — hardly, in 1822, a safe asylum for liberals — and Ledo escaped to Buenos Aires with the help of the Swedish consul. On 11 November, José Bonifácio called on all the juntas and *câmaras* to destroy cells of 'furious demagogues and anarchists who with neither principle nor scruple denigrate the undoubted constitutionalism of the emperor and his most faithful ministry'.[2] Colonel Maler, watching from the wings, found it all as good as a play.

Metternich would have approved of this chief minister who labelled democrats as *carbonari* and who devised a splendid ceremony for the crowning and sacring of the now suitably chastened emperor on 1 December, the anniversary of Dom John's acclamation. He chose freely from the ceremonials used to crown Napoleon I, the Austrian emperor and the King of Hungary. The emperor in green and gold, clad in a mantle of rose-red toucan feathers and wearing a crown weighing six pounds and encrusted with diamonds worth half a million cruzados, swore before the altar to observe and maintain to his last breath the Catholic Religion and the Constitutional Laws of the Empire. The coronation and foundation of a new chivalric order of the Southern Cross (O Cruzeiro do Sul) were marked by the Latin American premières of Rossini's *Elizabeth of England* and *The Italian Girl in Algiers*.[3]

Dom Pedro then proceeded to São Cristovão, where, like Zamorna in his palace on the Calabar, he stood at the head of a corridor of flunkeys in green tail-coats with gold galloons and extended his hand to the lips of Grandees of the Empire and Commanders of Christ and of the Southern Cross. José Bonifácio encouraged Dom Pedro to play his royal role like his father before him, while he stung the Portuguese with a flight of decrees, sequestering the property of absentee *reinóis*, banning investment in the *Reino*, increasing the duty on Portuguese goods and licensing a *guerre de course* against Portuguese shipping if, within four months, Portugal had not recognized Brazil's independence. He set spies to watch his old cronies in the São Paulo junta even though they were far too sedate to be *carbonari*. He placed Father Feijó, one of the Paulista deputies returning from the Cortes in Lisbon, under surveillance for openly criticizing the ministry for doing violence to its principles. Only the return of his brother, Carlos Antônio, in January 1823, glorious as the leader of protest in Lisbon, could refurbish the sagging image of the Andrada ministry. At long last, on 3 May, after many delays not of the ministry's making, the Constituent Assembly met. The auspices for true democracy were poor. Some of the deputies elected for Rio de Janeiro were in exile and only four deputies from Bahia managed to reach the capital. There were no deputies from Piauí, Maranhão and Grão Pará, whose juntas had stayed loyal to the Cortes. Those who did assemble met with a resolve to survive. Meanwhile, on 13 March, Thomas Cochrane had arrived in Rio 'to raise dread and terror among their enemies'.[4]

The battle squadron he was to command was, almost miraculously, ready for sea, the flag-admiral's cabin on the *Pedro I*, of 74 guns, being even upholstered in green and gold. Three frigates, two corvettes and four brigs comprised the force at his command, and the indefatigable navy minister, Cunha Moreira, had assembled supplies sufficient for three months. But he had not worked the same miracle with the crews. The musters were still predominantly Portuguese, their numbers made up with convicts, impressed vagrants and slaves. Cochrane was not ready to sail at once, not because he thought his ships poorly manned but because he wanted to be sure of his undisputed command and of his pay. Dom Pedro and José Bonifácio, chafing at the delay, agreed at once to all his demands, for no less than the winning of the north was expected of him, followed by a blockade of Lisbon and Oporto.[5] So that the seniority of the prickly *reinol* admirals who had elected to serve Dom Pedro should not be disturbed, the Scottish interloper was given the new rank of first admiral with pay worth £500 a year more than an English admiral commanding-in-chief.[6] At that moment two ships arrived with 200 thirsty British tars and six officers. The emperor and empress visited the dockyards, where the sailors were already drunk. But as Dona Leopoldina graciously explained, it was the custom of the north, whence brave men came. They did not disappoint her.

On 29 March the blockade of Salvador was proclaimed and on 1 April the squadron sailed. The ensuing saga has been often told, most loudly by Cochrane himself, of the attack on the squadron of Félix de Campos on 4 May, rendered futile by undisciplined and disaffected crews, of the solitary combat of the *Pedro I*, whose gunners could not fire straight and whose powder-boys had been locked below deck, of the cartridges that had to be stuffed with shredded bunting to stop them from exploding and decapitating the gunners, of crews so divided in loyalty that one half of the squadron had to be detached to watch over the other.[7] When Campos, having retired into the inner reaches of the Bay of All Saints, would not come out again, Cochrane put all his British and North American sailors in the *Pedro I* and enforced an effective blockade while he publicly prepared fireships to repeat his now world-famous exploit at the Basque Roads (1809) and at Callao in Chile (1822). He was to command the explosion vessel himself. Madeira knew when he was beaten. His fresh provisions were exhausted and all intercourse with the outside world had been suspended for months.

On 2 July the squadron and convoy, carrying the remnants of the Portuguese garrison, sailed out of the bay, while the motley and ragged patriots surged into the city they had beleaguered for a year. Once Campos was clear of the bay, the Brazilian squadron closed in. The frigates cut out the transports while the *Pedro I* shadowed the Portuguese armed ships. As Cochrane could neither spare nor rely on the loyalty of prize crews, the guns of the captured transports were cast into the sea, their water casks staved in, their masts cut and the vessels set on a course for Salvador. Six ships trying to make for São Luiz were rounded up and disabled. Cochrane sailed north to ensure that Madeira and Campos did not change tack and sail for the other 'constitutional' redoubt in Maranhão, while the chase continued to the mouth of the Tagus, where Captain Taylor in the *Niteroi* frigate burned four ships under the noses of the Portuguese. Altogether 16 of the original convoy of 70 ships and half the Portuguese garrison of Salvador, about 2000 men, were taken, and Taylor was to capture another 18 prizes in a *guerre de course* in Portuguese waters. Not a single sailor or mercenary in Brazilian service was lost in offensive action. It was a schoolboy wonder, the romance that escaped Byron two years later in Greece. The empire was saved.

After Bahia, Maranhão. The majority of the voters there being Portuguese merchants closely tied by consanguinity and commerce to Portugal, the São Luiz junta had ruled the city in obedience to the sovereign Cortes and defied the patriot *ordenanças* from Ceará, which spent their energies revolutionizing the interior. But when in July 1823 it received the astonishing news that on 5 June Dom John had dissolved the Cortes in Lisbon, the junta felt that royalist action in Lisbon had now removed the cause of civil war and proposed an armistice to the patriots. It was refused. When, therefore, the *Pedro I* sailed into São Luiz on 26 July, flying the Portuguese flag, she was received with undisguised relief as the expected reinforcement from Portugal.[8] Her true identity was revealed only after she had taken a position commanding the city, whence Cochrane announced that he was the precursor of a Brazilian force, hot from the liberation of Salvador. The junta bowed to the inevitable. Dom Pedro was acclaimed emperor in São Luiz on 28 July.

The liberation was not entirely free from trouble. When the merchants realized how they had been tricked and that there was no such force in the offing, they tried to restore the *status quo*, but they were no match for the cutlasses of the crew of the *Pedro I* and its Anglo-Saxon officers. As soon as the city was indisputably 'liberated', Cochrane presented the astonished junta with his bill. Interpreting the imperial decree of 11 December 1822, which had been intended to encourage the enlistment of mercenary seamen, as licence to secure his prize-money, Cochrane claimed the entire contents of the provincial treasury, the value of all stores in the arsenal, the property of all absentee Portuguese, the merchandise in the custom-house and the slaves on board ships flying Portuguese colours, all to be shared among the city's liberators. The junta was appalled. São Luiz was not an enemy town to be despoiled. It was a Brazilian city which had made a more or less spontaneous declaration for 'Independence and Empire'. Cochrane now met his match in the president of the new junta, a lawyer of partly Scottish descent, Miguel Freire de Bruce, who was to prove too sharp for the Scottish laird. If anyone had a claim to these preposterous prizes, it was Dom Pedro not Cochrane's motley sailors of fortune. The 'several million dollars' which the first admiral, who had no good opinion of either the generosity or the honesty of Latin American governments, had expected to be the first fruits of his campaign, proved to be as elusive as the other riches of Eldorado.

For the rampageous patriots from Ceará and Piauí had to be paid off before they marched on São Luiz to seize their share of the spoils, and there was not enough specie in the city to meet even two-thirds of the value of his sequestrations. Freire, moreover, was determined that the city should not be bled white by its liberators, and language, the intricate relationship of *mazombo* and *reinol* and the interplay of family and faction proved between them too baffling for Cochrane. Rivalries between the patriots in the interior and the lukewarm imperialists in São Luiz led to mini-coups, purges and fresh elections, all costing

money and time, so that on 20 September the first admiral sailed for
Rio de Janeiro to have his claims adjudicated in the capital. He was to
return a year later to try to collect his dues. In the interval, Maranhão
celebrated constitutional empire with a further coup, counter-coup,
civil war and a flirtation with republicanism. But in Rio de Janeiro
Dom Pedro dubbed Cochrane Marques do Maranhão, the first patent
of nobility conferred in the new empire.[9]

Belém do Pará, the last stronghold of Portuguese loyalty in the
country, fell to Cochrane's flag-lieutenant, John Pascoe Grenfell. The
Amazonian city had been the first to declare for constitutionalism and
the Cortes and for two years had enjoyed comparative peace in easy
subservience to Lisbon. Dom Pedro's partisans were kept at arm's
length. With the dissolution of the Cortes, the junta did not know
what to do and decided to wait for orders from *El-Rei*. On 10 August
Grenfell arrived in the *Maranhão* brig, repeating Cochrane's ruse
at São Luiz, and the junta decided to make common cause with
independence and empire. These rich Vicars of Bray were not, in
the event, to enjoy their dinners undisturbed by *mazombo* resentment.
On the 15th crowds began to loot the warehouses of Portuguese
merchants, while the largely Brazilian militia stood by in studied
indifference. They had reckoned without Grenfell. In a few minutes
the crew of the *Maranhão* cleared the streets and rounded up the
looters in droves. The sequel was to surpass the worst horrors of
the slave-trade. For the seditious Paraenses were too numerous for
the gaols. Five, the lucky ones, were shot as ringleaders. Two hundred
and fifty-six were then transferred to a ship in the harbour and packed
into the hold. There, through the equatorial night, the frenzy of free
bodies close confined in darkness and in heat sounded like a mutiny.
The hatches were battened down, a few shots being fired into the
seething mass by nervous guards hoping to restore order. In muffled
silence the frightful scene worked itself out. By next morning only
four men were still alive. Three subsequently died and the fourth,
a youth of 20, went mad. The shock to people normally far from
violent was traumatic. The riot of 15/16 October may have seemed
to the nervous junta like a 'horrible monster vomited up by the furies
of black Avernus', but how much worse the monster bred by their
fear, whose 255 patriot victims could be seen laid out on the river
bank. The *mazombo* opposition took itself off to Cameta, breathing
revenge against the *marinheiros*, and before the threat of civil war
as many as 1000 people left Amazonas. Grenfell sailed for Rio on

3 March 1824, to join his chief, heartily sickened by the nightmare that had followed so quickly upon the dream of independence. He was accused of deserting his post, court-martialled and honourably acquitted.[10]

Grenfell's error was to prove the worst loss of life in the whole saga of Brazilian independence. Dom Pedro had now been acclaimed in every province at a cost in lives ridiculously low when compared to the slaughter in New Granada and Upper Peru. The threat from Portugal now seemed faint and José Bonifácio could turn his efforts to securing international recognition.

On 3 May 1823, Dom Pedro, mantled on this occasion in a cape of parrots' feathers, had solemnly inaugurated the Constituent Assembly. He repeated the warning given at his coronation. He would accept a constitution only if it were worthy of Brazil and of himself, which meant, in the view of the Paulista Strafford, if it created insurmountable barriers to royal, aristocratic or popular despotism which had in one form or another overwhelmed the constitutions of revolutionary France and of post-war Spain, Naples and now Portugal. José Bonifácio promised that the Brazilian version should be based on a bicameral legislature but that the emperor should be able to exercise an absolute veto. Nothing that the Braganzas were to do on either side of the Atlantic shook his conviction that Brazil should be a constitutional monarchy. He had, moreover, high hopes that the example would spread, but this confidence was misplaced.[11] Neither an Emperor Bolívar nor an Imperial Union of Brazil, Buenos Aires and the Banda Oriental (both chimeras with which he tried to mesmerize the Austrian minister, Marschall) showed any signs of materializing, and the Emperor Agustín I of Mexico abdicated on 19 March 1823, and was shot when he tried to return to power. None the less Metternich was persuaded that independence and empire were inevitable and indissoluble and that a constitution was inescapable.[12]

That constitution was obstinately slow in appearing. The deputies, mostly magistrates, small-town lawyers and minor clergy were for the greater part men of unadventurous spirit, but there was a leaven of small landowners and priests with republican experience, led by the two veterans of the Lisbon Cortes, Father Feijó and Canon Muniz Tavares, the historian of the Recife rising of 1817. They were determined to establish the sovereignty of the assembly. If the emperor did not like it he should abdicate.[13] Like the unlamented Cortes, the Constituent Assembly worked through committees; it changed its president every month and aired each subject so exhaustively that the promised constitution receded at every session. An opposition formed by the *exaltado* rump of the Grand Orient and a wavering centre party led by Brazil's first imperial grandee, the Marques de Sant'Amaro, found themselves allied against the Andrada trinity and their partisans, known as the 'Ministerialists', for whom Carlos Antônio, representing São Paulo, was chief spokesman.[14] They clashed most bitterly over the disenfranchised and still exiled *exaltados* and their comrades still in custody. Then, on 30 June 1823, Dom Pedro fell from his horse and broke a rib. A stream of visitors made its way to the imperial sick-bed, and the emperor, who loved the warmth of human sympathy and interest (Metternich's 'ephemeral popularity', the badge of royal turpitude), insisted on receiving all comers from the assembly. Such unexpected access to the royal ear was a chance not to be missed, and soon the confined emperor had heard a woeful tale of Andrada oppression. Some of their opponents in São Paulo had been in custody since May 1822. Of what civil liberties, then, had Dom Pedro said he was the Perpetual Defender? He ordered the justice minister to order the release of all those arrested for their political views. When José Bonifácio could not persuade him to retract the order, the two Andrada brothers resigned on 15 July.

This time it was different. The 'comedy' of 30 October 1822 was not re-enacted. Dom Pedro might pay a glowing tribute to his services in the decree announcing his resignation, but José Bonifácio was no longer a popular idol. For the moment the crowd believed Dom Pedro when he announced that despotism and arbitrary rule were anathema to him. The reading public, small though it was, had sensed in the silence of the broadsheets and the absence of pasquinades the sterile hand of censorship. Now that Dom Pedro had invoked the inviolable rights of individual security, the air was once again thick with words. This time the Andradas were in opposition. The freedom of the press was one of the rights that Dom Pedro had promised to guarantee and in *O Tamoio* and *A Sentinela do Pão de Azucar* (*The Sugar Loaf Sentinel*) the two brothers brought to Brazilian journalism a bite and bitterness beyond the range of pro-government hacks. From power to opposition they moved with the aplomb of seasoned politicians. *O Tamoio*, so named from the Indian tribe originally native to the Bay of Guanabara, singled out those men at court and in the ministry who had been born in Portugal. The most important of them was the emperor himself.

Dom Pedro wisely chose a *mazombo* to replace José Bonifácio. José Joaquim Carneiro de Campos was, however, wholly inexperienced in affairs of state and no match for the opposition leaders who had learned their parliamentary skills in the Lisbon Cortes and whose declamatory eloquence stunned and mesmerized their listeners. His inexperience was put to the test almost at once. In September two emissaries arrived from Dom John to propose the suspension of hostilities, followed closely by two commissioners to negotiate a reunion of the crowns. The Andrada press immediately prophesied a *reinol* sell-out and Campos had to refuse to treat. Since the commissioners had no powers to recognize Brazil's independence, there was no point in their coming ashore, and as they entered Guanabara bay flying a hostile flag, their corvette was impounded as a prize of war. The commissioners had in fact wide powers to grant Brazil pretty well all that her deputies had originally demanded in the Cortes, but as they were not allowed to deliver Dom John's letters to his son, no one knew this. Within three weeks they were sent home ignominiously in a packet-boat. Campos breathed again. His ministry had survived the test with dignity if not with honour, and the emperor had not weakened at the first breath of reconciliation from the old country. No one could say, except Carlos Antônio, that Dom Pedro was in secret thrall to the monarchs of the Holy Alliance.[15] The commissioners on their return could tell Dom John nothing about his son, except that he had treated them shabbily. It was not news calculated to bring forward the day of peace and recognition.

On 2 September, the first constitutional project was at long last presented to the assembly in a draft signed by, among others, José Bonifácio and Muniz Tavares. It had 262 articles, based largely on the 1812 Spanish constitution. José Bonifácio, who still had access to the emperor, urged him to surprise the world, accept the project and, as soon as the northern provinces were stable, dissolve the assembly and give the nation a charter. To Dom Pedro's almost priggish ears such seasoned advice sounded like cynicism. Instead he welcomed the project warmly and hoped that he could be warmer still when it was converted into a constitution. He readily signed the first batch of laws the assembly sent up at the end of the month, but as the vexations of public life continued, he began seriously to ponder the advice he had been given by his former chief minister. The public attacks on Cochrane, the ceaseless philippics of the Andrada press with their increasingly racist tone, were impertinent, even seditious.

The *reinóis*, soldiers, merchants, government clerks, jurists and priests, who had in the heady days of 1821 first demonstrated for constitutional government, were pilloried, their honour and motives daily impugned. They shrank further under the shelter of the emperor on whose protection they now relied and in whose name they manifested their resentment. It was only a matter of time before there was an incident.

It came on 5 November, when two Portuguese army officers, convinced they had identified the author of an anonymous libel, burst into the shop of one Davi Pampluna and drubbed him soundly. They had identified the wrong man. Pampluna appealed to the assembly where Carlos Antônio and Martim Francisco, his younger brother, urged the deputies to become the judges in his cause. Their rhetoric and the ensuing uproar put timid souls in mind of the Paris Assembly in June and July 1792. Dom Pedro was threatened with the fate of Charles I of England in the columns of *O Tamoio*, while *A Sentinela* called on the Portuguese-born to return to Portugal as 'Dionysius to Corinth so that Brazil will be happy'.[16] The ministry fell to pieces.

Campos was replaced by another Brazilian, Francisco Villela Barbosa, a former deputy to the Cortes who had not actually resigned from that assembly until Dom Pedro's declaration of independence. That failure of foresight now made him suspect as a friend of Portugal. His test was to come very soon. On 11 November the deputies learned that the garrison of mainly Portuguese officers and men were under arms again, demanding satisfaction for attacks on their honour and on the dignity of the emperor. Villela was able to persuade their leaders to withdraw to barracks, but the deputies, under the leadership of Carlos Antônio, voted to stay in permanent session while the more fearful of them, remembering Easter Sunday, 1821, queued up before their clerical colleagues for confession and absolution. Villela offered peace: if *O Tamoio* and *A Sentinela* were silenced, and their editors disciplined, the soldiers would stay in their quarters.

During the all-night debate that followed, the moderates proposed that the assembly might debate a law moderating the licence of the press if the troops were firmly restrained, but when on 12 November Villela appeared in the uniform of a colonel of engineers, complete with sword, the symbolism, in the wake of counter-revolution in Lisbon, was not lost upon the deputies. He required the expulsion of the Andradas from the assembly as troublemakers, and when the house declined to discuss the proposition he withdrew. The deputies then refused to deliberate until all threat of military intervention had been withdrawn and vowed never to allow the assembly to be dissolved. But when voices affirmed that the emperor was acting in an illegal, even unconstitutional, manner, Dom Pedro's mind was made up. He ordered the dissolution, promising in the same decree that he would himself give Brazil a more liberal constitution than any that the assembly might devise.[17] As the troops surrounded the chamber, Carlos Antônio bowed to the inevitable. 'We have nothing more to do here,' he said, and as he left he saluted the guns ranged against the wall. 'I obey His Majesty the Cannon, the sovereign of the world.' He was arrested along with Martim Francisco and three other deputies. The others filed out silently between drawn swords. The Perpetual Defender told his people that he had saved the nation from 'the folly of men bewitched by pride and ambition'.[18]

The public was stunned. No Brazilian came to the *beija-mão* that marked the emperor's birthday. José Bonifácio, Muniz Tavares and Vergueiro were also arrested. The emperor, willy-nilly, was now the cynosure of the Portuguese, mostly soldiers, for power throughout Latin America was flowing from the barrels of guns. His courtiers paraded their conviction that the attacks on them had been motivated by jealousy and greed, jealousy of the Emperor's birth and dynasty, greed for the Portuguese gold that 'belonged' to Brazilians. There were many ready to believe that they had just escaped a Sicilian Vespers.

On 16 November Dom Pedro justified his 'constitutional' action. What monarch when compared to kings who had been deposed and decapitated would have done otherwise? The assembly had, after all its proud words and sanctimonious speeches, failed to produce a constitution and others besides José Bonifácio thought that the emperor might do better himself. It is the privilege of autocrats to steal the clothes of their democratic critics and Dom Pedro proceeded to do just that.

17· Survival, 1823–4

'It is clear that the firmness which prevailed during the administration of M de Andrada has not been maintained by his successors, but that a series of concessions is gradually depriving the new Emperor of the authority which he had acquired' —

George Canning to Henry Chamberlain, 8 January 1824

'The moment has come. Let us save our honour, our fatherland, our liberty. Long live the Confederation of the Equator!' —

Manoel de Carvalho País de Andrade, Recife, 2 July 1824

Dom John had dissolved the Cortes because it had made a hash of running the *Reino*. An assembly that had driven Brazil to separation, imposed as authoritarian a regime as it had overthrown, humbled the king and upset in turn the nobility, the church and the merchants, without doing very much to improve the country's parlous economy, did not deserve to survive. It collapsed when civil war threatened, and when Dom John asserted himself surprisingly to choke the rebellion of his wayward second son, Dom Miguel, and his estranged wife, he found it also surprisingly easy to dissolve the Cortes.

Across the Atlantic it looked like the triumph of reaction. José Bonifácio himself had in fact very little time for either the Cortes or the Constituent Assembly and feared that, given its head, the second might go the same way as the first. He had always hoped for something better. But he had been chief minister for barely 19 months when he resigned and he resented the way that he had been manoeuvred from power by the Portuguese round the throne, convinced that it was because he was a Brazilian. To his mind the Portuguese in Brazil had never been able to accept that two principal ministers in Dom Pedro's ministry should have been *mazombos*. Because he had thundered from the Paulista heights against the perfidy of the Cortes and had been the first to proclaim the liberty and independence of Brazil, he was accused of driving a wedge between the colony and the mother country. For that there could be no forgiveness.[1] It was true that he had made little effort to understand the complicated susceptibilities of those Portuguese who had rallied to the emperor. Because he believed in limited constitutional monarchy 'as the only system that can preserve in unity and solidarity the majestic example of social architecture from the Plate to the Amazon', he could not risk sole sovereignty falling in the hands of a few inexperienced but vocal lawyers, merchants and priests. In his view, the true enemies of the empire were not the Portuguese across the water but the republicans and democrats in the Grand Orient, nearly all Portuguese, like Gonçalves Ledo.

In the months following Dom Pedro's dramatic agreement to stay in Brazil, he found it easy to believe that the Lusitanian party supporting General Avilez was united to the *exaltados* in an unholy alliance to have the prince sent back to Portugal so that 'Independence should wear not a crown but a Phrygian cap'.[2] Even after Avilez had been bundled out of the country he could still believe that the Portuguese constitutionalists and 'democratic anarchists' between them wanted to reduce Dom Pedro to no more than the powerless president of a provincial junta. But, he told *O Tamoio*, he had seen through their plot, and after his return to power in October 1822 he had purged the *exaltados*, to the obvious satisfaction of the Brazilian man in the street. What confidence could be placed in those Portuguese-born democrats who had once cheered the rhetoric of Gonçalves Ledo and his fellow-masons but who in July 1823 supported the emperor in dislodging a popular ministry? 'However liberal a Portuguese may be in his own land, he is completely twisted [*profundamente corcunda*] in Brazil.' For the Portuguese-born, the first loyalty must always be to Portugal. Why else had they temporarily reconciled their differences to seduce the emperor with promises of an accommodation with Portugal once he had got rid of his Brazilian minister?[3]

José Bonifácio came late to politics, and like so many national leaders who lacked a national base or political formation, he relied too much on his family or on cronies, whose loyalty was greater than their political sense. Personally incorruptible and entirely without self-interest — when he stuck his salary into his hatband only to have it stolen off his head he refused to allow the emperor to authorize its payment again[4] — he had a vindictive impatience of criticism and the complete politician's interest in power. In power, he destroyed the 'democratic' opposition. In opposition, he ensured that there would be no rapprochement between the father who had dissolved the Cortes and the son who had turned the Patriarch of Independence out of office. No successor would be allowed to ignore José Bonifácio and the forces he represented, no ministry to tamper with national unity — 'the Brazil of 1815'. He had no quarrel with Dom Pedro, but he feared the effect of weak ministers on that impressionable, warm-hearted and impulsive youth. He was oppressed by a persistent nightmare that the emperor would be forced to flee the capital to beg the support of the provinces, a pale spectre compared to that confident hero of the Minas Gerais and São Paulo sorties of 1822, while democrats and absolutists contrived the dismemberment of the empire, the destruction of independence and a return to absolutism, the fate that had overtaken the patriots of Naples, Spain and Portugal. Only Brazilians, particularly the planters and farmers who were in effect the props of the Brazilian economy, could be trusted to see that none of this happened. The *reinol* had shown himself democrat, constitutionalist and absolutist by turns. And Dom Pedro himself, the pupil he had hoped to teach to be a good Brazilian, was a *reinol*.

So, for the most part, were the officer corps, the court officials, the Bishop of Rio, who had been the first president of the Constituent Assembly, the ministers of justice and of war, the royal household, the senior magistrates and the richer merchants, not only those in the north but also those in the capital, who controlled the new nation's credit. Most of the privileged positions in the empire were still held by *reinóis*. To all of them the Andradas' rudeness and contempt had become increasingly intolerable the longer they stayed in power, and proved wholly insupportable in opposition. Yet the most irreconcilable differences could not sever the affection and trust that had grown up between the imperial Telemachus and his Paulista mentor, and while José Bonifácio lived in France in generously pensioned exile, Dom Pedro discovered that he could trust no one like the man who had for two years filled the gap his father left when he sailed for Lisbon.

There was a certain inevitability about Dom Pedro's dissolution of the assembly so soon after the short-lived Cortes of 1821–3, but it did not mean that he had turned against constitutionalism. José Bonifácio resigned in July 1823, when the emperor exercised the constitutional rights that the minister had always insisted that he should enjoy. He was too committed to the concept of monarchy to turn against the institution; the emperor had fallen into bad company and must be made to realize it. Without his leadership, however, the

Constituent Assembly had outlived its usefulness and could be wound up. What influence José Bonifácio still had on the radical instincts of the young emperor were exerted in persuading him to dissolve it and give Brazil the more liberal charter he knew Dom Pedro favoured. While the patriarch withdrew from public life to write his masterwork on mineralogy, his friends reduced the alternative ministries to futility. The leading voice in opposition was that of his more conceited and more brilliant brother, Carlos Antònio, whose polemical skill propounded principles he had resisted while he was, first, a deputy in the Portuguese Cortes and, later, a lion in his brother's ministry. When he urged the assembly to be the judge in Pampluna's cause, did he remember his spirited defiance of the Cortes when it wished to arraign the authors of the Paulista manifesto? When he played to the galleries in Rio, did he recall his contempt for Borges Carneiro, who had raised the Lisbon public against the Brazilian deputies? But consistency is the hobgoblin of politics; more serious was the racist prejudice that overcame the champion of Brazilian rights in the Cortes, who now boasted an indelible hatred of all Europeans and who could not extend to the *reinóis* the magnanimity he had expected of them in Lisbon.[5]

It was Andrada policy to ensure that the emperor could not form an effective government from among their opponents. Those opponents were determined to keep the Andradas out of office. They succeeded in driving a wedge between them and the emperor by playing expertly on his conceit that he was the one serious democrat in the Luso-Iberian world. He reacted aggressively to insinuations against his honour which he equated to his capacity, and he dissolved the assembly in a flurry of self-righteous indignation. José Bonifácio had realized in his schoolmasterly way that the emperor's easy accessibility and unstudied carelessness, both of which endeared him to his subjects, were the weakness of a man who wanted to be popular. Dom Pedro's processions to Minas Gerais and São Paulo in 1822 had been simplicity itself. He had endured the hideous discomforts of the road like a seasoned naturalist, and his unpretentious entourage stepped straight out of a novel by Anthony Hope. But this simple camaraderie also exposed Dom Pedro dangerously to men (and women) who wished to influence him. While José Bonifácio had time to be constantly at hand, his influence was paramount, but his enemies appeared assiduously at the *beija-mão* and flocked to the imperial sick-bed, and were quick to turn the royal ear against his chief minister. They were aided and abetted by the Portuguese-born household, and in that sense José Bonifácio was right to distrust it.

The person who should have been closest to him, his wife, was as good a Brazilian as any, and better than most, but by an irony of bad taste that same household detested 'the foreign woman' and used a colonial beauty to reduce her influence over the impressionable emperor. The fortunes of the Paulista, Domitila de Castro, whom Dom Pedro had first met on his historic visit to São Paulo, were badly viewed by the majority of her countrymen, who had a proper regard for the sterling qualities of their empress, but they could do nothing about her rapid rise to Pompadour status. Between September 1822, and 31 May 1824, when Domitila gave birth to Isabel Maria de Alcântara Brasileira, she secured posts, titles and pensions for her family and shed her husband. She was subsequently created Marquesa de Santos and, crowning insult, first lady of the empress's bedchamber.[6] Dona Leopoldina never wholly lost her influence over her husband, since she was nearly always pregnant, but her vigorous constitution was exhausted by childbearing and the idleness of a tropical court, so that she became dowdy and plain, of which sad decline from healthy youth her undeniably beautiful rival took full advantage. The unhappy empress consoled herself with sketching and botanizing and reading about the continent that was slowly destroying her. In October 1824, her one friend, Maria Graham, was elbowed from her post as governess to the Infanta Maria da Gloria after only a month by a *camarilha* of palace servants who disliked the Scots widow's obsession with fresh air, mental activity and good manners, and who managed to convince the emperor that she lacked respect for his daughter. The future author of *Little Arthur's History of England* may have hoped to be a Brazilian Anna Leonowens, but São Cristovão was not the court of Siam, even though the infanta was obliged to take her bath in full view of palace slaves and sentries, the point on which Mrs Graham rebelled.[7]

There were moments of reconciliation between emperor and empress, particularly at the birth of the future Dom Pedro II in December 1825, but gloom finally settled on Dona Leopoldina, who filled her empty hours with a pair of William Carey's mineral balances, a case full of geological specimens and boxes of books dutifully sent from London by Mrs Graham, while Domitila thrust her bastard into the royal nursery. Leopoldina, 'that divine woman whom all Brazil worshipped', died in 1826, aged 29, from complications in childbirth.

There were many who thought that, had she lived, Dom Pedro would not have lost his throne.[8]

For the emperor appeared to have embarked upon the slippery slope. From November 1823 he was dangerously reliant upon Portuguese-born soldiery, many of whom had brought Dom John to the Largo do Rocio to swear to the constitution on 26 February, and had dispersed the parochial electors on the night of 21/22 April in 1821. When the chips were down, they had chosen loyalty to their prince and not to their commanding officer, but with Avilez's departure the *reinol* soldiers had not so much made a commitment to Brazil as to the emperor, a Braganza and a Portuguese, and also heir to the throne of Portugal.[9] For the Andradas all ministers prepared to support the man who had dissolved the Constituent Assembly were, if not actually *reinóis*, little better than Portuguese at heart.[10] The jibe stung Dom Pedro, who was resolved to show that he was not in league with the monarchs of the Holy Alliance. With surprising speed he presented his charter to the Council of State on 11 December 1823. The British envoy in Buenos Aires, three years later, was to write in grudging admiration, 'Dom Pedro hates liberty, much as Sir Toby Belch did water, but he is vain of his political science.' With Benjamin Constant in hand, between breakfast and dinner, 'out came the constitution, now the Palladium of Lusitania, the despair of Spain and the envy of the Turk.' Lord John Ponsonby was also obliged to concede that 'this constitution of such facile parturition is much better than the elaborate productions of French philosophers'.[11]

It was, in fact, more liberal than José Bonifácio's constitutional project (except in its intentions towards the slaves). It promised religious freedom, the abolition of all privileges except those of office, habeas corpus, taxation of income regardless of rank, equal citizenship to all free-born Brazilians and to all Portuguese who had lived in Brazil for 12 years or more. With Benjamin Constant to the fore, the legislative power was to be invested in two elected chambers, both able to initiate legislation and to sit together in a general assembly. The deputies were to be elected by provincial electors, themselves elected by all males, except monks, domestic servants or slaves, earning more than 100 *milréis* a month. Senators would be elected into lists, from which they would be nominated by the emperor. The moderative power was the emperor's right to convoke the general assembly, to dissolve the chambers, to nominate and to dismiss ministers. Executive power was vested in ministers responsible to the emperor, advised by a council of life councillors. The judicial power would be exercised by independent and immovable judges. There would be trial by jury, a civil and criminal code and regular constitutional review. Torture was also to be abolished. All this was more than a morning's excursus. Dom Pedro, it was said, had been delving into the 1812 constitution, the Code of Norway, the constitution of the Netherlands, the 1791 Constituent Assembly in France and Constant's proposed modifications to the Bourbon Charter granted France by Louis XVIII.[12]

He had certainly vindicated José Bonifácio's advice to scrap the assembly and produce something better. An income of 100 *milréis* a month excluded most of the Brazilian population from voting and the system of indirect elections made popular representation even more elusive, but these considerations did not prevent the charter from being the despair of Spain and the envy of the Turk. The disenfranchised were not, after all, the vocal minority which had demanded a constitution repeatedly since 1821. The charter, moreover, distributed power between the *mazombo* oligarchs, the agricultural and business interests and the bureaucrats who had most to gain from it. Provided they had the representation, the emperor could write in general human rights for everyone else.[13]

The provincial *câmaras*, even more susceptible to the power of the local bosses, were invited to comment. Very few accepted, but Salvador da Bahia unexpectedly approved the charter on the third anniversary of the *pronunciamento* in favour of the Constitutional Cortes, 10 February 1824. On 25 March it became the Fundamental Institution of the state. Like an omen, a fire broke out in the theatre after the celebrations had concluded, symbolic of the dangerous uncertainties of *de facto* independence without international recognition.[14] This door had not yet been opened and George Canning, who held the key in London, did not know in which way to turn it.

Britain's price for her good offices in securing recognition by the mother country had always been a promise by Brazil to abolish the slave-trade with Africa. In continuing to demand this, Canning was acting like Cupid with a quiverful of poisonous arrows. For 'there were not ten persons in the whole empire who consider the trade a crime'.[15] José Bonifácio's constitutional project had only dared to promise that no Brazilian should be obliged to give involuntary, unpaid, personal labour — a measure aimed at protecting the Indian not at emancipating the African; and the architects of independence persisted in the view that Britain's insistence on destroying a wealth based on plantations worked by black slaves was a plot to reduce the empire's fragile economy to total dependence upon her. They feared with almost too much justification that abolition would lead to the secession of the northern and north-eastern provinces and the break-up of the empire.[16] Canning's defence of hundreds of Africans not yet enslaved in the Americas, moreover, did not seem to be entirely disinterested. By tying an unacceptable price to his intervention, he was delaying the final and irrevocable loss of Brazil which could spell the collapse of Dom John's shaky government in Lisbon, expose Portugal to civil war and prompt the ultras to come back to power on Spanish bayonets. If that happened, Britain would be in treaty bound to come to Dom John's rescue. Such a call on her obligations was to be avoided if possible.

Early recognition by Britain could not be counted on, yet the longer it was withheld the more dangerous the situation became. But the Brazilians held some powerful cards. Canning deeply distrusted French intentions. French 'protection' of the young emperor might work on Brazilian fears of the Holy Alliance to such an extent that they would reject the Portuguese connection for ever by declaring themselves a republic or, worse, a balkanload of republics.[17] His superb diplomatic skill must now be exercised in reconciling two independent states with a common dynastic monarchy before Britain's recognition of Brazil unilaterally was forced from her from motives no nobler than those of perfidious France — the need to renegotiate the 1810 treaty of commerce with an independent Brazil in order to retain Britain's trading privileges.

Brazilian recognition thus forced itself to the top of the foreign secretary's preoccupations. His first idea was that Brazil and Portugal should share the same monarch, who would commute between the two capitals, but it was very quickly clear that Brazil would be independent under nothing less than an emperor, and to vulgar minds emperors stood above kings.[18] How, then, to persuade Dom John to accept his son's imperial title with honour? Dom John's foreign secretary was once again the experienced Dom Pedro de Souza Holstein, Conde de Palmela, who worked skilfully on British distrust of France. Surely Mr Canning must see that Portugal, bereft of her principal overseas possession, would be driven to increased reliance on the French connection? Could he not persuade Dom Pedro to accept the title of viceroy or regent with rights of succession to the throne of

Portugal?[19] He could not. Instead, he invited father and son to send plenipotentiaries to London to negotiate a settlement which would not compromise Portugal's sovereignty. For if Portugal obstructed Brazil's legitimate aspirations, she would destroy the monarchy that was the sole hope of reconciliation, and Great Britain could only deprecate 'the greater mischief which must attend on obstinate perseverance' in such a course. It was now Palmela's turn to demur. Independence, far from consolidating the monarchy, must tear it apart.[20]

In January 1824, the Council of Ministers in Lisbon took out and dusted the invasion project of 1822. Four thousand men ought to be sufficient to rally Portuguese supporters in Maranhão and Pará, supported by a naval force stronger than Cochrane's, all to be paid for by duties levied on the trade with the northern provinces that would be restored to Portugal. That anyone should have thought that a force smaller than that with which Avilez had been forced to leave Rio de Janeiro, escorted by a naval squadron no bigger than that of Félix de Campos, which had been chased ignominiously back to Lisbon, had any chance of success was due to the widely shared belief that Dom Pedro could not keep Brazil united.[21] The dual monarchy required one monarch, or it must break up like the Spanish viceroyalties into separate republics. If she acted resolutely, Portugal might at least save for the mother country the former colony of Maranhão.[22]

Dom Pedro's dissolution of the Constituent Assembly was a signal to Lisbon that creole nationalism had been rebuffed, suggesting that the pro-Portuguese faction had now triumphed. Palmela agreed to British intervention for a settlement. Unconditional surrender was quietly dropped; only justice should be done to Portugal's legitimate interests, which included keeping the independence fever to Brazil alone. The British envoy in Rio was mightily relieved. Dom Pedro had lost a lot of support when he dissolved the assembly, and his Council of State was composed of inexperienced Brazilians who commanded very little popular support. The danger of Balkanization was far from over; indeed, the process might already have started, for Recife was once again in the throes of republican revolt.[23]

The iron hand of Luiz do Rego had alone kept Pernambuco steady while the provinces to the north had declared giddily for the Cortes and constitutionalism. Before he left Recife on 26 October 1821, he had arranged a tolerably peaceful handover to a Brazilian junta prepared to acclaim Dom Pedro first as regent, then as emperor. In December 1823, the Pernambucan deputies to the Constituent

Assembly returned to Recife, still hoping to salvage something from the apparent wreck of their constitutional hopes. The province was soon split into royalist and republican factions, and from the latter a new tribune was to emerge on 21 February 1824. Manoel de Carvalho País de Andrade was intendant of the naval dockyard, and in 1817 had been the short-lived republic's agent in the United States for the purchase of arms. He had never made any secret of his republican ambitions, and now he had defeated the royalist candidate in the election for presidency of the local junta. To the government in Rio, a republic in Recife was as intolerable in 1824 as it had been in 1817, more so, in fact, as the emperor had just declared his excellent charter the Fundamental Institution of the state.

John Taylor, commanding the *Niteroi* and *Piranha* frigates, was at once dispatched to Recife to persuade the junta to reverse the vote and accept the royalist candidate. When it refused, he declared the port blockaded on 8 April. Manoel de Carvalho was undismayed. Indeed, with the stirring of sympathy in Paraíba and Ceará, he began to dream hazily of being not just the president of a provincial junta but of a new republic as large as Gran Colombia, which at that time incorporated what is now Colombia, Venezuela and Ecuador. On 28 June, Taylor was ordered to lift the blockade and join Cochrane, who was concentrating his forces against the threatened expedition from Portugal. At once the junta declared the emperor a despot and friend to despots, who was plotting to revoke Brazilian independence with the aid of Portuguese troops and English mercenaries. Four days later it declared Pernambuco a free republic and invited the neighbouring provinces to join an equatorial confederation. He sent two ships, commanded by a Maltese deserter from the Royal Navy, to seize his loyalist rival, who had taken refuge at Barra Grande, but they were both taken on the 25th by an imperial schooner.[24] In Rio, Dom Pedro, like his father before him, supervised the embarkation of the expedition which left with Cochrane on 2 August. The First Admiral landed his troops at Alagoas on 10 August and stood off Recife, where he met Maria Graham, the widow of his old shipmate, on her way from Britain to be governess to the princess imperial. He asked the redoubtable Scots widow to try to convince the rebel leader that he really would bombard the city if it refused the hand of peace, but in reply Carvalho offered to buy his services. 'Your not having been rewarded for your first expedition [to Bahia and Maranhão] affords a justifiable inference,' he wrote insolently, 'that you will get nothing for the second.' The Confederation of the Equator, on the other hand, would pay him 400 *contos* (£80,000) to change sides.[25]

The confederation collapsed in mid-September when the loyal troops overran the city and Carvalho fled to HMS *Tweed*. The planters, who had in 1817 rallied to the republic, this time withheld their support, and the handful of frustrated intellectuals who had launched the revolt had no stomach to fight their own countrymen. Some blood had to be shed, but there were not the proscriptions that followed 1817. The Maltese, Mitrovich, and two other seamen were shot in Rio, while 11 rebels, of whom the most prominent was the Carmelite friar, Frei Caneca, died in Recife. The latter had spent from 1817 to 1821 in a Salvador prison following his part in the first Recife rising, but he was left by this experience a more convinced republican then ever. He had become Carvalho's right-hand man and had to be shot when no one could be found to hang him. Carvalho escaped because the captain of HMS *Tweed* refused to hand him over. He spent the years of Dom Pedro's reign in exile and returned during the minority of his son to become an imperial senator, another republican to end his days as a pillar of the empire.

If the empire remained intact, the equatorial sun was going down on the fortunes of its prime liberator, Thomas Cochrane. So many of his seamen had either deserted or been arrested for debt that, when the news of Carvalho's coup reached Rio, he could not put the squadron to sea. Had they been paid their share of prize-money, he told Dom Pedro, he could have sailed at once, and indeed they returned to the flag as soon as the emperor ordered an advance payment of £37,000, a tenth part of what Cochrane estimated was owing to them, from the loan being raised in London. After the suppression of the confederation, Cochrane returned to São Luiz to press his claims there, and when he found Freire Bruce still awkward, had him removed on charges of conspiring to defraud the navy (and thus himself). But even with a cowed and compliant successor, his claim was still too huge to be settled and he had to agree to settle for about a quarter, the equivalent of £21,000. On 18 May, putting it about that his health was undermined by 'harassing and uncertainty', he suddenly sailed in the *Piranha* frigate for an unknown destination. On 26 June, to the astonishment of the port admiral, he sailed into Spithead, where his salute was returned gun for gun, the first — accidental — recognition of Brazil's independence by Great Britain.[26] The Brazilian government summoned him to Rio to account for his action, and when he refused to move it suspended him from service.

It was a sorry end to an association made glorious by feats unequalled in the history of sea warfare, but Cochrane could not live on glory alone, despite a handsome salary. The rich fortune he expected constantly eluded him, for the seamen of successful navies, he reminded Dom Pedro more than once, lived in hopes of the prize-money that would make them rich and pay their debts.[27] The Council of State might agree to pay him the full value of prizes taken before 13 February 1824, valued by independent assessors, Dom Pedro might promise in July that claims would in future be judged more expeditiously, the navy minister might promise him that he and his widow would receive half-pay for life as soon as the war was won, but it was not enough.[28] A new cause in a sea traditionally rich to privateers, the liberty of Greece, was a siren call to this romantic mercenary. The terms he was being offered were not as good as those the Brazilian empire guaranteed him, but he had no illusions left about the generosity of new governments, and when he sailed for Spithead he had no intention of returning.[29]

The wrangle over prize-money and dues continued unabated for several months, and Cochrane was convinced that he was the victim of those councillors of state who wanted an accommodation with Portugal. It was no surprise to him to hear that the court of commission had decreed the 'unqualified and arbitrary acts of the most audacious daring were committed under his command, occasioning to the national treasury enormous losses, particularly by the heavy indemnification of an infinite number of bad prizes'.[30] As his claims were obviously to be sacrificed to the cause of peace between Brazil and Portugal, there was no point in continuing to serve a government so unwilling to keep its promises. Dom Pedro's administration tried to do its best by Cochrane, but it had no understanding of how the naval prize system worked. To the struggling bureaucrats of the still uncertain empire, Cochrane's peremptory demands were outrageous and insulting. But his services to Brazil were as great as his claim and in the end Brazil recognized her debt and discharged it. Cochrane was not the first technical expert to astound his poor employers by the price of his services.

18· Recognition, 1824–6

'By reconciling the acknowledgement of that independence with the feelings and the honour of His Majesty's ancient ally, to render it a source of new strength and splendour rather than of weakness and distraction to the illustrious house of Braganza' —

Canning's instructions to Sir Charles Stuart,
15 January 1825

'What a jolly act of gallantry to let old John the Donkey have the nominal title of Emperor and to get Peter the Puncher to agree to it!' —

José Bonifácio to Antônio Vasconcelos de Drummond,
14 November 1825

On 26 May 1824, the United States of America recognized Brazil as a sovereign independent state. President Monroe had none of Canning's scruples about Dom John's titles and had everything to gain in the way of commercial opportunity by early recognition. But he could not believe that the empire would last. Indeed, when Dom Pedro's envoy, José Silvestre Rebello, announced on arrival that there were not six convinced republicans in Brazil, John Taylor had just declared the blockade of Recife.[1] The publication of the constitution of 25 March gave Rebello his cue to remind the American government that it had recognized Mexico, Chile and Peru, none of which had constitutions and one of which, Peru, still had a Spanish army on her soil. Secretary of State Quincy Adams, realizing that Britain must sooner or later recognize the empire and after Britain the world, advised the president to receive Rebello officially on 26 May. When the Portuguese minister objected, he was reminded that the US government, by extending *de facto* recognition, was only confirming a separation created by Dom John himself when he proclaimed the United Kingdom of Portugal and Brazil in 1815.[2]

In London, however, the recognition talks had run into the sand. In April, Dom John had barely survived a military coup engineered by Dom Miguel by taking refuge on a British man-of-war in the mouth of the Tagus and calling on loyalists to support him. The vulpine prince was stripped of his honours and withdrew to Madrid. Dom John's authority was shakier than ever and could collapse altogether if Brazil were lost for good. The Portuguese envoy in London could only agree to an independent administration for Brazil, appointed by His Most Faithful Majesty.[3] This was no good for Canning. In 1825, the 1810 Anglo-Portuguese treaty of friendship and commerce which the Brazilian government had scrupulously observed, and which ensured British merchants their most favoured nation status in the former colony, would need to be renegotiated and Britain could only negotiate with sovereign governments. If Britain were not to imitate the United States and further weaken the fragile hold Dom John still had on his remaining throne, some concession would have to be wrung out of Lisbon. Even Austria, that stronghold of legitimacy, counselled recognition and conciliation, while France was ready to recognize a strong monarchy in South America to neutralize the republicanism of the Spanish successor states.[4]

On 12 August Canning produced his own draft proposal. The crowns of Portugal and Brazil should be separate, Dom Pedro should renounce his succession to the throne of Portugal in favour of one of his children to be chosen by a Cortes. (This clause was a secret one, to be kept from Dom Miguel and the ultras.) Treaties of commerce and friendship would provide for the indemnification of Portuguese property and Portuguese merchants could be granted even more favourable trade privileges in Brazil than those enjoyed by the British. Brant was prepared to sign at once, but his Portuguese opposite, Vila Real, refused to handle it. Canning had to send it to Palmela by courier with a warning that irresistible commercial reasons would in 1825 compel Britain to act unilaterally. 'The abandonment of such an Empire without a struggle,' Palmela told the British envoy glumly, 'would be a dishonour to the Portuguese nation.'[5] Canning must see that Brazil without Portugal would fall into the hands of extreme republicans, Portugal without Brazil into those of the ultras! The foreign secretary in reply urged Palmela to face facts not bad dreams. Britain would recognize Brazil in 1825. It would be less embarrassing for the ancient alliance if Brazil had already been recognized by the mother country.[6]

Palmela was not yet ready to take that advice. He was sure that the

Confederation of the Equator proved his thesis about the instability of the Brazilian empire, and he produced a counter-proposal. Dom John should formally assume the title of emperor and make Dom Pedro his surrogate as ruler of an independent Brazil. In that way Dom John's honour would be satisfied. He foolishly revealed his idea to the foreign envoys in Lisbon, thus appearing to show a lack of confidence in British mediation. Though Canning was obliged to suspend negotiations, he recognized in the plan the germ of a solution.[7] It was time, perhaps, to put a little pressure on Rio de Janeiro. British public opinion, after seven years of comradeship in arms, would not take kindly to brusque treatment of Dom John and the pride of his indomitable little country. If Dom Pedro could come to terms with his father, he could free the way for recognition by the Court of St James, an accolade bestowed in December 1824 on Mexico, Colombia and Buenos Aires.[8] Canning, convinced that London was no longer the right place for continued negotiations, since endless time was lost in reference to Rio and to Lisbon, hit on an ingenious solution. A British diplomat should be designated to go to Brazil to negotiate a new trade treaty, thus implying recognition of the new state, and on his way he should call at Lisbon to reach a general understanding with Dom John on what concessions the king would make to his son. He should then proceed to Rio de Janeiro as Dom John's plenipotentiary and there negotiate recognition.[9] He chose for this unusual mission Sir Charles Stuart, Knight Grand Cross of the Order of the Turret and the Sword and a former (1810) ambassador in Lisbon. It was an inspired choice.

Dom John could hardly refuse. In Britain's debt for the preservation of his throne, he ruled only under the watchful guns of British warships on the Tagus. The king only asked that Stuart should come in a warship escorted by a little squadron *para Brasileiros ver*. Dom Pedro also agreed to receive him as his father's envoy. What the emperor did not know was that Stuart had orders not to leave Rio de Janeiro without a new commercial treaty and, if possible, agreement to end the slave-trade. As neither of these could be achieved without recognition, Stuart left England with it in his briefcase. Dom John, moreover, knew that, if the war continued, a Brazilian fleet was now more likely in the Tagus than a Portuguese army in Maranhão, and Britain could not protect him from it under its ancient treaty obligations unless he converted Brazil into a foreign power against whom the aid of Great Britain could be invoked. The options were closing.[10]

By April, Canning had enlisted the support of Chateaubriand: France would only recognize Brazil after Portugal and Britain.[11] But the success of the mission was not to be immediate. Stuart arrived in Lisbon on 25 March to find that Dom John insisted on being called Emperor of Brazil and being indemnified for the loss of all his property in the empire. Brant had already rejected the first. Emperors were elected and the title had been conferred on his son by the unanimous choice of the people of Brazil. How could Dom John also be emperor? The old king was resolved, however, that if he were to lose Brazil he should do so in the full panoply of power. Only if he were *de jure* Emperor of Brazil could he legally grant unfettered sovereignty to his son.[12]

In London Brant thought that if Dom John only held the title for life as a former King of Brazil, the proposal might not stick too fast in Dom Pedro's craw, and he returned to Rio himself to try to explain the father's obsession with titles.[13] When Stuart reached Rio on 17 July, the emperor was not obstinately opposed to allowing his father an imperial title, provided that the two countries were never united under the same monarch. He knew that he would never be accepted as Pedro IV or I; he also knew that Dom John wanted to ensure that his second son, his wife's clerical and reactionary darling, did not succeed him as King of Portugal. In Stuart's 'Portuguese Project' of 13 May there was no proposal that the Brazilian emperor should renounce his rights of succession. Stuart advised him not to give up what he was not asked to renounce, but Dom Pedro knew that he would never be properly accepted as Emperor of Brazil if he retained his claim on the throne of the mother country. Why should not Dom John solve his succession problem by recognizing Dom Pedro's daughter, Maria da Gloria, as his heir?[14] These preliminaries over, the emperor left the negotiations to his councillors, who did what they could to secure better terms. But their hands were tied behind them by sentiment. Dom Pedro insisted on a settlement by the third anniversary of the declaration of independence, and Stuart carried the day.

Dom John became Emperor of Brazil and instantly recognized his son as emperor as an act of royal and family grace. Brazil agreed to indemnify Portugal for her losses in the war of independence and assumed responsibility for Portugal's loan, raised in London, to enable her to reconquer her former colony! A secret protocol promised to pay Dom John a further £250,000 for his royal properties in Brazil.

If Dom Pedro had a surviving son, the heir would enjoy the joint title of Prince Imperial of Brazil and Prince Royal of Portugal and Algarve. The treaty was signed on 29 August 1825. On 7 September, Dom Pedro dramatically tore from his arm the band he had worn since he had opted for 'Independence or Death' on the bank of the River Ipiranga three years earlier. But informed Brazilians feared that the price of recognition was excessive. What with Dom John's indemnification for property he did not own and the balance of the Portuguese loan of £1,400,000, independence had cost 5 *patacas* a head. What annoyed them most was that Dom John's *Carta Regia*, issued on 15 November, while using his new title before his old, referred to his son as nothing more noble than prince royal and called the convention a treaty of peace and friendship, not of independence. Dom Pedro talked angrily of annulling the treaty and renouncing his rights of succession. He refused his hand to Portuguese at the *beija-mão:* 'You are foreigners. This is a favour I grant only to my subjects.'[15]

Dom John's subjects for their part also thought that the price was high. Though their king had given away something he did not possess, they had lost an empire. They could not see that Brazil had conceded anything and accused Stuart of following his master's voice and selling them down the Amazon.[16] Furthermore, nothing had been settled about the succession to the throne of Portugal. A question-mark hung over the future, and for the present the Portuguese had not even gained more favourable trading concessions in Brazil than the English were now free to renegotiate. Dom John's legs, those barometers of his health, had never been quite so bad, and as he had reached the dangerous age for Braganzas, it was feared the treaty might kill him.[17] But the old man (he was 58) was to survive until the following March and recognition of Brazil followed swiftly through the comity of nations. Only Spain refused to follow suit for nine years, unable to come to terms with the new order in South America before 1834.[18]

Stuart, by Dom John newly created Conde de Machico,[19] now put aside his Portuguese persona and presented his government's bill for services rendered. The Brazilian negotiators had hoped to persuade him to ask no more than Britain had asked of Buenos Aires or any other Spanish American successor state, but the British envoy would not tolerate such ingratitude. The negotiations cost Dom Pedro his chief minister, who resigned rather than capitulate, but on

18 October Stuart signed a new treaty of commerce and a convention abolishing the slave-trade. Anglo-Brazilian friendship was proclaimed as permanent and import duties were to continue for another 10 years at 15 per cent *ad valorem* on dry goods (not 18 per cent as Brant had hoped). Those 10 years were bought at the expense of some 80,000 Africans, for as a *douceur* Stuart agreed to allow the Brazilians four years in which to make abolition effective.[20]

The story was not quite finished. Stuart, patrician, self-opinionated and arrogant, was not one of Canning's men and interpreted his powers too liberally for a foreign secretary who required his envoys to understand his policies clearly, to follow his instructions closely and, if there were an unforeseen gap in their orders, to think like him. Stuart had agreed to things Canning could not accept.[21] So Stuart had to be taught his lesson. Canning repudiated the treaty and invited the Brazilians to renegotiate with Stuart's replacement. Robert Gordon was a young diplomat of Strangford's stamp, and upon his arrival in October 1826 he set about securing the agreements Canning wanted. The abolition of the slave-trade was not to be dependent upon the approval of Dom Pedro's Legislative Assembly, which must surely reject it. The trade must end on 23 November 1830. No other nation except Portugal should pay duty on dry goods as low as 15 per cent. Like the 1810 treaty, which it closely resembled, the 1827 treaty was subject to review (in 1840), and could only be terminated then if one of the contracting parties gave the other two years' notice.

Canning's famous boast that he had called the New World into being to redress the balance of the Old was not mere parliamentary rhetoric. Modern Brazil is one of his achievements. When he urged Dom John to go west in 1807 and found a new empire, he intended to secure advantages for Britain. He may not have expected the hegira of the Brazilian court to transform the colony into a sovereign state, but on his return to office in 1822 he recognized that this was what had happened and that, if the new country were not to be plunged into the anarchy of its Spanish American neighbours and fall prey to *caudillismo*, it must be united and independent under one head. Dom Pedro was that natural head and Canning's policy had but one object: to see that Europe's support for Portugal did not put his throne to hazard. His methods were Pavlovian, alternating intimidation with blandishment, but they were effective. As Member of Parliament for Liverpool, Canning believed without the encroachment of a doubt that Britain should secure the maximum commercial advantage from her power. He was the indirect cause of many a ruined fortune in the crazy speculation that greeted the British irruption into the markets and mines of South America, but he was also the instrument that wrote on the State of Brazil the words 'Made in England'.

19· The End of the First Empire, 1826–31

'Having maturely reflected on the political situation in this Empire, I know that my abdication is now necessary, desiring nothing more in this world than glory for myself and happiness for my country.' —

Dom Pedro I, Boa Vista, 6 April 1831,
the tenth year of independence

'Plante-se a acácia, o símbolo do livre, Junta as cinzas do forte. Ele foi re — e combateu tiranos — Chorai, chorai-lhe a morte.' (Plant the acacia tree, symbol of the free, near the ashes of the strong. He was a king and enemy of tyrants, weep now for his death.) —

Alexandre Herculano de Araújo (1810–77)

Dom Pedro reigned for only five more years. Peace with Portugal was followed almost at once by a renewal of the bloody and fruitless war in the Banda Oriental when, in December 1825, an Argentinian 'army of observance' crossed into Brazilian-held territory, while Admiral William Brown, a more canny if diminished Cochrane, kept the Plate closed to Brazilian ships. Lecor was soon walled up again in Montevideo, while Felisberto Brant, now Marques de Barbacena, tried his severely limited hand at a new career. His troops were half-mutinous from lack of pay, held together by a corps of hated German janissaries. They faced an army of creole invaders and irregular *gaúcho* bands fighting for independence. Before long Barbacena had retreated into Rio Grande do Sul and only political upheavals in the republic and a shortage of horses saved his army from annihilation.

In April 1827, the Argentines offered peace on the basis of an independent Uruguay. Canning, who feared that this unnecessary war might kill the Brazilian empire so painfully brought to birth, returned to mediation. Only the exhaustion of both sides brought the conflict to an end on 27 August 1828, for the Argentines were struggling for national unity and Dom Pedro for his throne. The incompetence with which the war had been conducted had damaged the imperial government irretrievably, for more soldiers had died from diseases induced by starvation and from wretched conditions than from wounds. The motley crew of officers, Portuguese, mercenary and Brazilian, failed by their dismal leadership to show what their men showed by their endurance — that they were the heirs of the army that had fought Masséna and Soult. The cost of the war had beggared the young state, the Bank of Brazil was bust and that Portuguese Potosí had only produced a clatter of copper coins extravagantly valued above their real purchasing power.

Dom Pedro's ministers, moreover, dignified by resounding titles, had proved inadequate to the tasks of financing a war and creating a continuously acceptable administration. Between 1826 and 1831 there were seven different ministries, and the chief portfolio of the empire twice changed hands three times in the course of one administration. Even so, the six ministries were shuffled among a dozen or so *mazombos* and a small clutch of faithful *reinóis* who had formed the post-Andrada governments. Between them they satisfied neither the emperor nor the assembly. The presence in one of them of a former tribune, now lion under the throne, the Portuguese-born José Clemente Pereira, the former president of the Rio *câmara*, seemed proof to the patriot opposition of pro-Portuguese sympathies at São Cristovão, where the emperor's personal household was held in the gravest suspicion as a nest of vipers. Particularly unforgivable was their petty persecution of Dona Leopoldina and their protection of the royal strumpet, Domitila de Castro. Dom Pedro could not escape the popular hatred that slopped off from them. The appointment at last of a wholly Brazilian-born ministry in 1829, headed by Barbacena, and a royal pardon for the Andradas helped to restore some of his waning popularity, but the improvement was not to last.

Dom Pedro's meagre credit waned disastrously when it was discovered how deeply he had involved himself in the problems of the *Reino*. Dom John died in March 1826. The Regency Council, determined to prevent the succession of Dom Miguel, proclaimed the Emperor of Brazil as Dom Pedro IV of Portugal. Knowing that his brother was the favoured son of the nobility and church hierarchy, and certain that his own subjects would never accept a union of the crowns, Dom Pedro had one of those master ideas of which he was capable at moments of crisis. He would abdicate in favour of the eight-year-old Maria da Gloria. She should marry her uncle as soon as she was old enough to do so. To avoid giving him the substance as well as the shadow of power, Dom Pedro would, while he was still king, grant Portugal one of his famous constitutions. But if the emperor was barely in control of events in Brazil, he was a powerless *deus ex machina* in the distant *Reino*.

British troops helped to beat off a Spanish-sponsored invasion headed by Dom Miguel in 1827, but the new Chamber of Deputies could get no reforms past the upper chamber of hereditary peers — both brought into existence by the constitution — and Dom Miguel refused to collect his bride until he had been formally appointed regent. All seemed to be well, however, when on 26 February 1828 the prince swore in Lisbon to uphold the charter and Dom Pedro confirmed his unconditional abdication. By April Dom Miguel had dissolved the chamber and in June the Ancient Estates of the Realm, specially convoked for the purpose, declared Dom Pedro's succession and his abdication null, absolved Dom Miguel from his oath and on 11 July proclaimed him king. Ten days earlier the 10-year-old queen had left Rio for Lisbon with Barbacena, in the forlorn hope that the European powers, especially Britain, would bring her uncle to heel. But Canning was no longer secretary of state and the Duke of Wellington refused either to provide British troops to support the constitutionalists or to allow arms to be bought in Britain. On 16 October 1829, Maria da Gloria was back in Brazil, accompanied by a new bride for Dom Pedro. She had not proved easy to find, for Habsburg disapproval of an unsatisfactory son-in-law had not been encouraging to minor princes. In the end, Barbacena had lighted upon a hard-up beauty, Amélie de Leuchtenberg (1812–73), the daughter of Eugène Beauharnais. Thus Napoleon's step-granddaughter, on 17 October 1829, succeeded his sister-in-law as Empress of Brazil. Amélie's 17-year-old charms immediately eclipsed the Marquesa de Santos, whose fall from grace was meteoric, but as the new empress and her stepdaughter arrived so too did rumours that some of the bride money Barbacena had raised in Europe had found its way into the hands of Maria da Gloria's partisans in the Azores. The empire had not made an ignoble peace with Buenos Aires to release cash and supplies for the emperor to win his daughter a throne.

Painful peace in the south, fearful involvement in a dynastic struggle in Europe, threatening bankruptcy and a continuing commitment to a large standing army, many of whom were German and Irish mercenaries who had once terrorized Rio in a revolt against mindless ill-treatment and subhuman conditions — had the emperor allowed himself to fall once more under the malign influence of the country's secret enemies? Despite his bitter complaint that 22 years in Brazil had given him a right to be called a Brazilian, he found himself dogged by that old suspicion that he was still Portuguese in blood and sympathies. The 1830 July Revolution in France provided new slogans for the 'patriotic' opposition, and when the liberal editor of a São Paulo broadsheet was assassinated, it was the Pampluna case all over again. Everything the emperor touched seemed to turn to ashes, and in a desperate bid to revive the spirit of 1822, Dom Pedro left Rio in December 1830, to find the pulse of the nation in Minas Gerais.

What he found beat sluggish and unsure. His appeal to the *Mineiros* to rally against those who wished to destroy the precious unity of the constitutional empire seemed only to convince his critics that he meant to abrogate the constitution himself. The national cockade reappeared, not as a badge of loyalty to the emperor but as a symbol of solidarity with the *mazombo* opposition. Vergueiro, now a senator, plotted a coup. Portuguese officers met with mutiny among their men; *reinóis* in court and garrison were accused of being either Miguelines or Marians, engaged in an issue irrelevant to Brazil. Even Dom Pedro's friends, like Barbacena, talked of abdication. When, on 5 April 1831, he dismissed his latest, month-old ministry of liberals and constitutionalists for a ministry 'he could trust', composed of six senators all recently ennobled, events in the capital were reminiscent of 1821. A great crowd of Brazilians, supported by *mazombo* militia and regular troops, gathered in the Campo Sant'Ana demanding a popular ministry. The garrison officers, unable to count on the loyalty of the few remaining troops under arms, counselled Dom Pedro to agree. The emperor, however, knew that the promise he had made to the soldiery in the Largo do Rocio on 5 June 1821, 'that I shall not come here a third time', must now be kept. Neither his honour nor the constitution allowed him to bow to mob rule, and it was almost with relief that at two o'clock in the morning of 7 April he handed a decree to one of the officers still in attendance at São Cristovão. 'Here is my abdication,' he told him solemnly. 'I hope you are content. I shall return to Europe and quit a land I have loved and will continue to love dearly.' Appointing José Bonifácio, once again in Brazil, as guardian to his five-year-old son, he went to the child's bedroom, where Dom Pedro II was sleeping peacefully. He stooped to kiss the boy's forehead gently, then as an afterthought he kissed his hand. It was the unconscious child-emperor's first *beija-mão*.

'He knew better how to abdicate than to reign,' was how the French ambassador described the final act of abdication, which he witnessed with his British colleague. But the emperor had been toppled by a mutiny not a revolution, and no one expected him actually to go. At once all parties drew back from the brink of anarchy, a Council of Regency was elected and the child-emperor put under the tutelage, as Dom Pedro had wished, of the Patriarch of Independence. Dom Pedro II reigned until 1889, when he too abdicated at the age of 64 to make way for a military republic, his long reign witness to the fundamental conservatism of Brazilian society before the end of slavery. The years of his minority were marked by political squabbles as bitter as any in his father's reign, by mutinies and separatist risings in Pará and Rio Grande do Sul, coming so thick and so fast that Carlos Antônio went to Oporto in 1832 to beg Dom Pedro to return. For the *exaltados* of the liberal left, hostile to the conservative policies of the Andradas, were as determined to remove Dom Pedro II as they had been to remove Dom Pedro I from their influence, while the former Andrada partisans, disillusioned by the continuing ineptitude of ministers and the vacuum of power in the regency of three regents, plotted the emperor's return. But Dom Pedro had abdicated in favour of his son and had other business on hand. As soon as this was settled, he might return to act as regent until Pedro II was of age.

He never came. The business in hand was the recovery of his daughter's throne. He had left Brazil with Maria da Gloria and his new wife on board HMS *Warspite*, but he had nowhere to go. He received nothing but polite sympathy from Britain and France, and could have settled in either as a private citizen, but in early 1832 he arrived in the Azores to join the refugees from Dom Miguel's coup. From there he sailed in July with 7000 ragged loyalists to seize Oporto. The civil war that followed was an adventure in the 19th-century tradition hallowed by Garibaldi. But by April 1834 there was a queen, too, in Spain beset by an openly reactionary rebellion, led by her uncle, Don Carlos. Palmerston, anxious to strike a blow against the Holy Alliance in the east, converted Britain's clandestine assistance to the Queens of Portugal and Spain into open resistance under a Quadruple Alliance of Britain, France and the legitimate governments of Portugal and Spain against the two pretenders. While

Dom Pedro held Oporto with veterans from the war in the Banda and several hundred British mercenaries, Admiral Sir Charles Napier, like Cochrane before him, destroyed the Migueline navy. By May Dom Miguel's game was up. In return for an amnesty for his supporters (for which Dom Pedro's coach in Lisbon was stoned by a liberal mob cursing him for being a Brazilian), Dom Miguel left the country clear for his brother's constitution and constitutional daughter. By September Dom Pedro was dead. The privations of the siege of Oporto had brought on a galloping consumption which his normally sturdy frame was too weak to resist. He chose to die as he had chosen 'Independence or Death', with an appropriate gesture, yielding up his spirit in the arms of a trooper who had endured the siege by his side in the defence of liberty and legitimacy. Childe Harold had come to the Dark Tower. Even his enemies reproached him for dying so young.

Why could Dom Pedro not have died in his bed as Emperor of Brazil? It was not for want of experience, for he had learned in a hard school, during the days of his regency in 1821–2. 'I prefer to leave the throne with honour,' he is reported to have said at the time of his abdication. 'My Brazilian-born subjects do not want me any more because I am a Portuguese.' His son would not suffer from that disability! But was that all it was? He suffered much from the defects of his own temperament, for, as Dona Leopoldina had quickly noticed, he had a passion for all things new. He loved action, surprising his friends and confounding his critics, just as he had done when he produced a constitution more liberal and more durable than that of the so-called professionals in the assembly. What he found intolerable was the repetitiveness of political crisis and the continuous barrage of criticism. It cut him to the quick to be accused of tyranny, of wanting to rule unconstitutionally, of being more Portuguese than Brazilian, but his angry reaction was to behave more autocratically and cleave more closely to his largely *reinol* friends. He had the panache to found the only lasting constitutional monarchy in Latin America but not the stamina to work the system. Towards the end his attention was certainly distracted by events in Portugal, and too many of his loudest partisans were the Portuguese-born who resented the privileges and power of the old colonial classes entrenched in the new empire. The *Primeiro Reinado* ended, almost symbolically, on a British warship. The man who, when he heard that he had been removed as the guardian of the young emperor, wrote to José Bonifácio that 'intrigue, envy and ignorance have triumphed over honour, paternity and patriotism, and despotism, demoralization and tyranny rule instead of reason, law, good faith, morality, security and liberty', might have been writing about the Portugal to which he had returned after 25 years. His fallen pride found relief in the action of war, but at 35 his death was a fulfilment not the betrayal of promise.

VICE ROYALTY OF NEW GRANADA

FRENCH
GUIANA

Cayenne

ATLANTIC OCEAN

Rio Negro

R. Japura

Rio Solimões
(Amazon)

Manaos

Belém do Pará

São Luiz do Maranhão

Rio Içá

Rio

Rio Madeira

Rio Tapajós

MARANHÃO

CEARÁ

RIO GRANDE
DO NORTE

G R A O   P A R Á

Rio Xingú

Rio Araguaia

Rio Tocantins

PIAUÍ

PARAIBA

PERNAMBUCO

Recife

VICE
ROYALTY OF
PERU

M A T O
G R O S S O

GOIÁS

B A H I A

ALAGOAS

Cuiabá

Rio

Goiás

S. Francisco

Salvador

Rio Jequitinhonha

MINAS GERAIS

ESPIRITO SANTO

Rio Doce

Rio Paranaíba

SÃO PAULO

Rio Paraíba do Sul

PARANÁ
(PART OF
SÃO PAULO)

São
Paulo

Rio de Janeiro

Santos

MISSÕES

Rio Paraná

RIO GRANDE
DO S. PEDRO

SANTA CATARINA

Porto Alegre

VICE
ROYALTY
OF
THE PLATE

BANDA
ORIENTAL

Buenos
Aires

Montevideo

R. Plate

BRAZIL
—1808—

Disputed area of the Missions

SCALE

miles
0 100 200 300 400 500 600 700

0   200   400   600   800 1000 km

List of References

Note: References that appear in more than one chapter are given in a short form in the notes and in full in the Bibliography (page 214), which also contains a list of the abbreviations used.

Chapter 1: Nemesis, 1807–8.

1. Cook, James, *The Journals*, ed J. C. Beaglehole, *The Voyage of the Endeavour, 1768–71* (Cambridge, 1968), vol 1, p 28n.
2. Cheke, Marcus, *Carlota Joaquina, Queen of Portugal* (L, 1947), p 8.
3. Freitas, vol 1, p 47; Monteiro, pp 46–7.
4. Manchester, *British Pre-eminence*, p 62.
5. Freitas, vol 1, p 82.
6. Lima, *D João no Brasil*, vol 1, p 46.
7. Junot, Laure, *Memoirs of the Duchess d'Abrantes*, 2nd English ed (L, 1833–5), vol V, p 378.
8. PRO FO 63/56 No 103: Strangford to Canning, 20 November 1807.
9. For the events of the hegira: Brandão, Raul, *El Rei Junot*, (Lisbon, 1912), p 105; O'Neill, Thomas, *A Concise and Accurate Account of the Proceedings of the Squadron under the Command of Rear Admiral Sir Sidney Smith KC in effecting the Escape and Escorting the Royal Family to the Brazils on 29 November, 1807* (L, 1809), pp 24–6; Lima, *D João no Brasil*, vol 1, 53–4; Junot, *Memoirs*, vol VI, pp 9–12; Manchester, *Transfer of the Portuguese Court*, pp 148–84.
10. Barrow, Sir John (ed), *The Life and Correspondence of Admiral Sir William Sidney Smith* (L, 1848), vol 2, p 269.
11. Santos, vol 1, p 206.

Chapter 2: Brazilian Welcome

1. J. P. Robertson, vol i, p 138.
2. Henderson, p 57.
3. Prior, p 95.
4. Prior, p 96.
5. Marrocos, p 97: letter of 29 August 1812.
6. Roberto Macedo, *História Administrativa do Brasil* (R, 1964), vol 6, part viii, pp 119–23.

Chapter 3: Discovering Brazil

1. In 1866, Perdigão Malheiro in *A Escrivadão no Brasil*, vol 2, p 26, estimated that at the end of the 18th century free Brazilians totalled 1,666,000, of whom 1,010,000 were white, 406,000 free coloured and 250,000 Indian. The enslaved population he put at 1,582,000, of whom 1,361,000 were black and 221,000 mulattos; see also Bethell, *Abolition*, ch 3. Other statistics varying from Malheiro are in Walsh, vol 1, p 329; Rugendas, p 150; Simonsen, Roberto, *História Econômica do Brasil, 1500–1820*, 5th ed (SP, 1967), vol 2, p 56; Alden, Dauril, 'Late Colonial Brazil', in CHLA (Cambridge, 1984), vol 2, pp 602–9.
2. Koster, p 268n.
3. Prior, p 101.
4. Andreoni, João Antônio (Padre André João Antonil SJ), *Cultûra e Opulência do Brasil*, text of 1711, ed A. P. Canabrava (SP, 1967), pp 315–16.
5. For Minas gold in the 18th century: Walsh, vol 2, pp 90–230; Luccock, pp 460–92; Spix and Martius, I, 4, i, pp 311–20. Caldcleugh, vol 1, p 58, certainly overestimated the annual value of gold mined in 1821 at £900,000. Eschwege, in *Pluto Brasiliensis*, vol 2, p 34, reckoned in 1814 that the total extracted in Minas Gerais was 800 kilos with negligible amounts from elsewhere, In 1753, the quint was levied on gold weighing 1,770,000 kilos. After 1812 it was scarcely 360 kilos. See Spix and Martius (as above). Albert F. Calvert, in *Mineral Resources of Minas Geraes* (L, 1915), pp 15–16, using the records of the quint, calculated that the total Brazilian production from 1700 to 1820 may only have been 530,000 kilos or some 4,500 kilos a year.
6. Almeida Prado, p 145; Leithold, p 30.
7. Saint-Hilaire, *S Francisco*, vol 1, pp 338–40.

Chapter 4: First Steps, 1808–11

1. Celso Furtado, *Economic Growth of Brazil: a Survey from Colonial Times*, trans by R. W. Aguiar and E. G. Dugdale of *Formação Econômica do Brasil*, (California, 1968), p 102.
2. For the 18th-century *Inconfidências*, see Maxwell, pp 201–3, who contests with vigour the contention that the 1789 *Inconfidência* had little contemporary significance, as argued by J. H. Rodrigues in his preface to the 4th ed of Capistrano de Abreu's *Capítulos de História Colonial, 1500–1800* (1954), pp 35–7.
3. PRO FO 65/6: Portugal 18: Strangford to Canning, 30 November 1807.
4. Vieira, pp 109–11; Santos, vol 1, pp 275–6.
5. Rubio, p 23, quoting *O Correio Brasiliense*.
6. Freitas, vol 1, pp 216–17.
7. Humphreys and Graham, pp 8–9: Sir Sidney Smith to William Wellesley Pole, Secretary to the Admiralty, 24 August 1808.
8. Street, p 106: Strangford to Canning, 30 January 1809.

9. PRO FO 63/59: Portugal 18: Canning to Strangford, 2 September 1808.
10. Humphreys and Graham, p 19: Smith to Pole, 26 September 1808.
11. Presas, pp 160–61.

Chapter 5: Brazil Observed, 1811–16.

1. Robert Southey, *Letters*, ed Maurice Fitzgerald (Oxford, 1912) p. 307: Southey to Chauncey Townsend, 20 July 1819.
2. Southey, pp 302–3, letter to Walter Savage Landor, 7 May 1809.
3. Darwin, *Beagle*: 1 March 1832.
4. Rugendas, p 21.
5. Rugendas, p 25.
6. Lindley, p 272. For conditions in the 'Big Houses', see also Graham, *Journal*, p 135, and Freyre, *Mansions*, ch 4.
7. Henderson, p 64.
8. Monteiro, Tobias do Rego, *O Primeiro Reinado*, 2 vols (Rio, 1939, vol 2, p 212; S Buarque de Holanda, *A Herência Colonial*, HGCB, II, vol 1, pp 32–3.
9. Armitage, vol 1, pp 16–17.
10. Freyre, *Mansions*, p 15.
11. Luccock, p 96.
12 For São Cristovão in general: Almeida Prado, pp 145–6, 190; Debret, vol 2, pp 192–4.
13 Caldcleugh, vol 1, p 62; Leithold, p 14.
14. Marrocos, pp 93, 159: letters of 3 July 1812 and 28 November 1813.
15. Araújo, Mozart de, 'Sigismund Neukomm', in *Revista Brasileira de Cultura* (Rio), ano 1, no 1, July-September 1969, pp 68–73.
16. Henderson, pp 50–51; Hill, p 7.
17. Rubio, pp 171–2; Street, pp 158–9.
18. Manchester, *British Pre-eminence*, p 86.
19. Marrocos, pp 78, 181: letters of 19 May 1812 and 25 January 1814. Almeida de Castro had been given the Brazilian title of Conde das Galveas.
20. Santos, vol 2, p 537; Marrocos, p 184: letter of 22 February 1814.
21. PRO FO 63/167: Portugal 7.

Chapter 6: Black Gold

1. See ch 3, n 1.
2. Luccock, p 435; cf Schwarz, S.B., *Elite Politics and the Growth of Peasantry in Late Colonial Brazil*, apud Wood (ed), *From Colony to Nation*, p 150.
3. Azevedo, p 369.
4. Coutinho, José Joaquim da Cunha de Azeredo, *Obras Econômicas*, ed S. Buarque de Holanda (São Paulo, 1966), pp 260–61, 354–7.
5. Boxer, *Golden Age*, p 174. Kidder and Fletcher, p 132, reckoned that a plantation slave would survive for 5 to 7 years.

6. Tollenare, vol 2, p 483: 16 February 1817.
7. Blacklaw, A. Scott, 'Slavery in Brazil', in *South America Journal*, July 1882, *passim*.
8. Walsh, vol 2, pp 479–91.
9. Tollenare, vol 2, p 480: 16 February 1817.
10. Mathison, p 156.
11. Walsh, vol 2, p 324.
12. Caldcleugh vol 1, pp 82–3; Bethell, *Abolition*, p 71; Donald Pierson, p 36; Prior, p 98.
13. Debret, vol 2, Plate 24: 'Intérieure d'une Résidence des Gitanes'.
14. For the development from the original slave religion to the alternative church in Brazil, see ch 11, page 107–8.
15. Koster, pp 446, 402–3.
16. Stein, p 138.
17. Coaracy, Vivaldo, *Memórias da Cidade do Rio de Janeiro*, (R, 1965), vol 3, p 366.
18. Wood, *Fidalgos*, p 142.
19. Koster, p 423.
20. Luccock, p 591.
21. Rugendas, pp 142–3.
22. Burlamaque, Frederico C., *Analytica acerca do Comercio d'Escravos e acerca dos Malês de Escrivadão Doméstica* (R, 1837), p 3; Conrad, *apud* Hanke, vol 2, p 208; Stein, p 159; Davis, p 256.
23. Walsh, vol 2, pp 361–2.
24. Hesketh, *apud* Hanke, vol 2, p 30; Debret, vol 2, p 216.
25. Koster, p 391; Rugendas, p 76. Both tell the same story; it clearly had a wide currency.
26. Saint-Hilaire, *S Francisco*, vol 2, p 93.
27. Bethell, *Abolition*, p 4; Bastide, Roger, and Florestan, Fernando, *Brancos e Negros em São Paulo*, 2nd ed (SP, 1959), p 16; Klein, Herbert S., 'The Colored Freedman in Brazilian Slave Society', in the *Journal of Social History*, 111, no 1, 1969, pp 31–52.

Chapter 7: The Trade Ends

1. Hesketh, 'Correspondence', in Hanke, vol 2, p 32. The experience of slave breeding in North America and the Caribbean is illuminated by the calculations of Fogel and Engerman, vol 1, pp 153–7, on the economic break-even age among slaves in the USA during the ante-bellum decades. Because of the high cost of capital and a 40 per cent death-rate before age 19, the accumulated expenditure by planters on slaves was greater than the average accumulated income up to and including age 26. After that the position was reversed. This high break-even age induced planters to encourage slave fertility. Contrastive studies in Jamaica indicated that the life expectancy of a slave there was some half a decade lower than the break-even age, so that planters preferred to buy adult slaves in Africa rather than rear them. The

Brazilian model may have been not unlike Jamaica's. Certainly the strong support for the trade suggests that the economics of slavery dictated a constant recourse to the transatlantic sources of supply. These economics could have been reversed had not Brazil been so used to absorbing the lion's share of the trade. Between 1500 and 1870, about 3.6 million Africans were taken to Brazil in bondage, compared to 400,000 to the USA. From 1807 to 1851 the proportion of the Brazilian trade to the whole rose from 38 to 60 per cent, and in the 19th century Brazil and Cuba between them received 8 out of every 10 Africans sold away from their homes. See Curtin, Philip, *The Atlantic Slave Trade: A Census*, (Wisconsin 1969), pp 47–9.

2. Conrad, p 16.
3. Verger, pp 13, 326–7; Rodrigues, Nina, *Os Africanos no Brasil*, 2nd ed (SP, 1935), pp 61–107; Pierson, p 36.
4. Graham, *Escorço Biográfico*, pp 132–3.
5. Leithold, pp 35–6.
6. Walsh, vol 2, pp 354–5.
7. Marrocos, p 73: letter of 3 April 1812.
8. Walsh, vol 2, p 358.
9. Rocha, Manoel Ribeiro, *Ethiope Resgatado, Empenhado, Sustentado, Corregido, Instruido e Liberado, passim*; Boxer, *Race Relations*, pp 111–13.
10. Stein, p 136.
11. Conrad, 'Abolition', in Hanke, vol 2, p 211.
12. Rugendas, p 146: Stein, p 137.
13. Verger, p 506; Saint-Hilaire, *S Francisco*, vol 1, p 108; Koster, pp 390, 446; Lindley, p 176; Spix and Martius, I, 2, i, p 113.
14. Boxer, *Golden Age*, p 306.
15. Freyre, *Mansions*, p 266; Genovese, Eugene D., 'Rebelliousness and Docility in the Negro Slaves: a Critique of Elkins's Thesis', in Lane (ed), p 54.
16. Harris, Marvyn, 'The Myth of the Friendly Master', in Foner and Genovese, p 43.
17. Klein, pp 35–52; Mathieson, W. L., *Great Britain and the Slave-Trade, 1839–65* (L, 1935), p 2.
18. Lindley, p 234.
19. Luccock, p 470.
20. Robertson, J. P., vol 1, p 165.
21. Pierson, p 45; Davis, *Problems of Slavery in Western Culture* (Harmondsworth, 1970), p 254.
22. Freyre, *Mansions*, p 131.
23. Stein, pp 133–4. For slaves in the jerked-beef industry of Rio Grande do Sul, see Ianni, pp 134–49, 282–5.
24. Darwin, *Beagle*: 3 July 1833.
25. Conrad, Destruction etc, in Hanke, ii, 210–1.
26. Hill, ch 4 *passim*.
27. Hill, p 120; Rodrigues, José Honório, *Brasil e Africa: Outro Horizonte* (R, 1961), pp 117–23.
28. Bethell, *Abolition*, p 152.

29. Davis, p 258; Conrad, 'Destruction', in Hanke (ed), p 26.
30. The debate on whether slaves were better treated in Latin than in British America started with Frank Tannenbaum's *Slave and Citizen: The Negro in the Americas* (NY, 1947). He claimed (pp 53–8) that both the law and the church secured for the slave respect for his 'humanity' and provided him, if he were frugal or fortunate, with a chance, however small, of freedom. Stanley Elkins developed this thesis in *Slavery: a Problem in American Institutional and Intellectual Life*. In his view, the 'Sambo' image, of a dazed, obsequious and passive moron, was not typical of South as it was of North American slavery. In refining Tannenbaum's thesis with the hypothesis that the Brazilian system in particular gave the slave a margin of hope for a better and freer life, he proceeded to make a comparison between the slaves on a North American plantation and the inmates of a Nazi concentration camp in the 1940s: both suffered from similar conditions of shock, deprivation, cruelty and hopelessness. The Tannenbaum-Elkins thesis was challenged by Eugene D. Genovese in 'The Treatment of Slaves in Different Countries', in Foner and Genovese, *Slavery in the New World*, pp 202–10, and in 'Materialism and Idealism in The History of Negro Slavery in the Americas', pp 238–55, both in Foner and Genovese: *Slavery in the New World*. He did, however, endorse (on p 240) one part of Tannenbaum's thesis — that slaves in Brazil had a greater prospect of freedom. But Marvin Harris in 'The Myth of the Friendly Master', in *Patterns of Race in the Americas* (NY, 1964), pp 65–78, found no evidence of better treatment in Brazil and held that the laws and rights to which Tannenbaum and Elkins referred were so much moonshine. D. B. Davis, in *The Problem of Slavery in Western Culture*, (Harmondsworth, 1970), pp 262–3, refuted Gilberto Freyre's description in *Mansions and Shanties* of *Casa Grande* paternalism and explained why Brazil really did earn her sobriquet of being a hell for blacks, easy replacement leading to a callous indifference to life, and manumission being in most cases the heartless casting away of worked-out bodies. Elkins's riposte 'Slavery and Ideology', in Lane (ed), *The Debate over Slavery*, pp 334–43, does not modify his main thesis that it was comparatively easy for a slave in Brazil to acquire freedom. The high rate of manumissions and the ever-increasing number of free blacks could not have left the main body of slaves unaffected. This rather than more humane physical treatment made the institution of slavery in Brazil the 'mildest' in the western hemisphere.
31. Neiva, p 216. The representation, of which these are the closing words, was intended for the Constituent Assembly but never delivered owing to its premature dissolution.
32. Webster, vol 1, p 222: Chamberlain to Canning, 2 April 1823.
33. *Diário do Governo* (Rio): unsigned letter, 22 April 1823.
34. Ramirez, p 204: Hippolyt von Sonnleithner, 7 January 1859; cf Ianni, pp 261–3.
35. Mathison, pp 18–51; Santos, vol 2, pp 701–4.
36. Ramirez, p 193: Sonnleithner, 14 May 1856.
37. Leithold, p 32.

Chapter 8: Staying On, 1814–17

1. Marrocos, p 222: letter of 10 April 1815.
2. Webster, vol 1, p 170: Strangford to Castlereagh, 7 July 1812.
3. PRO FO 63/9 Portugal 14: Strangford to Castlereagh, 1 December 1814.
4. Santos, vol 2, p 513.
5. Street, p 282.
6. Webster, vol 1, pp 176, 179: Chamberlain to Castlereagh, 20 July, 29 August, 8 October 1816; Street, p 288.
7. Webster, vol 1, p 185: Chamberlain to Castlereagh, 16 June 1817.
8. The acclamation is described in minute detail in Debret, vol 3, pp 64–73; Santos, vol 2, pp 615–56.
9. Darwin, *Beagle*: 1 June 1832.
10. Almeida Prado, p 19.
11. Monteiro, pp 162–3.
12. Ramirez, p 10.
13. Almeida Prado, p 3.
14. Spix and Martius, II, 5, i, p 238.
15. Manizer, G. G., *A Expedição do Acadêmico GI Langsdorff ao Brasil* (SP, 1967), p 51.

Chapter 9: Indians

1. Santos, vol 1, pp 276–9.
2. Malheiro, p 126.
3. Saint-Hilaire, *S Francisco*, vol 1, p 301; Spix and Martius, II, 7, iii, p 450; Ianni, see notes to ch 8, pp 54–8, 152.
4. Spix and Martius, II, 7, iii, pp 448–9.
5. Seidler, p 129.
6. Malheiro, pp 98–117.
7. Saint-Hilaire, *S Francisco*, vol 2, pp 108–10.
8. Santos, vol 1, pp 409–10.
9. Hemming, *Amazon Frontier*, pp 162–71. Two lives of Marlière: Franco, Afrânio de Melo, *Apóstolo das Selvas Mineiras* (R, 194), and Oiliam, José, *Marlière, o Civilizador* (Belo Horizonte, 1958). See also Saint-Hilaire, *Rio de Janeiro*, vol 2, pp 122–7, where he describes the work of Commandante Julião Fernandes Leão among the Botocudos; as does Wied-Neuwied, p 236.
10. Neiva, p 180.
11. Saint-Hilaire, *Rio de Janeiro*, vol 1, p 56.
12. Pohl, J. E., *Reise im Innern von Brasilien in des Jahres 1817-21*, 2 vols (Vienna, 1832), trans by Milton and Eugênio Amado as *A Viagem no Interior do Brasil* (SP, 1976), p 152; cf Spix and Martius, III, 7, iii, p 268.
13. Prado, p 115.
14. Almeida Prado, p 263.
15. Spix and Martius, III, 8, iv, p 182.

16. Seidler, p 122.
17. Spix and Martius, I, 4, ii, p 345, describing the Puri dances in Minas Gerais.
18. Spix and Martius, III, 9, iv, pp 291–2.
19. Spix and Martius, III, 8, iv, pp 184–620.
20. Saint-Hilaire, *Rio de Janeiro*, vol 2, pp 190–91; Spix and Martius, III, 9, iv, pp 355–6.
21. Santos, vol 2, p 615; see also Skidmore, Thomas H., *Black and White: Race and Nationality in Brazilian Thought* (Oxford and NY, 1974), pp 6–7.
22. Saint-Hilaire, *Rio de Janeiro*, vol 2, p 186.

Chapter 10: Rebellion, 1817

1. Maxwell, pp 218–23.
2. Barreto, Célia de Barros, 'Ação das Sociedades Secretas', in HGCB, II, i, p 192.
3. For the Olinda seminary as a nursery of liberals, see Azevedo, F. de, *Brazilian Culture*, p 370; Mota, Carlos Guilherme, *Nordeste, 1811: Estruturas e Argumentos* (SP, 1972), p 257; Quintas, Amaro, 'A Agitação Republicana do Nordeste', in HGCB, II, i, pp 209–10.
4. Tollenare, vol 2, p 546: letter of 9 March 1817.
5. Two eye-witness accounts form the main sources for the 1817 *Inconfidência*. *A História da Revolução de 1817* by Canon Muniz Tavares was written shortly after the event (but first published in 1840) from the standpoint of a dispassionate partisan of the republic, who later was a loyal servant of the empire. The edition with notes by Oliviera Lima (republished in 1969) is used for this chapter. *Notes Dominicales prises pendant un Voyage en Portugal et au Brésil en 1816, 1817, 1818* by Louis François Tollenare, ed Léon Bourdon (P, 1972), vol 2, pp 550–633, is the Sunday diary of a French cotton factor in Recife, in close contact with the revolutionary junta, whose members consulted him on precedents from the French Revolution in the 1790s.
6. Mota, p 35: letter dated 12 March 1817.
7. Tavares, p 132.
8. Quoted by Pedro Moacyr Campos in *Imagens do Brasil no Velho Mundo*, in HGCB, II, i. 55.
9. Luccock, pp 554–5.
10. Humphreys and Graham, p 200: Commodore Willam Bowles to Lord Fitzharris, 26 May 1817.
11. Tavares, p 33.
12. Luccock, p 560.
13. *Documentos, Lisboa-Rio*, vol 1, p 224: Moraes, Melo, 'Apontamentos da História dos Ministérios e Causa que determinaram o Regresso da Familia Real para Portugal'; cf Monteiro, pp 206–12. The most active and seditious association was the *Sinédrio* in Oporto, at which, after 1818, army dissidents plotted how to succeed where Gomes Freire had failed, and rid Portugal of her English general staff.

Chapter 11: The Kingdom of Brazil: Church

1. Capistrano de Abreu, p 66; Robertson, J. P., vol 1, pp 166–9.
2. Lindley, p 277.
3. Ianni, p 147; Verger, pp 329–30; Bastide, p 91.
4. Walsh, vol 2, pp 380–81; Debret, vol 2, pp 219–22 and Plate 33: 'Scène de Carnaval'.
5. Carrato, pp 70–71; Capistrano de Abreu, p 316.
6. Koster, p 244.
7. Mawe, p 204; Luccock, p 380.
8. Saint-Hilaire, *S Francisco*, vol 2, p 25.
9. Spix and Martius, I, 4, ii, p 332.
10. Caldcleugh, vol 1, p 75.
11. Saint-Hilaire, *S Paulo*, p 95.
12. José Bonifácio's draft speech for the Constituent Assembly can be found in his *Obras Científicas, Políticas e Sociais*, 3 vols (Santos, 1965), vol 2, p 139.
13. Haring, C. H., *Empire in Brazil: A New World Experiment* (Cambridge, Mass, 1966), p 114.
14. Prior, p 104.
15. Rugendas, p 116.
16. Buarque de Holanda, S., *Raízes do Brasil* (SP, 1947), p 26; Carrato, p 32.
17. Walsh, vol 1, p 378.
18. Kidder, p 145.
19. Koster, p 85.
20. Saint-Hilaire, *S Francisco*, vol 1, p 100.
21. Walsh, vol 1, p 324.
22. Staunton, vol 1, p 160.
23. Santos, vol 1, p 55.
24. Thales de Azevedo, *Cultûra e Situação Racial no Brasil* (R, 1961), p 89.
25. For the *Congadas* and devotion to Our Lady, see Koster, pp 273–4; Debret, vol 2, p 225: Plate 20: 'Divers Convois Funèbres'; Saint-Hilaire, *Rio de Janeiro*, vol 2, pp 203–5; Bastide, pp 182–3; Ianni, pp 165–6.
26. The origins of spiritism are explored in Bastide, pp 83–6, 157–8; Pierson, pp 306–7; Carneiro, Edison C., *Candomblés da Bahia* (R, 1960), pp 77–98. Between Salvador and Rio there are differences in the attribution of *orixás*. In Salvador, Ogun is St Anthony and Our Lady of the Apparition is Oxun. There are also differences in spelling between *tereiros* or temples of the adept. See Nunes, Atila, 'Sincretismo', *Correio da Manha*, Rio, 7–8 January 1970.
27. For the *Irmandades*, see Wood, *Fidalgos, passim*; Debret, vol 3, p 143. And for the *Santas Casas*, see Wood, *Fidalgos, passim*; Graham, *Journal*, pp 306–7; Kidder, pp 109–110.
28. Marrocos, p 60: letter of 27 February 1812.
29. Spix and Martius, I, 3, iii, pp 283–4.
30. Saint-Hilaire, *Rio e Minas Gerais*, vol 2, p 302.

31. Debret, vol 2: Plate 46: 'Le Chirurgien Nègre'.
32. Saint-Hilaire, *S Francisco*, vol 1, p 101.
33. Spix and Martius, II, 6, ii, 254.

Chapter 12: The Kingdom of Brazil: State

1. Debret, vol 3, p 51.
2. Azevedo, p 355.
3. Carrato, pp 148–9.
4. Presas, p 178.
5. Caldcleugh, vol 1, p 66; Graham, *Journal*, p 301: 23 September 1823.
6. Saint-Hilaire, *S Francisco*, vol 1, pp 303.
7. Caldcleugh, vol 1, pp 76–7.
8. Marrocos, p 163: letter of 28 September 1813; Prior, p 105.
9. Luccock, p 548.
10. Walsh, vol 1, p 489.
11. Tollenare, vol 2, p 414: 29 December 1816.
12. Debret, vol 3, pp 25–6; Saint-Hilaire, *S Francisco*, vol 1, p 42, quoting from Eschwege, *Brasilien, die Neue Welt*, vol 2, p 49.
13. Koster, p 197.
14. Mawe, p 283.
15. Luccock, p 81.
16. Delso Renault, *O Rio Antico nos Anuncios no Jornais* (R, 1969), p 54.
17. Saint-Hilaire, *S Francisco*, vol 1, p 316.
18. Luccock, p 80.
19. Maria Graham met her on 29 August 1823: *Journal*, pp 292–4.
20. Johnson, John J., *The Military and Society in Latin America* (Stanford, 1964), pp 180–82.

Chapter 13: Constitution, 1820–21

1. Almeida Prado, p 89.
2. For the diplomatic community, see Almeida Prado, pp 85–90, 92–4. For the French artists as spies. see Lima, vol 1, pp 244–5; Cahú Sylvio de Mello, *A Revolução Nativista Pernambucana de 1817* (R, no date), p 93.
3. Bagot, vol 2, p 309, quoting Lord John Ponsonby, the British envoy in Buenos Aires, to Canning, 17 October 1826.
4. Francisco Gomes da Silva's *Memórias Oferecidas à Nacão Brasileira* were published in London in 1831.
5. Webster, vol 1, p 186: Chamberlain to Castlereagh, 4 October 1817, quoting the finance minister, João Paulo Bezerra.
6. Webster, vol 1, p 204: Castlereagh to Thornton, 15 November 1820.
7. Monteiro, p 256: *parecer* of 2 January 1821.
8. Varnhagen, vol 6, pp 29–30: *parecer* of 7 January 1821.
9. 'Le Roi et la Famille Royale de Bragance, doivent-ils dans les circonstances présentes retourner au Portugal ou bien rester au Brésil?', in *Documentos, Lisboa-Rio*, vol 1, pp 201–8; its rebuttal, pp 208–15.

10. Webster, vol 1, p 205: Thornton to Castlereagh, 31 January 1821.
11. Varnhagen, vol 6, p 346; Raiol, vol 1, pp 16–19.
12. Varnhagen, vol 6, pp 261–3.
13. Tavares, pp 222–8.
14. Varnhagen, vol 6, pp 37–8, 41–2; Monteiro, pp 291–2, 298–300: Palmela to Dom John, 24 February 1821.
15. Documentos, Lisboa-Rio, vol 1, p 239; Varnhagen, vol 6, p 45; Monteiro, p 309.
16. Monteiro, p 360; Graham, Journal: 'Sketch of the History of Brazil', p 65.
17. Webster, vol 1, p 209.
18. Lima, O Movimento da Independência, p 68.
19. Monteiro, pp 353–4.
20. Webster, vol 1, p 210: Thornton to Castlereagh. 4 May 1821.
21. Vieira, p 13.
22. The versions of what Dom John said to Dom Pedro vary slightly: cf Varnhagen, vol 6, p 57, with Armitage, vol 1, p 36.
23. Varnhagen, vol 6, p 57.
24. Debret, vol 3, p 269.
25. Azevedo was a successful capitalist not a fidalgo, who, for loans to the crown believed to total 348 contos, had been ennobled in 1812. He advanced another 300 contos for the return to Lisbon. He stayed behind in Brazil and became even richer. His wife, said to be the daughter of an Irish washerwoman, was a close friend of Maria Graham's. See Almeida Prado, p 117; Monteiro, pp 327–8.
26. Documentos, Lisboa-Rio, vol 1, p 260.

Chapter 14: Defiance, 1821–2.

1. Rizzini, pp 238–9; Miranda, J. A. de, Memória Constitucional e Política (Lisbon, 1820), p 38.
2. Documentos, Lisboa-Rio, vol 1, p 336: Antônio José de Paiva Guedes d'Andrade, 'Considerações sobre o Manifesto aos Soberanos e Povos da Europa'.
3. Varnhagen, vol 6, pp 62–3.
4. Varnhagen, vol 6, p 82; Documentos, Lisboa-Rio, vol 1, p 354: Conde das Casaflores, Spanish minister in Rio, to the secretary of state in Madrid, 6 June 1821.
5. Cunha, P. O. Carneiro da, 'A Fundação de um Império Liberal', HGCB, 11, i, p 163.
6. Monteiro, p 387; Armitage, vol 1, p 49; Varnhagen, vol 6, p 86.
7. Varnhagen, vol 6, p 93: Oliveira, p 91; Lima, O Movimento da Independência, p 131.
8. Oliveira, pp 98–102: 'Representação dirigida ao Principe Regente do Brasil pela Junta Provincial de São Paulo', 24 December 1821.
9. Barata, M., 'Viagens Científicos de J. B. Andrada', RIHGB, vol 260, July-September 1963, p 248.

10. The circumstances surrounding *O Fico* are exhaustively described in Monteiro, pp 418–41; Varnhagen, vol 6, pp 90–97.
11. Graham, *Journal*, p 180: entry for 10 January 1822.
12. Graham, *Journal*, p 192: entry for 24 February 1822.
13. Webster, vol 2, p 232: Chamberlain writing from Lisbon to the Marquess of Londonderry, 10 March 1822.
14. *Documentos, Lisboa-Rio*, vol 1, p 372: José Bonifácio to Martim Francisco de Andrada, 21 January 1822. For Dom Pedro to have selected a *mazombo* from so many vocal and importunate *reinóis* is at first sight unexpected. José Bonifácio's name may well have been suggested to the prince by the *Mineiro*, José Joaquim da Rocha (1777–1841), founder of the Distinctive Lodge, which met at Niteroi and of which Carlos Antônio was a member. Da Rocha had been elected a deputy to the Cortes but never left Brazil. Marschall believed he was the organizing mind behind *O Fico*. He certainly collected the signatures and mobilized the patriots, *fazendeiros* and slaves against Avilez. Dom Pedro owed him a debt of gratitude and José Bonifácio's admission to the ministry may have been its discharge. See Barbosa, Francisco Assis, 'José Bonifácio e a Política Internacional', RIHGB, vol 260, July-September 1963, pp 263–4. On the other hand, the junta of São Paulo under José Bonifácio had been the only one to recognize Dom Pedro as the fount of power when the other juntas recognized the Cortes. See Lima, *O Movimento da Independência*, p 101.
15. Neiva, pp 100-l.
16. Monteiro, p 477.
17. Lima, *O Movimento da Independência*, p 185.
18. *Documentos, Lisboa-Rio*, vol 1, pp 378–83: 'A Maçonaria no Movimento da Independência'.
19. Monteiro, p 495; Humphreys and Graham, p 355: Admiral Hardy to Croker, 13 June 1822.
20. Lima, *O Movimento da Independência*, p 72.
21. Lima, *O Movimento da Independência*, p 208; the sessions of the *Apostolado* continued until 15 May 1823.
22. Varnhagen, vol 6, pp 267–70.

Chapter 15: Independence, 1822

1. Monteiro, pp 618–19; Lima, *O Movimento de Independência*, pp 190–99.
2. Barbosa, Francisco Assis, 'José Bonifácio e a Política Internacional', in RIHGB, vol 260, July-September 1963, pp 260–61.
3. *Documentos, Lisboa-Rio*, vol 1, p 390: 'Decreto do Principe Regente de 1 de agosto sobre a Difesa do Brasil'.
4. Barbosa, p 262.
5. Monteiro, pp 525–8, saw the incident in political terms, but Varnhagen (vol 6, pp 121–3), who found the Andradas as a family antipathetic, ascribed Martim Francisco's dismissal to his unattractive personality. Both authorities agree that the Governor of São Paulo, Carlos de Oeynhausen, was deservedly popular and respected.

6. Carvalho, Gomes, *Os Deputados Brasileiros nas Cortes Geraes* (R, no date), p 37.

7. Monteiro, p 556.

8. Monteiro, pp 545–7; Varnhagen, vol 6, pp 137–8; Rio Branco, *Efemérides Brasileiras*, ed Rodolfo Garcia (R, 1946), pp 415–6; Cintra, Francisco de Assis, *Dom Pedro e o Grito da Independência* (SP, 1921), pp 211–20. All the eye-witnesses differ in minor particulars over what Dom Pedro actually said.

9. Gomes da Silva, Francisco, *Memórias* (R, 1939), p 65.

10. Varnhagen, vol 6, p 140; Webster, vol 1, p 216: Chamberlain to Canning, 10 February 1823.

11. The dates on which these masonic resolutions were taken are disputed; cf Varnhagen, vol 6, pp 136–41, ed Helio Vianna, nn 19, 29 and 30, with *Documentos, Lisboa-Rio*, vol 1, pp 395–8. Rio Branco, p 431, held that the sessions of 7 October took place in Dom Pedro's presence on 14 September, the night he returned from São Paulo.

12. Monteiro, pp 659–64.

13. Debret, vol 2, p 78; Varnhagen, vol 6, p 146.

14. Monteiro, pp 664–6.

15. Barbosa, p 264.

16. Bethell, *Abolition of Slave-Trade*, p 34.

17. Webster, vol 1, pp 220–21: Canning to Chamberlain, 15 February 1823. Brant nearly agreed to abolition *ex sua parte*, but drew back at the last minute because he did not feel he had the power to do so. *Arquivo Diplomático da Independência, Grâ Bretanha*, I, i, p 217: Brant to José Bonifácio, 20/30 November 1822.

18. Robertson, W. S., p 412.

19. Ramirez, pp 27–8: Dona Leopoldina to Francis II, 6 April 1823.

20. The Austrian minister in Rio, Marschall, describing Cochrane to Metternich, 17 May 1822.

21. Cochrane, vol 2, pp 7–8.

22. Gonçalves Ledo warmly applauded the choice of 'this man whom I knew in London'. See *Documentos, Lisboa-Rio*, vol 1, p 393: *parecer* undated, in August 1822.

23. Greenhalgh, Juvenal, 'José Bonifácio e a Marinha Nacional', in RIHGB, vol 260, July-September, 1963, p 229.

24. Graham and Humphreys, p 363: Commodore Hardy to John Wilson Croker, 6 February 1823.

25. Vale, 'Creation of the Brazilian Navy', pp 75, 79.

Chapter 16: War, 1822–3

1. Varnhagen, vol 6, pp 157–9.

2. Varnhagen, vol 6, p 169.

3. Debret, vol 3, pp 79–84; Varnhagen, vol 6, pp 172.

4. Monteiro, p 605, quoting Felisberto Brant.

5. Webster, vol 1, p 216: Chamberlain to Earl Bathurst, 22 November 1822.

6. Vale, 'The Creation of the Brazilian Navy', p 86.
7. Cochrane, vol 2, pp 27–31. Vale, 'Lord Cochrane in Brazil', 1, p 421, has established that two other Brazilian ships engaged the Portuguese line.
8. Friar Manoel Moreira of the Passion and Dolours of Christ, chaplain of the imperial squadron, in his diary entry for 25 July (in *Anais de Biblioteca Nacional*, LX [R,1938], p 245) recorded that the *Dom Pedro* flew the English flag. Cochrane in his Narrative, vol 2, p 60, says he hoisted the Portuguese colours. Vale, 'Lord Cochrane in Brazil', 1, p 435, supports Cochrane. According to the chaplain, however, the Portuguese-speaking crew were hidden away and the English officers walked the deck talking in loud voices, an odd thing to do if they were meant to be mistaken for *reinóis*. Cochrane's narrative has more drama, in the style of his old shipmate, Frederick Marryat, than the chaplain's diary, but Friar Manoel was a more professional truth-teller.
9. The Maranhão episode is described in full in Vale, 'Lord Cochrane in Brazil', 1, pp 437–8. For the political background, see Varnhagen, vol 6, pp 325–45; Raiol, vol 1, pp 26–38.
10. Raiol, vol 1, pp 53–83; Varnhagen, vol 6, pp 350–51; Vale, 'Lord Cochrane in Brazil', 1, pp 439–41.
11. João Cruz da Costa, 'As Novas Idéias', in HGCB, II, i, p 185.
12. Monteiro, pp 744–6.
13. Armitage, vol 1, p 120.
14. José Egidio Alvarez de Almeida, Marques de Sant'Amaro, was the son of a *capitão-mor das ordenanças* in Bahia. He had been Dom John's secretary in 1809 and stayed to serve Dom Pedro. A member of the committee which decided on the form of the acclamation, he was made a grandee on 9 January 1823, the anniversary of the *Fico*. He refused José Bonifácio's ministry during his short-lived resignation in October 1822.
15. Varnhagen, vol 6, p 203.
16. Varnhagen, vol 6, p 212.
17. The last days of the assembly are described in detail in Rodrigues, José Honório, *A Assembléia Constituente de 1823*, (Petropolis, 1974), pp 198–224.
18. Varnhagen, vol 6, p 219: decree of 13 November 1823.

Chapter 17: Survival, 1823–4

1. Extracted from an interview given to *O Tamoio*, carried in its issue of 2 September 1823.
2. Magalhães Jr, Raymund, 'José Bonifácio e a Imprensa', in RIHGB, vol 260, July–September 1963, p 210.
3. Rodrigues, José Honório, *Conciliação e Reforma no Brasil: un desafio histórico-político* (R, 1965), p 36.
4. Drummond, Antônio Menezes Vasconcelos de, 'Anotações a sua Biografia', in *Anais de Biblioteca Nacional, Rio*, vol 13, no 3, 1885/6, p 87.
5. Monteiro, pp 775–80: 'O Carácter dos Andradas'; Neiva, pp 265–9.

6. Harding, Bertita, *Amazon Throne: the Story of the Braganzas in Brazil* (NY, 1941), pp 111–52.
7. Graham, *Escorço Biográfico*, p 102.
8. Seidler, pp 76, 81.
9. *Documentos, Lisboa-Rio*, vol 1, p 42: Silvestre Pinheiro Ferreira to the Cortes, 19 July 1823. The news had not reached Brazil of the dissolution of the Cortes on 5 June.
10. In fact all of them had made an unmistakable commitment to the independence and survival of empire. The Marqueses de Caravelas (J. J. Carneiro de Campos) and Paranaguá (Vilela Barbosa) and the Viscondes de Cabo Frio (Cunha Moreira), Olinda (Aráujo Lima) and Cachoeira (Carvalho e Melo), were all Brazilian-born, while the Marqueses de Praia Grande (Caetano Pinto, former Governor of Pernambuco), Lajes (Vieira de Carvalho) and Baependi (Nogueira da Gama) were Portuguese-born. See Nasser, Alfredo (ed), *Organisações e Prográmas Ministeriais desde 1822 ao 1829: Regime Parlamentar no Império*, Arquivo Nacional (R, 1962), pp 7–10.
11. Bagot, vol 2, p 309.
12. Armitage, vol 1, pp 152–5; Costa, João Cruz, 'As Idéias Novas', HGCB, II, i, p 186, speculates whether Martim Francisco de Andrada 'fathered' the concept of the moderative power or whether Dom Pedro discovered it himself from Constant's *Cours de Politique Constitutionelle*.
13. Costa, E. V. da, *The Political Emancipation of Brazil, apud* Wood, *From Colony to Nation*, pp 86–8.
14. *Documentos, Lisboa-Rio*, vol 6, p 464: José Delavat y Rincon, Spanish envoy in Rio de Janeiro, to Madrid, 31 March 1824.
15. Webster, vol 1, p 233: Chamberlain to Canning, 31 December 1823.
16. Neiva, pp 209–16; Webster, vol 1, pp 222–3: Chamberlain to Canning, 2 and 26 April 1823.
17. Robertson, W. S., p 412.
18. Webster, vol 2, pp 13–14: Canning to Henry Wellesley, Vienna, 19 August 1823.
19. Webster, vol 2, pp 238–40: Sir Edward Thornton in Lisbon to Canning, 23 November 1823.
20. Webster, vol 2, pp 243–4: Canning to Thornton, 23 December 1823; Thornton to Canning, 5 January 1824.
21. *Documentos, Lisboa-Rio*, vol 1, pp 446–8: the dispatches of José Delavat y Rincon, 6 and 13 November 1823, who was sure that Pernambuco and Bahia would soon declare themselves independent.
22. *Documentos, Lisboa-Rio*, vol 1, pp 85–9: *relatórios* of Palmela, 9 January 1824; pp 91–7: *relatórios* of Subserra, 9 January 1824; pp 97–113: *parecer* of Tomás Antônio Vilanova Portugal, 12 February 1824.
23. Webster, vol 1, pp 240–41: Chamberlain to Canning, 15 May 1824.
24. The Maltese deserter, John Mitrovich, was the son of a Dalmatian corsair who flew the flag of the Order of St John in the perpetual war waged by the Knights of Malta against Islam in the 18th century. He followed his father's avocation and is believed to have joined a British man-of-war in 1814. George Mitrovich, Malta's champion in

the fight for a free press and a constitution in the 1830s, was the corsair's grandson and John's nephew. (I owe this information to Mr Roger Vella Bonavita of the University of Malta and to Mr P. Caruana Curran, from whose unpublished BA Hons thesis of 1973 I have learned the details of Mitrovich's parentage.)

25. Cochrane, ii, 162.
26. Ibid, 252
27. Ibid, 116: dispatch from Cochrane to the navy minister, Cunha Moreira, 6 January 1824.
28. *Documentos, Lisboa-Rio*, vol 1, p 457: Session of Council of State: 12 and 14 February 1824.
29. Vale, 'Lord Cochrane in Brazil', 2, pp 157–9.
30. Cochrane, vol 2, p 277.

Chapter 18: Recognition, 1824–6.

1. Accioly, Hildebrando, *O Reconhecimento do Brasil pelos Estados Unidos da América* (SP, 1945), p 113.
2. Accioly, pp 153–4. Condy Raguet was received by Dom Pedro as US consul in Rio de Janeiro on 29 October 1825.
3. *Arquivo Diplomático da Independência: Grâ Bretanha*, vol 1, p 98: Brant to Carvalho e Melo, 2 August 1824.
4. Webster, vol 2, p 252: Canning to Sir William à Court, Lisbon, 9 October 1824; Robertson, W. S., p 425: Grivel's dispatch of 25 May 1824.
5. Webster, vol 2, p 248: à Court to Canning, 25 September 1824.
6. Webster, vol 2, pp 251–2: Canning to à Court, 9 October 1824.
7. Canning was subsequently annoyed to learn that the Portuguese had made a secret and unsuccessful attempt to put this idea to Dom Pedro in Rio as early as May, while he was trying to negotiate a settlement in London.
8. Webster, vol 1, pp 249–53: Canning to Chamberlain, 12 January 1825.
9. Webster, vol 2, pp 262–3: Canning to à Court, 17 January 1825.
10. Webster, vol 1, pp 263–71: Canning's instructions to Stuart, 14 March 1825.
11. The French had, in fact, offered Dom Pedro immediate recognition in return for the trade privileges enjoyed by the British. The emperor refused to entertain the suggestion; the French subsequently denied that they had ever made such an offer. Freitas, vol 1, pp 189, 193; Webster, vol 1, p 60; Robertson, W. S., pp 428–9.
12. *Arquivo Diplomático da Independência, Portugal*, vol 6, p 64: *carta patente* of 13 May 1825.
13. Webster, vol 1, pp 281–2: Canning to Stuart, 14 June 1825.
14. PRO FO 13/4, Brazil: Stuart to Canning, no 53, 27 July 1825.
15. Webster, vol 1, p 294: Chamberlain to Canning, 7 January 1826.
16. Varnhagen, vol 6, pp 255–6.
17. Webster, vol 2, pp 273–4: à Court to Canning, 24 November 1825.

18. Brazil's Spanish American neighbours had not waited for Portugal. Mexico recognized her on 9 March 1825, and Buenos Aires had had a commercial agent in Rio de Janeiro since 1822.
19. Dom Pedro also created him Marques de Angra before he left Brazil, but this was also a Portugal title granted by the emperor after Dom John's death when he was briefly King of Portugal.
20. PRO FO 13/6, Brazil: Stuart to Canning, no 87, 21 October 1825.
21. In Stuart's treaty, Brazil's ships were to be granted exemption from search on the high seas if Britain were at war with a third party. Britain also abandoned her right to *Juizes Conservadores* and she extended reciprocity of trading privileges to Brazilians in Britain. All these concessions exceeded his brief.

Glossary

Aguardente: a spirit made from sugar cane, more often called *cachaça* (qv).

Alvará: a royal writ or warrant.

Bandeira: a party of explorers, slave-raiders or prospectors operating in the *mato* (qv).

Bandeirante: a member of a *bandeira*.

Batuque: a circular dance, accompanied by stomping and hand-clapping, a favourite among the slaves from Angola.

Botocudo: Indian tribe of Minas Gerais, Espirito Santo and Bahia, also known as *Aimoré*, who distended the lower lip with plugs of wood from the silk cotton tree. Believed to be cannibal.

Braço: literally 'arm', a farm-hand, usually a slave.

Cabildo: municipal council in Spanish colonial America.

Cabildo abierto: open session of a *cabildo*.

Caboclo: literally, 'copper-coloured', a half-breed of white and Indian, a term used of any half-breed backwoodsman or menial.

Cachaça: white rum, *aguardente*.

Cafuzo: offspring of an Indian and a black.

Calabouço: calaboose or lock-up, where slaves were punished.

Câmara, senado da: municipal or town council in colonial Brazil.

Campo: prairie country.

Candomblé: religious rites of African origin practised in Salvador da Bahia.

Capela Real: Chapel Royal.

Capelão-mor: court chaplain, also Bishop of Rio de Janeiro after the arrival of the court.

Capitania: jurisdictional division of colonial Brazil equivalent to a province, headed by a captain-general.

Capitão-do-mato: bush captain, leader of a gang sent to hunt down runaway slaves.

Capitão-mor: commander of the *ordenança* (qv) of the local militia.

Carioca: inhabitant of Rio de Janeiro.

Carta Regia: Royal Charter.

Carrasco: public executioner, responsible for public floggings, usually of slaves.

Chumbeiro: literally 'a lead pellet', *pé de chumbeiro* or leaden-footed was a pejorative term for a native of Portugal.

Comarca: judicial district in colonial Brazil roughly equivalent to a county.

Conto: a thousand *milréis* of Brazilian money.

Cortes: the three estates of the Portuguese nation meeting together as the supreme legislature. Used after 1821 to mean an elected national assembly in both Portugal and Brazil.

Crioulo: a Brazilian-born black, not used for a creole or Brazilian-born white, usually known as a *mazombo* (qv).

Cruzado: a gold unit of Portuguese currency, worth 400 *réis*.

Decreto: decree or edict.

Desembargador: judge of the Court of Appeal.

Desembargo do Paço: the main Court of Appeal of the realm.

El-Rei: customary reference to the King of Portugal.

Engenho: a sugar-mill in Brazil, sometimes used to include the plantation.

Escravo da rua: a slave permitted by his owner to ply his service for hire in the streets, usually as a chair-man or porter.

Exaltado: fanatic or radical, a name given to the republican politicians of the 1820s.

Fazenda: ranch or farm.

Fazenda Real: Treasury of the realm.

Feitor: slave overseer.

Fidalgo: noble or gentleman.

Fidalguia: nobility.

Gancho: hook secured to the collar on a runaway slave to make further escape more difficult in the undergrowth.

Gaúcho: horseman, native of Rio Grande do Sul and Uruguay.

Gegê: a black slave imported from Ouidah in Dahomey.

Iluminista: a member of the Illuminati or of a secret society dedicated to human or social regeneration.

Inconfidência: an act of defiance to royal authority, a rebellion.

Irmandade: charitable brotherhood or confraternity.

Jangada: a light raft used for the coastal trade of NE Brazil.

Juiz da fora: crown judge or magistrate.

Juiz ordinário: elected member of the *comarca* (qv) with minor judicial powers.

Macumba: variant of the religious rites of African origin, practised in Rio de Janeiro (qv *candomblé*).

Malê: a Muslim slave from West Africa.

Mameluco: offspring of white and Indian.

Marinheiro: literally a sailor, another pejorative for a Portuguese in Brazil.

Mascate: a pedlar, a term of abuse for a Portuguese shopkeeper or moneylender in Brazil.

Massapé: black, clayey soil of Espirito Santo and Bahia especially suitable for sugar cane.

Mato: open country, thick with tangling bush and scrub.

Mazombo: a Brazilian-born white, a creole, originally used of first generation Brazilians with foreign, usually Portuguese-born parents.

Mulato: offspring of black and white.

Nagô: Yoruba-speaking black slave imported from Lagos, Nigeria. It is one of the Yoruba words for the language spoken in the coastal areas of Nigeria in the 18th century.

Ordenança: rural militia or muster of all able-bodied males.

Orixá: the individual possessive deity invoked by *Candomblé* and *Macumba* adepts.

Ouvidor: crown or royal judge, senior judicial authority in a *comarca*.

Pau do Brasil: Brazil dyewood, *Caesalpina echinata*.

Pelourinho: whipping post, mainly for slaves.

Preto da ganha: slave allowed to earn his own living by plying a trade.

Procurador: an elected deputy or spokesman.

Quilombo: hiding place for runaway slaves.

Quilombola: a runaway slave living in a *quilombo*.

Quinta: country house.

Rancho: shelter for *tropeiros* (qv).

Recolhimento: asylum for the sick or aged.

Reconcavo: sugar-growing coastal area round Salvador da Bahia.

Registro: toll-point, turnpike.

Reino: metropolitan Portugal.

Reinol: an inhabitant of the *Reino*.

Réis: plural of *real*, a unit of Brazilian currency, as in *milréis*, 1000 reals.

Roceiro: small agriculturist, pioneer or frontier farmer.

Senzala: slave quarters.

Sertão: any large uncultivated or uncultivable area, primarily referring to the dry lands of the interior of NE Brazil.

Sertanejo: inhabitant of the *sertão*.

Tropeiro: driver of pack mules.

Tumbeiro: literally a hearse, the name given to a slave-ship.

Umbanda: an ethical Afro-Brazilian religious movement deriving from *Candomblé* and *Macumba* (qqv).

Vaqueiro: cowboy, stockman.

Vereador: alderman, municipal or town councillor, member of the *Senado da Câmara*.

Vintém: a coin worth 20 *réis*.

Bibliography

Note: The bibliographical details of any source quoted once only, or more than once in the notes of the same chapter, are given in the notes. Sources referred to in more than one chapter are listed below.

Abbreviations:
BA = Buenos Aires
CHLA = *The Cambridge History of Latin America*
HAHR = *Hispanic American Historical Review*
HGCB = *História Geral da Civilisação Brasileira*
L = London
PRO = Public Records Office, London
NY = New York
P = Paris
R = Rio de Janeiro
RIHGB = *Revista do Instituto Histórico e Geográfico Brasileiro*
SP = São Paulo

Almeida Prado, J. F. de: *D João VI e o Inicio da Classe Dirigente do Brasil, 1815–1889* (SP, 1968).

Armitage, John: *The History of Brazil from the Arrival of the Braganza Family in 1808 to the Abdication of Dom Pedro the First in 1831*, 2 vols (L, 1836).

Azevedo, Fernando: *A Cultura Brasileira*, trans by W. R. Crawford as *Brazilian Culture, an introduction to the Study of Culture in Brazil* (NY, 1950).

Bagot, Josceline F: *George Canning and His Friends*, 2 vols (L, 1909).

Bastide, Roger: *Les Amériques Noires*, trans by Peter Green as *African Civilizations in the New World* (L, 1971).

Bethell, Leslie: *The Abolition of the Brazilian Slave-Trade* (Cambridge, 1970).

Bethell, Leslie: 'The Independence of Brazil'; with José Murillo de

Carvalho; 'Brazil from Independence to the Middle of the 19th Century', both in CHLA, vol 3: *From Independence to c 1870* (Cambridge, 1985).

Boxer, Charles R.: *The Golden Age of Brazil, 1695–1750: Growing Pains of a Colonial Society* (California, 1964).

Boxer, Charles R.: *Race Relations in the Portuguese Colonial Empire, 1415–1825* (Oxford, 1963).

Buarque de Holanda, Sergio (ed): *História Geral da Civilisação Brasiliera tomo 2: O Brasil Monárquico*, in 2 vols: *O Processo da Emancipação* (SP, 1965) and *Dispersão e Unidade* (SP, 1967).

Caldcleugh, Alexander: *Travels in South America During the Years 1819, 1820, 1821, Containing an Account of Brazil, Buenos Aires and Chile*, 2 vols (L, 1825).

Capistrano de Abreu, João: *Capítulos de História Colonial, 1500–1800*, ed J. H. Rodrigues (R, 1954).

Carrato, José Ferreira: *Igreja, Iluminismo e Escolas Mineiras Coloniais* (SP, 1968).

Cochrane, Thomas: *Narrative of Services in the Liberation of Chili, Peru and Brazil*, 2 vols (L, 1859).

Conrad, Robert: *The Destruction of Brazilian Slavery, 1850–1882* (California, 1973).

Conrad, Robert: 'The Abolition of the Brazilian Slave-Trade, 1818–53', in Hanke (qv), vol 2.

Darwin, Charles: *The Diary of the Voyage of HMS Beagle*, ed N. Barlow (NY and Cambridge, 1934).

Debret, Jean-Baptiste: *Voyage Pittoresque e Historique au Brésil*, 3 vols (P, 1834–9), trans by Sergio Milliet as *Viagem Pitoresca e Histórica ao Brasil*, 4th ed in 2 vols: the original vols 1 and 2 of the Paris edition in vol 1 and vol 3 in vol 2 (references are given to this edition).

Documentos para a História da Independência, vol 1: *Lisboa-Rio* (R, 1962).

Elkins, Stanley: *Slavery: A Problem in American Institutional and Intellectual Life* (Chicago, 1969).

Elkins, Stanley: 'Slavery and Ideology', in Lane (ed), *Debate over Slavery* (qv).

Eschwege, Baron Wilhelm Ludwig von: *Brasilien, die Neue Welt, in topographischer, geognostischer, bergmannischer, politischer und statistischer hinsicht, 1810–21*, 2 vols (Braunschweig, 1830).

Eschwege, Baron Wilhelm Ludwig von: *Pluto Brasiliensis, eine Reihe von Abhandlungen über Brasiliens Gold, Diamanter un Anderen Mineralischen*

Reichtum (Berlin, 1833), trans in *Coleção Reconquista do Brasil* (Belo Horizonte, 1980), pp 58–9.

Fogel, R. W., and Engerman, S. L.: *Time on the Cross: the Economics of American Negro Slavery*, 2 vols (L, 1974).

Foner, L., and Genovese, E. D.: *Slavery in the New World: a Reader in Comparative History* (New Jersey, 1969).

Freitas, Caio de: *George Canning e o Brasil: influência da diplomacia inglêsa no formação brasileira*, 2 vols (SP, 1958).

Freyre, Gilberto: *The Masters and the Slaves: a Study in the Development of Brazilian Civilization*, trans from *Casa Grande de Senzala* by S. Putnam (NY, 1963).

Freyre, Gilberto: *The Mansions and the Shanties: the Making of Modern Brazil*, trans from *Sobrados e Mucambos* by Harriet de Onis (NY, 1963).

Graham, Maria: *Journal of a Voyage to Brazil and Residence there during the Years 1821, 1822 and 1823* (L, 1824).

Graham, Maria: 'Correspondência entre Maria Graham e a Imperatriz Dona Leopoldina e cartas annexas'; 'Escorço biográfico de Dom Pedro I com uma noticia do Brasil e do Rio de Janeiro', both in *Anais da Biblioteca Nacional*, vol 60 (R, 1938–40).

Hanke, Lewis (ed): *The History of Latin American Civilization: Sources and Interpretations*, 2 vols (L, 1969).

Hemming, John: *Red Gold: The Conquest of the Brazilian Indians* (L, 1978).

Hemming, John: *Amazon Frontier: The Defeat of the Brazilian Indians* (L, 1987).

Henderson, James: *A History of the Brazils comprising its Geography, Commerce, Colonization, Aboriginal Inhabitants* (L, 1821).

Hesketh, R.: 'Correspondence with Foreign Powers relating to the Slave-Trade', in Hanke (ed), *The History of Latin American Civilization* (qv).

Hill, Lawrence F.: *Diplomatic Relations between the US and Brazil* (North Carolina, 1932).

Humphreys, R. A, and Graham, G. S.: *The Navy in South America, 1807–23* (L, 1962).

Ianni, Octavio: *As Metamorfoses do Escravo: apogeu e crise da escravatura no Brasil meridional* (SP, 1962).

Keith, H. H., and Edwards, S. F.: *Conflict and Continuity in Brazilian Society* (South Carolina, 1969).

Kidder, The Revd Daniel P., and Fletcher, The Revd J. C.: *Brazil and the Brazilians portrayed in historical and descriptive sketches* (Philadelphia, 1857).

Klein, Herbert S.: 'The Colored Freedman in Brazilian Slave Society', in *Journal of Social History*, III, 1, 1969.

Koster, Henry: *Travels in Brazil in the Years from 1809 to 1815* (L, 1816).

Lane, Ann J. (ed): *The Debate over Slavery: Stanley Elkins and his Critics* (Chicago, 1971).

Leithold, Joh. Gottfr. Theodore Von: 'Minha Excursão ao Brasil ou Viagem de Berlim ao Rio de Janeiro e volta', trans from the German by J. de Sousa Leão Filho in *O Rio de Janeiro visto por dois Prussianos em 1819* (SP, 1966).

Lima, Manuel de Oliveira: *Dom João no Brasil, 1808–1*, 2 vols (R, 1908).

Lima, Manuel de Oliveira: *O Movimento da Independência, 1821–2*, 2nd ed (SP, 1922).

Lindley, Thomas: *Narrative of a Voyage to Brazil terminating in the Seizure of a British Vessel and the Imprisonment of the Author and the Ship's Crew by the Portuguese* (L, 1805).

Luccock, John: *Notes on Rio de Janeiro and the Southern Parts of Brazil, taken during a residence of ten years from 1808 to 1818* (L, 1820).

Malheiro, Agostino Marques Perdigão: *A Escravidão no Brasil: Ensaio Histórico-Jurídico-Social*, 2 vols (R, 1866).

Manchester, Alan K.: *British Pre-eminence in Brazil, its Rise and Decline* (North Carolina, 1933).

Manchester, Alan K.: 'The Transfer of the Portuguese Court to Rio de Janeiro', in Keith and Edwards, *Conflict and Continuity in Brazilian History* (qv).

Marrocos, Luiz Joaquim dos Santos: *Cartas, 1811–21* (R, 1939).

Martius, Carl Friedrich Philip von: see Spix and Martius.

Mathison, Gilbert Farquar: *Narrative of a Visit to Brazil, Chile, Peru and the Sandwich Islands during the years 1821 and 1822 with miscellaneous remarks of the past and present state and political prospects of those countries* (L, 1825).

Mawe, John: *Travels in the Interior of Brazil with Notices on its Climate, Agriculture, Commerce, Population, Mines, Manners and Customs, and a Particular Account of the Gold and Diamond Districts including a Voyage to the Rio de la Plata* (L, 1823).

Maxwell, Kenneth R.: *Conflicts and Conspiracies: Brazil and Portugal, 1750–1808* (Cambridge, 1973).

Monteiro, Tobias do Regû: *História do Império: a Elaboração da Independência* (R, 1927).

Neiva, Venancio de Figueiredo: *Resumo Biográfico de José Bonifácio de Andrada e Silva, O Patriarca da Independência do Brasil* (R, 1938).

Oliveira, José Feliciano de: *José Bonifácio e a Independência* (SP, 1955).

Pierson, Donald: *Negroes in Brazil, a Study of Race Contact at Bahia* (Chicago, 1942).

Prado, Caio, Jr: *Formação do Brasil Contemporâneo*, 2nd ed (SP, 1945), trans by Suzette Macedo as *The Colonial Background of Modern Brazil* (California, 1967).

Presas, José: *Memorias Secretas de la Princesa del Brasil, actual Reina Viuda de Portugal, la Señora Doña Carlota Joaquina de Borbon* (Bordeaux, 1831), trans by R. Magalhães Jr as *Memórias Secretas etc*, (R, 1940).

Prior, Lieut James, RN: *Voyage along the Eastern Coast of Africa to Mozambique, Johanna and Quilos to St Helena to Rio de Janeiro, Bahia, Pernambuco in Brasil in the Nissus Frigate* (L, 1819).

Raiol, Domingos Antônio: *Motins Políticos ou História dos Principais Acontecimentos da Provincia do Pará desde o Ano de 1821 até 1835*, 3 vols in *Coleção Amazonica* (Belém do Pará, 1970).

Ramirez, Ezekiel Stanley: *As Relações entre a Austria e o Brasil*, trans by A. J. Lacombe (from a dissertation for the degree of PhD of Stanford University, SP, 1968).

Rizzini, Carlos: *Hipólito da Costa e o Correio Brasiliense* (SP, 1957).

Robertson, John Parrish: *Letters on Paraguay*, 2 vols (L, 1838).

Robertson, William Spence: *France and Latin American Independence* (Baltimore, 1929).

Rubio, Julian Maria: *La Infante Carlota Joaquina y la Politica de España en America, 1808–12* (Madrid, 1920).

Rugendas, Johann Moritz: *Malerische Reise in Brasilien* (Mühlhausen, 1835), trans by M. de Goldberg as *Voyage Pittoresque dans le Brésil* (P, 1835); and by Sergio Milliet as *Viagem Pitoresca através do Brasil* (SP, 1940).

Saint-Hilaire, Auguste François César Prouvensal de: *Voyage dans l'Intérieure du Brésil*, in 4 parts of 2 vols (P, 1823–52). Translations used as follows: by C. R. de Lessa, *Viagem as Nascentes do Rio S Francisco e pela Provincia de Goyáz*, in 2 vols (SP, 1937), from *Voyage aux Sources du Rio S Francisco et dans la Province de Goyáz* (P, 1847); *Viagem pelas Provincias do Rio de Janeiro e Minas Gerais*, 2 vols

(SP, 1938); from *Voyage dans les Provinces de Rio de Janeiro et de Minas Gerais* (P, 1852).

Santos, Luiz Gonçalves dos (Padre Perereca): *Memórias para servir a História do Reino do Brasil*, 2 vols (R, 1934).

Seidler, Carl: *Zem Jahre in Brasilien* (Leipzig, 1835), trans by Bertoldo Klinger as *Dez Anos no Brasil* (SP, n.d.).

Spix, Joh. Baptist von, and Martius, C. F. Philip von: *Reise in Brasilien in den Jahren 1817 bis 1820*, 3 vols (Munich, 1823–31), trans by Lucia Furquim Lahmeyer as *Viagem pelo Brasil*, 3 vols (R, 1938), to which edition all references are made.

Staunton, Sir George: *An Authentic Account of an Embassy from the King of Great Britain to the Emperor of China . . . taken chiefly from the papers of HE the Earl of Macartney*, 2 vols (L, 1797).

Stein, Stanley J: *Vassouras: A Brazilian Coffee Country, 1850–1900* (Harvard, 1957).

Street, John: *Artigas and the Emancipation of Uruguay* (Cambridge, 1959).

Tavares, Muniz: *História da Revolução de Pernambuco de 1817*, ed Oliviera Lima (Recife, 1969).

Tollenare, Louis-François de: *Notes Dominicales prises pendant un Voyage en Portugal et au Brésil en 1816, 1817 et 1818*, ed L. Bourdon, 2 vols (P, 1972).

Vale, Brian: 'The Creation of the Brazilian Navy' in the *Mariners' Mirror*, vol 57, no 1, 1971, pp 63–88.

Vale, Brian: 'Lord Cochrane in Brazil', parts 1 and 2, in the *Mariners' Mirror*, vol 57, no 4, 1971, pp 415–42; vol 59, no 1, 1973, pp 135–59.

Varnhagen, Francisco Adolfo de: *História da Independência do Brasil*, ed Helio Vianna, being vol 7 of *História Geral do Brasil* (R, n.d.).

Verger, Pierre: *Flux et Reflux de la Traité de Nègres entre le Golfe de Benin et Bahia de Todos os Santos du 17ème siècle au 19ème siècle* (P, 1968).

Vieira, Dorival Teixeira: 'Política Financeira — O Primeiro Reinado do Brasil' in HGCB, II, i, pp 100–18.

Walsh, Revd Robert: *Notices of Brazil in 1828 and 1829*, 2 vols (L, 1830).

Webster, Sir Charles K.: *Britain and the Independence of Latin America, 1812–30*, 2 vols (L, 1938).

Wied-Neuwied, Prinz Maximilian zu: *Reise nach Brasilien in den Jahren 1815 bis 1817* (Frankfurt, 1820), trans by E. S. de Mendonça and F. P. de Figueiredo as *Viagem ao Brasil* (SP, 1940).

Wood, A. J. R. Russell: *Fidalgos and Philanthropists: the Santa Casa da Misericordia of Bahia, 1650–1755* (L, 1968).

Wood, A. J. R. Russell (ed): *From Colony to Nation: Essays on the Independence of Brazil* (Baltimore and L, 1975).

Index

demand for Brazil's sugar. For the past three decades prosperity had returned to the north-east. Moreover, Dom John's arrival in Salvador was marked by the occupation of the last French colony on the American continent when, in January 1809, troops from Pará, assisted by Captain Yeo in HMS *Regis*, overran Cayenne. Though the occupation was in the name of King Louis XVIII and Portugal promised to return it at the end of the wars (in which a closely related personal union was purchased), one of the Cayenne ships, when was imported for the same time into Brazil. Originating from Tahiti and reelaborated, Mauritius, Cayenne cane grew thicker, taller and faster than Creole cane, which had been transplanted from Madeira, and could be cut not once but twice a year. Brazil once again became the foremost sugar producer in the world and a new golden age first dawned. It was to have only a brief life. The sugar, developed in several ports, Europe to beat the British blockade and renewed competition from Cuba and the British West Indies, were to bring their attendant problems ... Coffee, not sugar, which was Brazilian, however, came was to save the country from ruin.

Since 1727 it had in some cases been possible to raise coffee trees in Rio Garden from beans smuggled from French Guiana. It was not until 1774, however, when the United States cut its supply from Haiti, that another thought it might be useful merchandise from enterprising planters round Rio de Janeiro were planting coffee in such the space available to them. All they had to do was to keep the trees from being overcultivated ... first crops could be harvested in four to five years. A tree yielded on average 2 pounds of coffee a year and one slave could tend up to 2000 trees, collecting 32 pounds between them. Selling richer, and requiring labour than other crops, coffee began to provide the large profits which followed its immense cultivation in the southern Paraíba Valley between Rio and São Paulo. By the middle of the 19th century a coffee planter's wealth ... in proportion with one of the railways came to Brazil to shift the beans to the port of Rio de Janeiro. The richer owners in numbers, the ... to their plantations and ... and future ...